The Manchus

The Peoples of Asia

General Editor
Morris Rossabi

Published

The Manchus
Pamela Kyle Crossley

In preparation

The Koreans
Martina Deuchler
Pak Youngsook

The Georgians
Tamara Dragadze

The Persians
Gene Garthwaite

The Turks
Colin Heywood

The Peoples of Mughal India
Harbans Mukhia

The Japanese
Irwin Scheiner

The Sinhalese
Jonathan Spencer
John Rogers
Charles Hallisey

The Afghans
Willem Vogelsang

The Chinese
Arthur Waldron

The Manchus

Pamela Kyle Crossley

First published 1997

2 4 6 8 10 9 7 5 3 1

Blackwell Publishers Inc
238 Main Street
Cambridge, Massachusetts 02142
USA

Blackwell Publishers Ltd
108 Cowley Road
Oxford OX4 1JF
UK

Library of Congress Cataloging-in-Publication Data

Crossley, Pamela Kyle.
The Manchus/Pamela Kyle Crossley.
p.   cm. – (The Peoples of Asia)
Includes bibliographical references and index.
ISBN 1-55786-560-4
1. Manchus – History.   2. China – History – Ch'ing dynasty, 1644–1912.
I. Title.   II. Series.
DS731.M35C75   1996   96-17702
951'.03 – dc20   CIP

British Library Cataloguing in Publication Data

A CIP catalogue record for this book is available from the British Library.

Typeset in 11 on 12½ pt Sabon
by Best-set Typesetter Ltd., Hong Kong
Printed in Great Britain by Hartnolls Limited, Bodmin, Cornwall

This book is printed on acid-free paper

For Joseph Francis Fletcher, Jr,
who should have written it

Contents

Plates

Maps

Preface

It is probably not usual for a writer in this series to have to alert readers to the dangers of reading her book. But as readers who continue beyond this page will discover, the frontier of knowledge of Manchu history and culture is receding so quickly that it is hazardous indeed to pretend to write down anything about it for a general audience, or for any member of that audience to be willing to believe what she or he reads. On the other hand the Manchus are so important – and in one form or another have been on our minds so long – that it really is time to proceed. My fellow specialists will feel, as I have, that many complex points have been simplified here, though I would maintain that the result has not been misrepresentation. Those who are not specialists may find themselves hacking through apparently hindering detail, but I hope they will find a clearing at the end of the trail.

At first glance it might be difficult to distinguish the Manchus from Chinese history in general, but I must rush to alert the reader that what is enclosed in these pages is not in any way a history of China (of which many excellent accounts have now been written). A portion of it is devoted to the history of the Qing empire, of which China was a part, but which, as I suggest, might really be better understood through a comparison with its contemporary Eurasian land empires, particularly those of the Romanovs and the Ottomans. Still, the Qing empire is only a passage in the history of a people – really, a set of peoples – with whom most of us are more familiar than we realize.

The inspiration for this book was not my own, but that of Morris Rossabi, who probably imagined something slightly different and must not be considered co-conspirator in any of my misdeeds. Nor indeed can John Davey, who with Morris checked the manuscript for readability and basic sense. Fiona Sewell has snared an astonishing number of silly errors, though some may have escaped even her wily eye, while Brigitte Lee, Sarah McNamee and Emma Gotch have shepherded the book through production. Yu Chen, Elizabeth Mawn, Gary Jan, and Nancy Toth have helped with some tedious tasks necessary to prepare the final manuscript, and I hope they are satisfied with the final product.

This has been part of a small flock of projects that have been completed – when they have been completed – during a personal crisis. There will never be pages enough allowed me to display the names of all those who, on different occasions and in different forms, provided the help that quite literally made it possible for things to be done, including but not limited to the writing of books. But at a minimum I must publish the following: Lillian M. Li, Margaret Hennigan Bloom (and A.H.B. III), Yeeleng Rothman (and Joshua), Fae Myenne Ng, Susan Naquin, Kandice Hauf, Odile Hourani, Paula Harris, Evelyn Rawski, Johanna Waley-Cohen, Jonathan D. Spence, Charles and Susan Wood, Susan Blader, Yan Peng, and those I should identify only as P.N. and G.B. I owe a very particular debt to Susan Reynolds, and as a satellite of that to her guests at La Bergerie in 1995, who showed me so many kindnesses and still have me ruminating on the hypothesized phenomenon of "holiday." And I am mindful of the editors from various presses who, to my advantage, have shown more patience than sense: Sean Wakeley, Beth Welch, John Davey, and Sheila Levine.

So many friends and colleagues at Dartmouth have provided personal and professional aid beyond any call of duty: Gail Vernazza (and Thomas) who makes all things possible, Marysa Navarro, Gene Garthwaite, Mary Kelley, James and Susan Wright, Paphanh Sithavady, and Jon M. Holbrook are among those to whom this book, specifically, is due.

Finally, for distractions, demands, emergency management skills, support while I've been at home and while I've been away, and miscellaneous kindesses I am grateful to those living in or about the mystical Kedron Valley, of whom only a few can be cited: Deborah Donahue, Constance Dowse, Paul Kendall, Chip Kendall, Annah Abbott, Charlene A. Shepard, and most especially two who will never understand that they have helped make the book, never read it, never care that it exists, and would only bolt away if presented with it: Aisha and Rosie.

Note on Transliteration

This book is written for those who are not specialists in Manchu, Chinese, or Mongolian studies, but for all readers the following should be noted regarding transliteration and style: Most Chinese names and terms are in *pinyin* romanization, which has been conventional in many English-language publications since 1979. Where words and terms are likely to be familiar to readers, they are kept in the familiar form: Genghis Khan, Peking, and so on. Reign periods and emperors as individuals are as far as possible kept distinct. I have spared readers the chore of dealing with the personal names of the emperors (except in appendix I, for cross-referencing with other works), but the rulers are referred to by the formula of, for instance, "the Kangxi emperor," meaning the emperor of the Kangxi period (in this case, 1662–1722). In many publications readers will find this individual referred to as "Kangxi" (or "K'ang-hsi"), as if this were his personal name (which in reality was Xuanye). This convention, in my view, obscures a vitally important aspect of the Qing (and earlier) rulers' contemporary identities, and clashes far too much with the usage of the original documents. This is one point on which I would prefer to change rather than cheerfully adopt popular usage. Another is the usual "Taiping Rebellion," which appears to trivialize a civil disorder of the highest magnitude. Here, as elsewhere, I have referred to it in English as the "Taiping War," which strikes me as a starker and more accurate description.

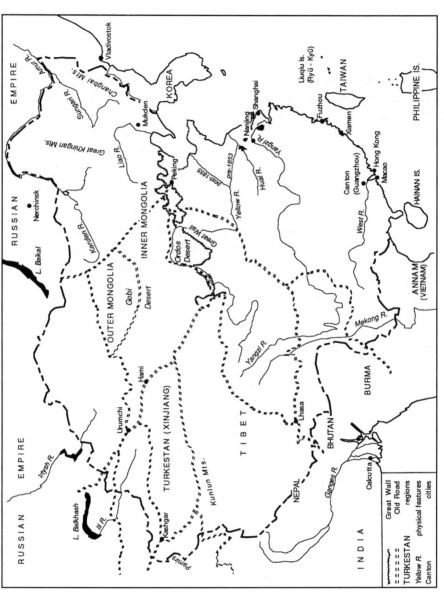

Map 1 *The Qing empire c.1750, as it ceased its era of expansion.*

1

The Paradox of the Manchus

The confusion of Mongols and Manchus under the name of "Tartar" is a handy starting point for consideration of the Manchus as a people and the Qing [Ch'ing][1] as the empire they founded. "Tartar" (*tatar, dada,* and variations) was the name of a Turkic-speaking medieval people of Central Eurasia. They became a significant element in the early Mongol federations of the twelfth century, and in the later middle ages Europeans commonly referred to the Mongols as "Tartars." Because the Turkic peoples settled in Crimea and near parts of the Caucasus were in fact called Tatars (and many writers correctly and strictly reserved the terms for this group), the corruption "Tartar" remained familiar in Europe. It was later applied to Timur ("Tamerlane") and his followers, and by the seventeenth century it was bestowed upon the newly-powerful Manchus, who were in the process of adding China to their Qing empire of Manchuria. In one form or another the practice of calling Manchus "Tartars" persisted at least until the destruction of the Qing empire in 1912, and in some quarters lingered even afterward.

"Tartar," then, was evidently a European and American commonplace for free-spirited, horse-riding Eurasian peoples who harassed and in select instances conquered sedentary cultures of sober repute. But it is interesting that even those who became well acquainted with the Qing empire, who visited it and came to understand well the culture of the ruling class, often continued to invoke the "Tartar" label.[2] Qing provincial military governors were called "Tartar generals," and the portion of the city of Peking reserved for Qing bannermen was known as the "Tartar City." Partly this is to be explained by an antiquarian impulse, a

REGNI SINENSIS
a
TARTARIS
devastati
ENARRATIO,
Authore Martino Martinii.

AMSTELÆDAMI.

Plate 1   *This cover to Martino Martini's account of the Qing conquest of China bears little relation to its contents, which describe the Mongol-style robes and boots of the Manchus and claim that in "their manners they resemble our Tartars of Europe, though they may be nothing so barbarous." (Lilly Library, Indiana University, Bloomington, Indiana)*

belief – or wish – that "civilized" people of modern times could still have access to the life of the great Mongols who ruled Eurasia in the middle ages by studying their modern reflection in the Manchus. Edward Gibbon, who never visited China, was clearly enchanted by such an idea, and used accounts from his own time of Manchu battue to reconstruct the hunt culture of the medieval Mongols.[3] The charm of this conceit could not have been completely unrelated to the romanticization in European popular culture of nomadic Tartars as "noble savages." Indeed, at the same time that popular theater in nineteenth-century America was capitalizing upon the stereotyping of native Americans as unspoiled foils for the satirizing of "civilized" pretensions, European theater was doing the same with the "trapping the Tartar" theme.

Eighteenth-, nineteenth-, and twentieth-century Western misapprehensions are not all that lie behind this connection of Manchus with "Tartars," however. Though the Manchus and the Mongols were very distinct as historical peoples – and as historical topics – their political histories and cultures were intertwined. Prior to the early 1600s, the ancestors of the people later known as Manchus were not called Manchus. A majority were known by some variation on the name of "Jurchen" (see chapter 2), but many who lived in close proximity to or in assimilation with the Mongols of eastern Manchuria were indeed known to the Ming Chinese as *dazi*, or "Tartars." Among the Jurchens themselves, a Mongol connection became increasingly important, and the early Qing emperors were inclined, as we consider in a later portion of the book, to declare their inheritance of the right to rule established by Genghis Khan and transmitted through successive Mongol regimes to the Manchus themselves.

This is not, however, to excuse modern historians who – most commonly out of a wish to simplify, and less commonly out of real ignorance – confuse Mongols and Manchus to the extent of referring to the early Manchus as "nomads." The forms of economic life among the Jurchens and the Manchus will be explored in later chapters. What is important to note here is that the Qing empire led by the Manchus was not nomadic in economic impulsion, in political organization, or in style. Comprehensive theories of nomadic conquest which attempt to include the Manchus inevitably go rather wrong. The problem of the Qing conquest regime and its evolution into a stable, long-lived empire is much more complex. When viewed as an empire and not as a dynasty, the Qing yields a more coherent picture and the possibility of illuminating comparisons with other great land-based empires of the early modern period – particularly the Ottoman, with which the Qing shared the ignominious distinction of being lampooned by the European press as the "sick man" of a continent in the early twentieth century.

Ethnicity and Causation in the "Manchu" Dynasty

In Chinese history writing of the first half of the twentieth century, the characterization of the Qing dynasty as "Manchu" was connected to the many misfortunes which China and its peoples suffered in the nineteenth century. The Qing was a regime of conquest, a result of the invasion of China and the destruction of the Ming empire in the middle 1600s. Many historians influenced by Chinese nationalists of the late nineteenth and early twentieth centuries argued that because the Manchus were foreign to China, they precipitated a series of social and political crises that in the nineteenth century resulted in China's impoverishment and quasi-colonization by the powers of Europe and the United States of America.[4] In this argument, the failure of the Manchus enflamed Chinese nationalism, leading first to the revolution which destroyed the empire in 1911/12, and second to the revolution which established the People's Republic of China in 1949.

More precisely, Chinese historians have pointed to the fact that in the 1600s and 1700s the laws of the Qing granted privileges to Manchu aristocrats and commoners, displacing Chinese from their lands and creating hatred of the foreign occupiers. In the nineteenth century, because the Manchus were themselves foreigners they were thought not to have had the will to resist foreign aggression. In such a view it would be predictable that after ignominious defeat in the first Opium War of 1839–42 the Manchus allowed a cascade of "unequal treaties" which left China helpless to control its borders, its revenues, or the increasing number of legal and economic privileges accruing to European and American residents in the country. Frustration over this situation was seen to have combined with local immiseration to incite the Taiping War, the stupendous civil war which wracked China from 1850 to 1864 and resulted in permanent political restructuring and demographic dislocation.[5] Indeed, the Taipings were distinguished for their vehement racial rhetoric against the Manchus, and when possible practiced a sort of "ethnic cleansing" which they associated with a patriotic wish to establish a Chinese government, serving Chinese interests. Nationalist historians considered the Taipings the precursors of Sun Yatsen and others who later established the Chinese republics.

Given this tendency to reason from the fact that the Manchus were foreign conquerors to the misfortunes of China in the nineteenth and twentieth centuries, it is not surprising that the earliest modern studies of the Manchus occurred in the context of the history of China since 1800. Indeed it was the Communist Revolution of 1946–9 in China that spurred historians to examine the Qing period for evidence of tendencies toward political or social radicalism, particularly those associated with nationalism. Under the terms of scholarship inspired by these ideas, China before exposure to the West had been in "decline." It was not capable of generating transformative energies. The road to epochal change in China, in this view, had been opened through the country's "response" to the West.[6] More precisely, a series of responses was perceived, in the earlier of which (response to the Opium Wars, suppression of the Taipings) reactionary forces had prevailed and in the later of which (the nationalist and Communist revolutions) revolutionary forces had prevailed. Through this entire saga, the forces of reaction, repression, and obscurantism had been represented not exclusively, but most vividly, by "the Manchus" – particularly the Empress Dowager Cixi (1835–1908), whose shortsightedness and corruption have become legendary throughout the modern world.

It is important to note in examining the historical treatment of the Manchus that a logical contradiction was happily tolerated. On the one hand, the Manchus were characterized as foreign to China and uninterested in its fortunes once the productivity of the country began to fall after 1800. On the other hand, the Manchus were described as having no important identity of their own remaining after conquering and settling in China. They were regarded as yet another example of what is reputedly China's ability to "conquer its conquerors." The "sinicization," or "sinification," as it is often called, of the Manchus was regarded as so inevitable and complete that it has been assumed that by 1800 the Manchu language was dead, the military vocation of Manchu men persisted only as a self-parody, and the Manchu elite had been so

"Confucianized" that they could be neatly assigned the roles of primary defenders of everything regarded as "Confucian" in this historical view – the suppression of the Taiping armies, the rejection of contact with the West, and the maintenance in China of an archaic social and political system. As we shall see, none of these simplistic and still conventional assumptions can be shown, by the historical evidence, to be true.

There was, in fact, no traditional "Manchu" culture or identity. Both were created simultaneously with the Qing empire in the 1630s. This does not mean that Manchu identity was inauthentic or illusory. It means that, like many peoples', Manchus' sense of themselves as a distinct nationality, with a history, language, and culture, could not be separated from the growth of the state which institutionalized the components of that identity. The primary institutional component in this case was what in English are normally called the "Eight Banners."[7] The banners in some form were organized long before the Qing state – certainly as early as 1601, and possibly earlier – and persisted, in some form, until 1924. They allowed registration of the early followers of the putative Qing founder, Nurgaci, to be categorized as "Manchu," "Mongol," or "Han" ("Chinese"), recorded all members of their households and what could be known of their ancestors, organized them into command hierarchies, granted educational opportunities, and allowed the distribution of wages, supplies, and land to the armies.

Most important, the Eight Banners became the foundation for the unified cultural identity of the conquest elite – not of Manchus exclusively – in the early Qing period. This is the key to understanding the role in the conquest and early occupation of a group usually called in English the "Chinese bannermen," but who would be better distinguished by a word that would not identify them with the Chinese. Elsewhere, I have suggested the term "Chinese-martial bannermen" (see appendix II). The origins of this group, who are identifiable in Manchuria from the late 1500s, are unclear, and were probably diverse. Some certainly originated in northern China, and via the Ming province of Liaodong[8] migrated to the Jurchen territories. Others were probably of Korean origin. But a large number were evidently of Jurchen ancestry, who were either the children of parents who had adopted many or all elements of Chinese or Korean culture, or were assimilated themselves. To contemporary observers, and to the forerunner of the Qing state, their outstanding characteristics were fluency in Chinese, strong personal associations with the Chinese towns of Liaodong, and, in a small number of cases, literacy. By the time of the Qing conquest of China in the middle 1600s, the numbers and the power of the Chinese-martial within the conquest elite had magnified tremendously. Though the early civil war known as the "Rebellion of the Three Feudatories" (1673–81) ended the political threat to the Qing throne of a group of Chinese-martial leaders, the remaining Chinese-martial bannermen maintained a degree of cultural identity with the other bannermen (*qiren*), and by the end of the Qing period were seen as indistinguishable from "Manchus."[9]

Also prominent among the conquest elite – and difficult at many junctures to distinguish from "Manchus" of various periods – were groups which were at one time or another called Mongols. This included not only Mongolian-speaking Mongol descendants living in Manchuria during the Ming period who were early recruits to Nurgaci's forces, but also descendants of early Jurchens, living in northern Manchuria, who spoke a distinct dialect, organized themselves politically in the Mongol fashion, and were called "Mongols" by Nurgaci and his followers – these included but were not limited to the famous Hūlun confederacy that dominated Manchuria before Nurgaci's rise. Finally, there were Mongols of Mongolia who submitted to Nurgaci or to his Qing successors, usually contributing potent new political titles and ideological ideas to Qing rule, while dramatically changing the strategic leverage of the empire. Many of these peoples were progressively enrolled in the Mongol divisions of the Eight Banners. Those earliest enrolled, including the Khorchins and the Kharachins, were most closely woven into the conquest elite, and to the end of the imperial period were most closely identified with the Manchus.

After establishment of the Eight Banners, all bannermen were born into the banner affiliation of their fathers, and women changed banner affiliation as they changed family affiliation, at the time of marriage. Though the term "bannerman" might be used most correctly to indicate a man actually serving in the military and receiving a monthly wage, in general social practice under the Qing empire all Manchus, Mongols, and Chinese-martial were referred to as "bannermen" if they had been born with a banner affiliation – whether or not they were actively serving, and whether or not they were receiving a wage. Thus "bannerman," a political status in the seventeenth century, became an ethnic identity by the nineteenth century.

The Qing Empire as a Historical Idea

There are several points to be made in dismantling established views of the Manchus, and framing the history presented in this book. First of all, though the Manchus certainly had a dynasty, it is a misleading – if quaint – feature of European writing on the Qing period to refer to the political regime as a "dynasty" exclusively. In fact, Qing was an empire, one of the largest, most powerful and influential of the early modern period. Along with the Romanov empire based in Russia, the Ottoman empire based in Turkey, and the Mogul empires of India, the Qing was one of the land-based empires which ruled Eurasia when Western Europe was a small and not obviously important outcropping of the greater continent. The Qing shared with the Ottoman empire a partial political inheritance from the Eurasian empire of the Mongols, and many trade contacts besides.

To the great empire of the Romanovs in Russia, however, the Qing was a formidable enemy. Beginning in the middle 1600s the Qing threatened to stop Russian expansion eastward toward the Pacific Ocean and North America, and two hundred years later, when the naval and marine forces of the British empire had created an international impression of the Qing armies as all but helpless, Qing forces were still effectively blocking Russian attempts to take territory south of the Amur river. In Central and Inner Asia, the Russian and Qing empires were at loggerheads until the completion of a border negotiation process that began in 1689 and was completed in 1727. Thereafter, the Qing continued to resist Russian penetration of Turkestan until they were displaced there by British agents in the nineteenth century.

As we shall see, the Qing empire was not only a formidable military presence throughout eastern Asia, but also a global cultural actor. It was in the Qing period that European enthusiasm for Chinese styles in porcelain, textiles, furniture, and wallpaper reached its height. Also during the Qing, Europeans and Americans developed a taste for and a huge trade in tea from China, creating the economic imbalances that drove the opium trade and led to the Opium War between the British and Qing empires in 1839.

Prior to these conflicts of the nineteenth century, relations between the Qing empire and Europe had not been acrimonious. Indeed European Jesuits, who had become familiar with the Chinese elite under the Ming, were instrumental in the establishment of Qing power in China, and continued to be influential advisors to the Qing emperors into the early eighteenth century. The Vatican welcomed the opportunity to establish Catholicism in China and other parts of Asia at a time when Western Europe was increasingly hostile to many of the church's ideas. But it was disturbed by the willingness of many Jesuits to become sympathetic to the religious ideas of the Qing elite and to attempt to reconcile Confucian and European beliefs. This created some debate between the Kangxi emperor and the popes, and with the decline of Jesuit influence worldwide in the eighteenth century the role of Jesuits at the Qing court changed. Many continued to live quietly in Peking, and a few distinguished themselves not as advisors to the emperors but as painters and designers in the imperial service.

A number of Jesuits became putative scholars of the Manchu language, and in addition to seeking to translate Christian scripture into Manchu, also presented European translations – or at least paraphrases – of Manchu works. One of these, in particular, was influential in the creation of an impression in eighteenth-century Europe of the Qing empire as a wealthy, enlightened, secular society ruled by a gentle philosopher-king. After the early 1700s, however, very few new Jesuits arrived in China, and in the 1800s European religious activists in China were almost exclusively Protestant missionaries attempting to succor and convert large numbers of commoners. Unlike the Jesuits, whose skills and sharp attention to the interests and culture of the elite had made them useful to both the Ming and Qing courts, the Protestant missionaries were met with hostility by the Qing rulers.

Understanding Qing as an empire also underscores its cultural diversity and political complexities. The ruling lineage may indeed have been Manchu – giving due consideration to the elusiveness of this as an ethnic title – but the conquest elite comprised peoples of many origins, including Chinese, Koreans, Mongols, the Turkic and Tungusic peoples of Manchuria, and, later, Central Asians. As early as the 1640s, when northern China was conquered by Qing forces, the composition of the invading armies can be shown to have included only a small minority of Manchus, and increasing numbers of people of Chinese descent or birth. Describing the Qing empire and polity as "Manchu" is in every way misleading, and tends to reinforce the simplistic interpretations of China's troubles in the nineteenth century.

New Windows on Qing History

Recent revisions in the overview of the Qing period have been inspired by and have in turn inspired a much wider exploration of documentation of the early Qing period in particular. Korean records — previously known but infrequently consulted – are increasingly used by scholars of the Qing to augment the narratives previously provided by the Chinese-language documents of the Qing state. Korean documents of the Yi period (1392–1910) and earlier are written in the Chinese script, and so those able to read classical Chinese may with slight additional training use them. Not only state annals of the Yi kingdom, but also the private narratives of ambassadors, students, merchants, and other travelers to the Qing empire, have been consulted with profit to understand matters often completely neglected by the official documents of the Qing.

One of the most compelling and immediate of these records is the memoir of Sin Chung-il recounting his visit in the winter of 1595/6 to Nurgaci's headquarters at Fe Ala. The manuscript was discovered in 1938 by the Korean Yi Yinsong, when Manchuria was under the rule of the "puppet state" – dominated by the Japanese military – of Manchukuo. Japanese scholars working in Manchukuo were great curators of Qing documents and architecture, and the next year Sin's report was published by the "Manchukuo University" in the capital, Mukden. It afterwards was reproduced under the title *Kŏnju jichŏng dorŏk*, in Korea.[10] Sin's account is used extensively in the first part of this book.

The Qing used three state languages – Manchu, Mongolian, and Chinese – and before 1800 Manchu was given pride of place. Until twenty years ago it was supposed by Qing specialists that all government documentation was produced simultaneously in Chinese and in Manchu (as well, sometimes, as Mongolian), and that reading the Chinese versions was sufficient. It is now known that this is not always the case. Many edicts, regulations, and compendia and some memorials indeed were completely rendered in two or three languages. But there are also instances of error, omission, and deliberate censorship in materials written in Manchu that were later translated into Chinese.

The training of scholars around the world in Manchu and in exploitation of these documents has not yet reached a point where Qing specialists as a community may claim easy command of the knowledge contained within them. This situation pertains despite the fact that Joseph Fletcher (1934–84) – the scholar of Mongolian history, early Manchu history, and Islamic history – strenuously urged Qing specialists to learn the national language of the empire, and not to rely on Chinese alone for their research.[11] Though the number of those reading Manchu in the West has increased since the time of Fletcher's admonitions, it is still small. As a consequence, the Qing is perhaps the last of the great empires for which vast stretches of central documents remain unreviewed, and for which major discoveries may yet be made.

There is evidence that emperors deliberately removed portions of the Chinese-language record from general access while leaving the Manchu-language documents in the files. As part of their normal procedures some departments – such as the State Historical Archives – were required to prevent documents from passing to related organs of the bureaucracy. The deliberate alteration of Manchu-language texts permitted to proceed to other departments was established by Mo Dongyin, who in 1958 pointed out that Nurgaci's original war oaths against the Ming were accompanied by a shamanic ceremony which was deliberately obscured when the passages were translated into Chinese. Certainly, to the end of the eighteenth century, emperors gave priority in their daily schedules to the perusal of edicts and other communications translated from Manchu into Chinese, so important to them was management of the transferal of information, ideas, and sentiments from one language to the other.

Just as the first access to palace memorials enabled scholars to realize through comparison how earlier documentary collections had been altered for political or ideological reasons, so the comparison of Manchu-language palace memorials with their Chinese counterparts can reveal the extent to which certain types of information were reserved for officials who could read Manchu. The use of Manchu as a security language applied routinely to military affairs. As late as the Taiping War (1850–64), banner officers used the language to communicate with the central government through a medium that was not widely understood by civilians or foreigners. This was perhaps a generalization of its use for secret communications that dated from the earliest period of the state. Manchu was also the primary language of the leaders of the Eight Banners, who were responsible for expanding the empire to its largest historical boundaries in the late seventeenth and eighteenth centuries.[12]

The early Qing emperors, as we shall see, encouraged translations into Manchu from Chinese histories and philosophical texts. They also sanctioned the translation of certain Chinese novels of the Ming period, most famously *Romance of the Three Kingdoms*,[13] thinking that the dramatic battle narratives would improve the strategic acumen of the nobles and bannermen. But there was clearly an independent, private world of Manchu literature, in which sexually explicit – and officially banned – novels such as *The Golden Lotus*[14] were also translated. Moreover, Manchu literature did not consist entirely of translations from Chinese. There were original Manchu prose works, poetry eulogies, memorial inscriptions, folk songs, and ballads. Part of the provenance of these forms can be found in traditional Jurchen/Manchu oral literature, which was not well documented before the end of the nineteenth century. Poems alternating Manchu and Chinese lines, as in the "drum-song" genre, testify to the profound and extensive Manchu impact on Peking's popular performing arts.[15] Although the court repeatedly promulgated regulations against the participation of bannermen in either street or more formal theater, it is well known that these regulations were disregarded not only by banner commoners but also by noblemen and imperial clansmen, some of whom dissipated their fortunes on the support of theatrical troupes and the commissioning of entertainments. What is often overlooked in this famous tradition, however, is that it provided an environment for the continued nurturing of Manchu in the folk arts.

Seen as an empire of world stature that endured for nearly three hundred years, expressed itself in half a dozen languages, and radically affected the fortunes of industrializing Europe and America, the Qing presents a very different profile to recent scholars than did the apparently ossified, denatured, paralyzed, and parasitic "dynasty" with which specialists of the later nineteenth century had made many readers familiar. It is part of the ongoing reassessment of the Qing period to seek a new understanding of how and why "Manchu" culture and identity are woven into the imperial history. Certainly, the traditional cultures of Manchuria had their reflection in the imperial culture of the Qing. On the other hand, to characterize the inner culture of the Qing court as an unmodified survival of ancient cultures of unconquered Manchuria would be a serious mistake – as bad a mistake as the previous depiction of the Manchus as "Confucianized," "sinicized," empty epigones of the great Chinese empires that had gone before them. "Manchu" identity and the Qing state revolved around one another, in a mutual gravitational pattern that was not broken until the late decades of the empire. This book is an exploration of both those histories, the ways in which their paths intersected, and the ways they finally diverged.

2

Shamans and "Clans": The Origins of the Manchus

What is known to us in the West as "Manchuria" is more or less what the Chinese call the "northeast" (*Dongbei*), and encompasses the modern provinces of Liaoning (normally called Liaodong prior to the seventeenth century), Jilin, and Heilongjiang.[1] But to reconstruct traditional Manchuria these provinces must be augmented by northern Korea about as far south as Hamhŭng (which was not within the boundaries of a Korean state until the end of the fourteenth century) and to the east by the Russian "Maritime Province" (Primorskii Krai). From the time of the Puyŏ people in about the first century BCE to about the fourteenth century CE, these were culturally coherent; Heilongjiang and the Maritime Province remained of a piece well into the nineteenth century.

The special geographical features of Manchuria have determined much of the pattern of its social development. It is essentially a system of lowlands stretching from Liaodong Bay on the Gulf of Bohai in a jagged pattern northeastward toward Khabarovsk. The modern Chinese cities of Shuangliao, Qiqihar, and Harbin roughly mark the triangular center of these lowlands, which continue eastward with the Songari river through Yilan and Jiamuse before expanding into another broad plain. From here they reach northward to the Russian city of Blagovescensk, and due south to Vladivostok, embracing Lake Khanka, which is today divided by the Sino–Russian border. On four sides this lowland system is bounded by mountains. To the west the Greater Xing'an Range and its southern extension divides Manchuria from Mongolia and northern China. To the north the Lesser Xing'an Range stands between the central lowlands of Manchuria and the Amur river. Far to the east, the Sichote Range cuts the valley of Lake Khanka from the Sea of Japan. And to the south lie the massive highlands which virtually cover northern Korea, topped at their northern end by Changbaishan – a sacred site in Qing imperial lore (see appendix III) – from which the Yalu river flows westward and the Tumen eastward to form the modern border with the Korean People's Democratic Republic.

Strictly speaking, there were no Manchus before 1635, which was the year the nascent Qing empire announced that a large portion of its followers would be known by a new national name. Most of those who were renamed as "Manchus" in that year had ancestors among earlier peoples of Manchuria, particularly the Jurchens, who had been known to the empires based in China since the time of the Tang empire (618–907). "Jurchen" in various forms may bear a more ancient connection to the "Wuji" name of the Northern Wei period (465–535). Certainly the Jurchens were related to or descended from the Heishui Mohe people of the Tang period, who in turn shared ancestry with the Parhae people of southern Jilin and northern Korea. A portion of the medieval Jurchens founded the Jin empire (1121–1234) that controlled Manchuria and northern China. In recognition of that early Jurchen empire, the later Jurchens under Nurgaci revived the Jin dynastic name in 1618, and historians today refer to the Nurgaci state as the "Later" or "Latter" Jin.

In the middle 1600s, the Later Jin state evolved into the Qing empire. "Manchus" were given a new identity by that state, in a clear program to distinguish them from the Jurchens who had lived in Manchuria for centuries. Political considerations aside, there was some justification in the new nationality. Jurchens were by this time so widely spread in geographical terms and so disparate in culture that the old name no longer had any real meaning. Nevertheless, Manchu culture showed in the early period, and continued to show, marked fundamental continuities with traditional life in northeastern Asia.

Prelude to the Manchus

The cultures of the Tungusic peoples have been very diverse in historical times. Settlement occurred first in the lowlands, and movement followed their outlines. The earliest settlers in the regions were immigrants from as far as Southeast Asia and the Pacific Islands, who made their way by sea northward, reaching Manchuria in later Paleolithic times. They first settled the islands and piedmonts of the Liaodong peninsula, later following the Liao River into the central lowlands. Beginning perhaps 2500 years ago, many of the peoples of what are now Manchuria and northern Korea began to be influenced by Chinese culture. They became farmers, and began raising livestock and working in ceramics. Many where traders, bringing the furs, pine seeds, and other products collected by the more traditional Tungusic peoples to China, and returning with silk, cash, and other Chinese goods. The ancestors of the Manchus were relatively late in arriving, following the Amur river southward into the eastern lowlands of present-day Khabarovsk in the last century BCE. The result was not the refinement of a homogeneous people and culture from heterogeneous sources, but the settlement of the uneven terrain of

Plate 2   *These indoor boots illustrate the legacy of the Manchus from the Tungusic peoples of Northeastern Asia. They favored padded robes, caps, and leggings against the brutal winter temperatures. Bright colors were highly valued in the dress of both men and women, and border patterns depicting animals and birds were common. These imperial stockings differ from those used by commoners only in that they are silk instead of cotton. Outdoors, they would be exchanged for felt or leather boots with thick soles for protection against muddy or icy ground. (National Palace Museum, Peking)*

the region by culturally diverse groups who on occasion wove their lineages and federations together.

The empires based in China began to establish military colonies in Korea as early as the third century BCE, which intensified the cultural and commercial exchange between China and Northeastern Asia. It was partly by these routes that Confucianism and Buddhism became influential in Korea by the third century CE, and from there were later transmitted southward to Japan. The "Four Chosŏn Commandaries," established in northern Korea by emperor Wu of the Han empire in the second century BCE, extended that influence into southern Manchuria.

The division of the peoples of Manchuria between sedentary and nomadic economies has never been clear. As early as the Paleolithic, there is confirmation that at least some of these northerly peoples had become accustomed to riding reindeer, which suggests at least a partly nomadic life. The Wuji, and later the Mohe and Parhae, all exported reindeer. But until the Tang period horses in the Manchuria were rare, as were cattle, and there is no evidence of large-scale pastoralism before the domination of the region by the empire of the nomadic Kitans in the tenth century. Instead, hunting, fishing, and gathering were the mainstays of the earliest economies, and agriculture was haltingly introduced into southern Manchuria from the Korean peninsula in the early centuries CE.

Slavery was an ancient institution among the Tungusic peoples. There is some evidence for the existence of slaves in the villages, particularly the agricultural villages, of the Mohe of Tang times. They were taken in battle against local peoples, and later in raids on Chinese and Korean towns established on the perimeters of Jurchen territory. By Jurchen times, slaves played a critical role in the hunt, since they did the surrounding of the prey's territory and the beating of drums which drove the animals into the shooting sights of their overlords (a universal form of Eurasian hunt, the battue). Over the centuries, the amassing of slaves as agricultural workers and household managers transformed the economic and social foundations of Manchuria. It even provided the primary political conceit, that of the master–slave relationship between headmen (who sometimes were and sometimes were not "khans") and their followers.

Korea was organized into small kingdoms in the second century, and not long afterward a larger society covered northern

Korea and southern Manchuria. This Puyŏ state would later be considered the ancestor of many of the kingdoms of Korea and Manchuria. It combined some elements of Central Asian culture – primarily a knowledge of Buddhism and the breeding of horses – with elements of Chinese culture such as Confucianism, and many of the economic and religious traditions of the Tungusic peoples. Puyŏ maintained relations with both the Korean kingdoms and the Chinese empires, until it dissolved in the fifth century. The name continued to be reflected in the federations of medieval times (the Fuyu, for instance, were closely associated with the Uriangkha), and in place names of the modern Chinese provinces of Manchuria.

After the evaporation of the Puyŏ domination in Manchuria, the Mohe peoples become prominent in the records. The most powerful of the northern Mohe groups were the Heishui (that is, Heilongjiang, for the Amur river), and the most powerful of the southern Mohe groups was the Sumo (that is, Songmo, for the Songari), whose territories reached as far south as Changbaishan. During the seventh century, the Sumo were subjected to constant military pressure from both the Koguryŏ state of Korea and the Tang empire. Around 700 a leader of the Sumo Mohes found a way to alleviate these pressures by cooperating with Tang forces in the suppression of a rebellion among the Kitans of northern Manchuria. As a reward, his lineage was recognized as local hegemons by the Tang, and permitted to establish a demi-state – a sort of principality within the empire. A few years later it assumed the name of Parhae (in Chinese, Bohai).

The Parhae were the first to develop urban centers and a political system recognized by their neighbors. Artisanal skills flourished among them. They were known for iron mining and smithing (skills they certainly learned from the Turks), and many of the local names of Manchuria retain the word for iron in memory of the Parhae industries. Tang records mention many other settlements among the Parhae that were famous for their vegetables and grains, or manufactured goods, or husbanded animals. Many of these – including pigs, horses, exotic long-haired rabbits, preserved vegetables (not unlike Korean *kimchee*), copper, falcons, pelts, pearls, and ginseng – would remain the foundation of the Manchurian economy for centuries.

Ruins of Parhae towns are still to be found in northeastern China and in maritime Russia, particularly in the vicinity of

Khabarovsk. By the standards of China or southern Korea they were modest establishments in size, but employed sophisticated work with brick, wood, and metal in their construction. The housing of common people shows a feature that is characteristic of the Tungusic peoples from their earliest appearance in the Chinese records. All-season houses, whether made of wood, bark, brick, or earth, tended to be semi-subterranean, which allowed them to retain warmth in the harsh climate of the region. The houses were normally round, with a central chimney hole. This style of house was very widespread throughout northern Eurasia. The Wuji had such houses, which they entered by a ladder through the chimney hole. Persians observed the medieval Turks building such dwellings, and into the twentieth century the Samoyeds were described as living in "half-subterranean caverns." These were not unlike many of the styles of housing found among the earliest settlers of North America, where evidence of round, semi-subterranean houses exists as far south as the Anasazi sites of Arizona.

Parhae had a bureaucracy which used Chinese characters to write the native language, distributed among a set of five cities which functioned as its capitals. The prince of Parhae and his large following of aristocrats inhabited these capitals in series each year, reinforcing their relations with the local magnates and collecting tribute. Both Buddhism and Confucianism were influential among the Parhae elite, many of whom traveled regularly to the Tang capital at Chang'an as ambassadors or students.

The Parhae class system, like those of the related kingdoms of Korea, was extremely rigid. Elites tended to be affiliated with large extended families and to have surnames (no evidence exists that this was the practice among commoners). This pattern had pertained in northern China, too, in very early times, but had virtually disappeared by the creation of the first Chinese empire in 221 BCE. In Manchuria, however, it persisted, and the power and cohesiveness of the aristocracy generally kept the power of rulers and their families in check. The system required a caste system of rank by birth, in which upward mobility for the common people was virtually impossible.

After the fall of the Tang in 907 the Kitans immediately established their Liao empire in Manchuria and Mongolia, and lost no time in moving against their old enemies, the Parhae. In 926 the Parhae principality was abolished, and Liao princes were given dominion over Manchuria. Parhae and many others of the southern Mohe descendants were resettled elsewhere or conscripted into the army. At first the Liao empire indicated no wish to conquer and administer the northern Manchurian territories, but frequent skirmishing with the northern Mohe forced the Liao empire into a carrot-and-stick policy that depended upon fierce military reprisals in combination with rewards and political recognition for Heishui Mohe willing to declare themselves neutrals – or, better, accomplices – in the Liao imperial enterprise. In this scenario, the Mohe, the forest-dwelling peoples north of Parhae, increased their influence, and gained some recognition from the Liao empire which continued to rule Central Asia and Manchuria in the tenth and eleventh centuries.

In the early 1100s a group called the Jurchens had emerged from among the Heishui Mohe, and their leader, Agūda, was invited to the Kitan court. Agūda was generally suspicious that the Liao intended to suppress the Jurchens, and was particularly outraged to discover that the Kitans expected him to dance for them as after-dinner entertainment (by tradition the function of a captive, degraded enemy). He refused, and later raised troops to rebel against Kitan rule in Manchuria. His war to unify the Jurchens and then to break the hold of the Liao empire was successful. In 1121 the Jurchens captured the Kitan capital and established a new empire, the Jin ("Gold") empire of their own.

The material culture of the Jurchens before the rise of their empire demonstrated their origins among the hunting and gathering peoples who came to occupy the banks of the Amur and Songari rivers. The round tent used in summer residence was common to the peoples of this region. So was the peculiar style of dress, based upon thick leather boots, knee-length tunics of felt or hide with bright appliqués of colored silk, cotton, or hemp, and the decorated apron, which up to the present has persisted as the costume of the shaman. The Jurchens were known for their consumption of raw meat and fish, and their liking for a strong liquor made from millet (*gaoliang*). Boats, sleds, and weapons of these peoples have shown marked similarities, as have certain household goods. One item has been regarded as unique: The curved, hanging cradle of the Manchus and Evenks, which often flattened the backs of infants' heads (later imagined to be a "genetic" quality of the Manchus). In spite of the occasional singular implement or style, the traditional peoples of Manchuria had remarkably similar cultures, and were not themselves inclined to distinguish one people from another on the basis of national names or concepts. Until the rise of the Qing empire, for instance, those peoples called by outsiders – including modern historians – Golds (in Chinese, Hezhe), Orochons, and Oroks all called themselves Nani, the name of the local tributary of the Songari river.

The Jurchens borrowed some elements of their empire from the Kitans. One was distillation of the society into national divisions, so that people living in the northern part of China (which the Jurchens, like the Kitans before them, ruled) were governed in Chinese and according to Chinese political tradition, while Jurchens lived in distinct territories, and were governed according to their own traditions. The emperors, in the fashion of the Kitans before them, transcended the regional divisions by legitimating themselves in all traditions, including Confucianism, Buddhism, and shamanic ritual.

As already noted, the Jurchens adapted Kitan script for the writing of their own language. Using this script as a medium, an entire educational and bureaucratic system in Jurchen was constructed, and major works of Chinese philosophy and history were translated into Jurchen. This permitted the introduction of a number of concepts that the earlier language would have found difficult to express – among them the word for "emperor" (*hūwangdi*, from Chinese *huangdi*), a notion of power concentrated in a single individual that was foreign to the decentralized political culture of Manchuria.

The Jin empire shared with its Liao and Parhae predecessors a system of multiple capitals. Chinese empires of earlier times had never considered Peking an imperial site, placing their imperial cities in the Wei river valley of Shaanxi province, far to the west. The Liao had first used Peking as an imperial capital, but, because of its position at the southern extreme of their empire, had called it not Peking ("northern capital") but Nanjing ("southern capital"). The Jin, whose territory eventually included China north of the Yangzi river, considered the city their central capital (*Zhongdu*), and probably built the earliest imperial complex from which the Forbidden City known in modern times evolved. They elaborated the pond built by the Liao into a small artificial lake (now part of the three artificial lakes of the Forbidden City) and a small islet that still exists. They constructed, late in the eleventh century, the Marco Polo Bridge (*Lugou giao*), which has been considered one of the world's engineering marvels since it was described in the *Travels*. They also built the first observatory in the city. The Mongols, the Ming, and finally the Qing all elaborated upon the Jin foundation, their efforts resulting in the enormous architectural treasure that now exists.

The Jurchens, like the Kitans before them and the Mongols after, faced the problems of formalizing folk cultures, authorizing and enforcing orthographic practices, and familiarizing some critical portion of their population with the necessary Chinese knowledges to govern. A critical choice before these regimes was whether or not to use the system of written examinations established in China during the Tang empire for the selection of government officials. In each case, choices were made respecting not only the style of education to which nobles and elites would be subjected, but also whether the examinations would be used to raise those perceived as "commoners" to the ruling class, or to limit access to the highest office to the hereditary elites.

The imperial bureaucracy of the Jin empire bore little similarity to that of the Kitans, and part of the reason is to be found in the basic socio-economic differences between nomadic and sedentary societies. The Kitans and Mongols retained, at least in official policy, a strong attachment to the principles of nomadic life among their peoples and a toleration for traditional segmented political structures. They appear to have been disinclined to effect drastic changes in their economic and social lives by linking status or achievement to time-consuming attainments in civil or literary pursuits. For this reason, they largely eschewed the Chinese institution of using written examinations to select and promote bureaucrats. Kitans were by edict barred from participating in the examinations held under the Liao, and the suspension of the examinations for the greater part of the Yuan empire left the question of Mongol achievement in the examinations moot.

In the case of the Jurchens, however, the establishment of bilingual examinations and official attempts to encourage participation in the examinations by the peoples in question are evidence of a very different state posture. Unlike the Kitans or the Mongols, the Jurchens were not given land grants in China proper, nor were they committed to cultural precepts or political structures that were characteristic of nomadism. Attempts to use the examinations for the promotion of commoners or for restricting aristocratic access to high office were consistent, in the Jin empire, with aggressive state programs to limit the privileges and the influence of the nobility, to centralize the state, and to prepare the dynastic constituency for a very broad role in the maintenance of a civil system. These practices were all forerunners of the bureaucracy of the Qing empire.

The cosmopolitan culture of Jurchen officials strengthened the early empire, but by the middle 1100s the Jin emperor Shizong (r. 1161–89) became concerned that the Jurchens were losing their distinct identities as conquerors and as soldiers. He instituted a program for the retraining of Jurchen elites in warfare, hunting, and the harsher life of Manchuria. Aristocrats were compelled to leave Peking and literally go to camp in Inner Mongolia or Manchuria, where constant hunting was supposed to develop their skills in riding, shooting, and generally becoming less dainty. His experiment, which was not a success, was considered both a model and a warning by the Manchu emperors who later ruled China. They were avid readers of the history of the Jin empire, and repeatedly referred to the dilemma of Shizong, who could neither force the Jurchens to return to their old ways, nor sanction the new culture they were developing for themselves in China.

Both the Liao and Jin had a hostile relationship to the Chinese empire of the Song (980–1227, Southern Song 1227–79), which was much smaller than the Tang. The Liao and the Song had reached an uneasy peace which required the Song to render heavy tribute to the Liao in order to avoid war. Once the Jurchens had destroyed the Liao empire, however, the Song refused to enter into a similar agreement with them. The continuous warfare and threat of warfare between the two states resulted not only in the stimulation of Song defensive technology, leading to major strides in the uses of iron and gunpowder, but also in the fatigue of the Song economy due to its enormous military expenditures. Despite the Song effort, in 1227 they lost control of territory north of the Yangzi river to the Jurchens.

When, in 1234, the Jin empire fell to the Mongols, a variety of fates befell the Jurchen people. Many Jurchens had remained in Manchuria during the Jin period, and continued to live in the traditional manner. Others had migrated to northern China as part of the conquest forces of the Jin empire. Of these, some had become acculturated, and were considered by the Mongols as Chinese. Still others were identified by the Mongols as Jurchens, whether they stayed in China – where many served as Confucian officials – or returned to Manchuria. The result was that the

Jurchens of Manchuria were alienated from the imperial culture and institutions of the Jin, and lived according to the older customs of Manchuria, with a superficial political influence from the Mongol Yuan empire.

The Yuan was destroyed in 1368, but Mongol influence among the peoples of Manchuria continued in many forms. Since even after the decline and fall of the Mongol empires the Mongolian language continued to function as a *lingua franca* in Eastern Asia, the Jurchens continued formal communications with both the Ming court in China and the Yi court in Korea. Certain forms of Buddhism, particularly that of the Sa-skya pa lamaist sect, became familiar to the Jurchens of Manchuria in the 1500s because of Mongol contacts. The result was a complex, multi-layered cultural milieu in which Mongolian political and cultural influences mixed with traditional Jurchen economic life and the radiating attractions of the Chinese trading towns of the Ming province of Liaodong. This was the world observed and described by the Korean bureaucrat Sin Chung-il at the end of the sixteenth century.

Distinctive Manchu Institutions

For most of the twentieth century, "clan" has been the normal English term for the lineage organizations of the Manchus, and indeed of the Tungusic peoples of which they are a part. The term has not only been used comfortably to describe Manchu social organization, but has been used famously in this fashion, for it was S.M. Shirokogoroff's seminal *Social Organization of the Manchus: A Study of the Manchu Clan Organization* (Shanghai, 1924), which – following earlier terminology used by Lewis Henry Morgan to describe native American societies – legitimated "clans" as critical generic social units. Not long afterward, the Chinese anthropologist Ling Chunsheng used Shirokogoroff's basic concepts in his exhaustively detailed and well-illustrated study of the Tungusic peoples in the region of the Songari River.

Despite its antiquity and peculiarities of method and expression, Shirokogroff's study has remained an indispensable source for anyone curious about the Manchu people. He defined the clan – proximately among the Manchus, but generally among all "tribal" peoples – as "a group of persons united by the consciousness of descent from a male ancestor and through male ancestors, also united by recognition of their blood relationship, having common clan spirits and recognizing a series of taboos, the principle of which is the interdiction of marriage between members of a clan, i.e. exogamy."[2] In practice, he noted "clan" members living, or attempting to live, within some proximity of one another; meeting together at least annually to mediate intra-clan disputes, sacrifice to clan spirits, and manage common property; and identifying themselves under a single clan name. This last characteristic was definitive, as Shirokogoroff reiterated in italics: "*The clan cannot exist without a name and this is an important character of the clan.*"[3]

Today there is resistance to generalizing a peculiar Scottish social institution to widely spaced and chronologically divergent peoples, as well as to the abstract notion of "clans" or "tribes" as marking types of human societies. Nevertheless Shirokogoroff's empirical complex of ideas associated with "clans" among the Manchus must be noted, for it is affirmed not only by anthropological studies in Manchuria since his time, but also in the social, cultural, and political history of the Qing: He associated clan identities with a "consciousness" of mutual descent, with regular meetings to conduct mutual property business, with worship of mutual spiritual patrons, and with the willing acknowledgment of a name. At no point did he say that those bound together by clan ties were actually descended from a real ancestor, or indeed that any proof of blood ties determined much at all about members of a clan, apart from whom they could not marry.

As envisioned by Shirokogoroff, Ling, and other anthropologists, the comprehensive nature of the clan was the salient aspect of the traditional life in Manchuria. It facilitated all economic activities. It mediated the spiritual and physical well-being of each individual. Intermarriage between clans ranked with trade and conquest as a means of cultural transmission. Cross-marriages were also a mechanism for the creation of new clans and, in some cases, new peoples. Clan alliance was the only institution of political amalgamation, and what we would recognize as a "tribe" was, in Manchuria, an extension of the clan. Using this concept, Shirokogoroff captured well the dynamism and discontinuities that had been evident in Manchu social life.

Nevertheless, it is probably best to think of Manchu social organization in the terms provided by the Manchu language itself, and to briefly examine the history of the words. Certainly as early as the twelfth century, when the Jurchens of the Jin empire ruled Manchuria and northern China, a word ancestral to the modern Manchu word *mukūn* was used to describe social cooperatives that appear to have been very much like extended lineages (see appendix III). Biographical entries, for instance, in the imperial history of the Jin with few exceptions indicate the *mukūn* to which an individual belonged, traced through his or her father, and it is clear that by this time the *mukūn* was regarded as a descent group. The earliest connotations of the word, however, had nothing to do with descent, or blood relationships; it was instead related to words meaning to live together (as in a village) or to move together (as in a herd of animals, a fleet of boats, or groups organized for hunting or warfare).

The associated meanings make sense. Brief descriptions of the Jurchens and their ancestors in the Chinese and Korean records indicate the preference for living together in fairly stable villages, and also that any village was a functioning cooperative that moved with a degree of hierarchical organization during the hunting seasons, or in time of war. Indeed the *mukūn* was the basic unit in the imperial armies of the Jin, since the most efficient and most reliable way of organizing a rapidly growing Jurchen military force was to enlist whole extended lineage groups as units, and to give each headman (*mukūnda* in Qing times) the rank of captain over the unit.

Though good for a war leader whipping together a conquest force, this is a difficulty for historians who would like to reconstruct the actual numbers of the armies involved. Each *mukūn* contained however many members were living together in the village or villages acknowledging themselves as members of the lineage unit. There were surely natural ceilings on the upward size a *mukūn* could reach. One upper limit has already been alluded to: Whether or not villages originated as kin organizations, they would tend to become lineages by the process of intermarriage over the course of time; when a majority within a village were kin of close enough degree, young men and women would necessarily be married out in order to observe the rule on exogamy. But another natural limits was the environment. Those very northerly villages dependent upon hunting and gathering had to remain small, and there is evidence scattered over Jurchen social history of the frequent outmigration of individuals or groups of individuals who felt the strain of resources; they invariably formed a new *mukūn*, and did not consider themselves associated any longer with their erstwhile relatives in the original group. In the southerly, increasingly agricultural regions, on the other hand, *mukūn* were more flexible in the sizes – and inevitably the shapes – they could assume.

It appears that the Jurchens had no native institution that went higher than the *mukūn*. In Jin times, *mukūn* were united for command purposes into superunits called *minggan* (from a Mongolian word for "thousand"), and incorporated into a newly-rigidified, formalized bureaucratic organization. Among the sixteenth-century Jurchens on the eve of the rise of Nurgaci, *mukūn* could be found allied under the leader of an *aiman* – from the Mongolian word *aimakh*, which is often translated as "tribe," but which indicated a confederation of *mukūn* groups. Even as the Qing state grew in size and complexity after 1630 and relied more and more upon a descent-group concept of *mukūn*, it could find no historically native term for organization above the level of the *mukūn*, and imposed an invented nomenclature in the organization of the Eight Banners.

Shirokogoroff hypothesized an original "matriarchy" among the Manchus, on the basis of his observation that maternal lineages were accorded great prominence in any individual's status and association, and in many cases the maternal uncle (*nakcu*) was the primary authority figure. There are indications that maternal uncles within the imperial family (most famously the Chinese-martial uncles of the Kangxi emperor) retained their special roles as disciplinarians, protectors, and spiritual sponsors well into the eighteenth century. Though there is in fact no evidence that Manchu society, its Jurchen antecedents, or indeed any society yet discovered had an authentic matriarchal history, there is much anecdotal evidence from the histories of the Jin and Qing empires to affirm that the prestige accorded maternal lineages was linked to a relatively high level of influence by women. Since mothers of adult men had more power than wives, this was truer of senior women, and particularly those who were members of influential families. In the Qing period, both the Kangxi (1662–1722) and Qianlong (1736–95) emperors were influenced by senior women of their courts. And among common women, the ban on the binding of the feet of Manchu women settled in China remained a symbol of their activity in the economic and political lives their communities.

In both the Jin and Qing cases, there was a loose paradigm of the conceptualization and functioning of the lineages that accompanied the transition from stateless life to state creation, and then the second transition from conquest states to governing orders. When referring to the period before the creation of the Jin state, for instance, the imperial history (written in Chinese) often referred to the forerunners of the lineages as "parties" (*dang*), meaning only that they were primarily recognized as groups – not exclusively as descent groups – in the management of economic life (including hunting and raiding), all consistent with early meanings of *mukūn*. As the state formed, these units – always having names, as Shirokogoroff remarked – became institutionalized parts of the army, and individuals adopted their *mukūn* names as surnames. As the armies stopped moving with the conquest of northern China and the population became more settled – and scattered, from Manchuria to northern China – the Jurchens regarded those having the same surnames as sharing actual descent from a hypothetical ancestor. Accompanying this progression was the transformation of the Jin-period *mukūn* from a working unit to a lineage concept.

A similar pattern can be seen, on a greater scale and in more detail, in the case of the formation and expansion of the Qing empire. Those documents of the seventeenth century that can dependably provide a retrospective of the previous century indicate that *mukūn* in the stateless regions of Manchuria were the primary working groups of the Jurchens; when, through small-scale warfare, some villages were absorbed, their members would also be absorbed into the conquering *mukūn*. But as increasing numbers of Jurchens immigrated to the towns and agricultural villages of southern Manchuria, as well as into the Ming province of Liaodong, *mukūn* affiliations were frequently changed or dropped altogether, as some Jurchens took up life in the style of the Koreans or Chinese, and adopted surnames appropriate to those cultures.

In Nurgaci's wars of unification, *mukūn* were again used as the fundamental organizational units. This worked well when Nurgaci expanded eastward and northward, absorbing villages and commissioning their headmen as captains in the armies. But from the earliest period it is clear that Nurgaci always had a certain number of individuals who were not really affiliated with a *mukūn*. In some cases, depending upon the immediate circumstances of the acquisition of the individual, he might simply be placed into an existing *mukūn*. But in an increasing number of cases, these individuals were placed with others like them, in the socio-military units that were the forerunners of the Chinese-martial banners. These units were called, early on, the *ujen cooha* – a term that for a long time has been translated by Qing specialists as "heavy troops," but which more likely meant "cherished troops" (see appendix II) in the sense that Nurgaci was the khan who "cherished the various peoples" (see chapter 3). At the threshold of the formation of the state, then, the *mukūn* became the fundamental criterion of identity, separating those who would later be known as "Manchu" (that is, those whose military units were based upon "companies" that were in origin *mukūn* organizations) from those who would later be known as "Chinese-martial" (whose military units were based upon created "companies").

As the conquests expanded and bureaucratic control over the Eight Banners intensified, the hold of the *mukūn* over the command of certain companies loosened – a process that took approximately a hundred years. When a majority of Manchus were eventually settled in China as a partially salaried occupation force, the original bonds of the *mukūn* deteriorated, and Manchus began to acknowledge *mukūn* ties as being primarily ancestral affiliations – though the ancestors indicated were generally no earlier than the time of Nurgaci, and many times no earlier than the occupation of China. In modern times, the *halamukūn* (a neologism of the Qing period indicating a super-relationship and a sub-relationship that in practice placed every individual within a cadet group of a large, historically romanticized lineage) emerged as a marker of Manchu identity – and status within that identity – and it is now regarded as an ancestral affiliation exclusively.

In this context it is no surprise to discover that in order for the early state of Nurgaci to use the very fluid *mukūn* as the foundation of socio-military organization, a certain amount of forgery, artificiality, and bureaucratic intervention had to be applied. It would not do for *mukūn* to be constantly formed and reformed by economic and environmental circumstance, as had traditionally been the case. When newcomers joined Nurgaci – and in Manchuria it was generally the case that the *mukūn* joined as a unit – their name would be recorded, and it would not change. Rewards, promotions, and eventually land grants went to the *mukūn* as a group. To establish the permanence of the *mukūn*, Nurgaci's servitors usually insisted a history of some kind or other be recorded, its truth or untruth being of no consequence.

In time, affairs originally managed by the *mukūn* exclusively, such as distribution of property, management of membership lists, and designation of the headman, became subject to the documentation and adjudication of the state. Historians specializing in the Qing period have belatedly realized that the regularized "300-man companies" of the middle Qing period did not reflect the original contours of the *mukūn*-based companies of the early Qing, and estimates of the conquest forces have as a result been revised numerous times. Equally important, until this process was understood, the extremely active role of the Qing state in controlling the criteria of identity for Manchus and others of the conquest elite was not fully appreciated.

Between the conquest of Liaodong in 1621 and the end of the seventeenth century, an enormous bureaucracy developed to keep track of banner genealogies, eligibilities for stipends, promotions and captaincies, trials and punishments, and rewards on the occasions of retirements, death, or proof of extraordinary service. These were not compiled into documents for general consultation until the eighteenth century, however, when the Qing court began to promote genealogies and nationalities as part of the imperial ideology. Then began a series of mass printings of banner histories, regulations, and genealogies that did not cease until the very end of the 1700s. These extensive documents, published in Chinese, may now be consulted – with due skepticism – on a variety of matters concerning the structure and functioning of the Eight Banners.

All these reflections apply equally to the imperial lineage of the Qing, which is usually referred to as the Aisin Gioro. As we shall see in chapter 3, the name and the history of the Aisin Gioro lineage was as artificial – and as necessary – as that of any other Manchu lineage. Nurgaci's *mukūn* group was certainly well formed in his own time, but it was not very precisely named, and its history had passages of obscurity despite the fact that it could claim an illustrious forebear. At what time the ancestral lineage claimed the exact name of Aisin Gioro is unclear (since the revised records maintain that it always had that name), but the reasons for its selection are more clear: In order to cut off more distantly-connected groups from claims to the rulership, in order to allow the formation of a state cult of shamanic worship based on the lineage, and in order to give the imperial history a motive.

During the height of the Qing, imperial lore attributed to Nurgaci an "intention to restore his lineage,"[4] and the campaigns of conquest were understood to be the pursuit of justice for the lineage among the Jurchens and for Jurchens ruled by the Ming empire. Since the lineage was the key to the coherence and success of the empire, it was justified in rewarding itself with the proceeds of conquest. Indeed the Aisin Gioro lineage itself became a large, highly-bureaucratized organization, with as many as thirty thousand members by the end of the nineteenth century. And that was only a fraction of the actual descendants of Nurgaci's father Taksi, since the state continually passed laws limiting admittance to the lineage, demanding expulsion of those convicted of certain criminal offenses, and striking off excessive collateral lines.

The state pursued its conquest by right of divine favor of the lineage, which maintained its righteousness by, among other things, continuing to observe shamanic communication with its patron spirits. Shirokogoroff used Tungusic culture and shamanism as his model for understanding shamanism in all societies. Though his analyses would not all be found persuasive today, it is nevertheless the case that his field studies of shamanism among the Tungusic peoples of Manchuria in the early twentieth century have left a profound mark on anthropology. Manchu shamanism in particular was regarded as such a vivid phenomenon that the vocabulary and much of the scholarship on it are irrevocably associated with the Tungusic peoples. The word "shaman," for instance, comes from the Manchu language – the only commonly-used English word that is a loan from this language – and is similar or identical to cognates from the other Tungusic languages. It described an individual believed to have experienced a spiritual death and rebirth, and as a consequence having the ability to travel to and influence the supernatural plane. This shaman, who in earlier times might be either a man or a woman, could perceive and intervene with the supernatural forces causing illness, drought, or the migration of animals. Because of the shaman's ability to ensure the success of a hunt or of a war party, it was imperative that all village or lineage leaders should be in intimate contact with shamans.

The importance of shamanism in Northeastern and Inner Asia in the centuries before and during the rise of the Jurchens is clear, and by the eleventh century the ceremonies showed the influence of practices that could be traced to the early Turkic empires, to the imperial lineage of the Tang empire (who were partly Turkic in descent and claimed dominion over some of the Turks of Central Asia), and to the Kitans. The Jurchens, like many peoples before them, knew the ceremony of sacrificing a white horse (to heaven) and a black ox (to earth) on mountain tops or other high places to commemorate auspicious events. They also observed annual sacrificial ceremonies in the spring and the fall, which had originally been associated with the seasonal hunts. And like the Kitans they practiced necromancy by shooting arrows into willow leaves, the results to be interpreted by the shamans.

Mukūn had protective spirits, and the shaman was the intercessor with those spirits for all members of the group. The connection between *mukūn* and spiritual protection was strong for all members, but was especially critical to the headman, whose position depended upon the assent of the shaman. Headmen and shamans needed to work cooperatively, and usually needed to be in proximity. Indeed a founding myth of the Jurchens insists that their archetypal early war leader was himself a shaman. His story, briefly recounted, is part of the epic cycle that is usually known today as *The Tale of the Nisan Shamaness.*[5]

During the Qing, the imperial lineage developed a complex of shamanic rituals. A special temple with imposing statuary was constructed in the palace complex at Mukden after it became the Qing capital in 1621, and once the imperial lineage was installed at the new capital at Peking in 1644, the Kunning Palace was outfitted for a variety of shamanic rituals, including being equipped with a special row of ovens for the cooking of sacrificial meats, and a "spirit pole" for the hoisting of sacrifices to heaven. Shamanic dances and processions were staged in the open areas of the Forbidden City (*zijin cheng*) on holidays, and often featured reenactments of Nurgaci at the hunt. In the eighteenth century the court even ordered the compilation of a sort of encyclopedia of its shamanic rituals, including detailed drawings of necessary implements (some of which were known only by Chinese terms, an indication that there was continuing innovation in religious practice by the imperial lineage, which needed loanwords to describe these items).

Shamanism, like many other elements of folk culture, is difficult to trace in the Manchu communities which in the Qing period were scattered from Manchuria to Central Asia and all parts of China. There is anecdotal evidence, however, that the Manchus of the provincial garrisons retained at least occasional shamanic practices, and many put up spirit poles in their private homes (as was the custom among the aristocracy in Peking) after they received permission in the eighteenth century to reside apart from the garrisons. In Manchuria itself, there evidently continued many traditions that had a strong connection to the ancient beliefs of the region. These cultural survivals made possible Shirokogoroff and Ling's field research. Similarly, the *Tale of the Nisan Shamaness*, though not redacted until the early twentieth century, clearly contains some very ancient elements, and, because it was recorded so late from an oral source, is also an indispensable monument of modern spoken Manchu.

The Manchu Language and the Altaic Idea

The Jurchen language was relatively closely related to Evenk, Gold, Orochon, Nani, and other languages of the hunting and fishing peoples of Northeastern Asia and the Russian Maritime Province. It was evidently but much more remotely connected to Korean, Japanese, and Okinawan. By the time of Nurgaci, the language spoken by his followers had been enriched by a vocabulary laced with words derived from Mongolian, Russian, Chinese, Turkic, Arabic, and, ultimately, Hebrew (as for instance *doro*, "law," from Mongolian *dörö*, from Hebrew *torah*). In Qing and modern times Manchu has had, apart from the standard language, one important dialect in Sibo (see appendix III), which is now recognized by the government of the People's Republic as a distinct language. Manchu proper has had many subdialects, from the earliest times to the present day, though the eighteenth-century Qing court did all it could to minimize dialects and other forms of cultural informality.

Because knowledge of medieval written Jurchen was abandoned by the Jurchen descendants in later centuries, examples of ideographic-script Jurchen have been preserved, without revision, for modern scholars to use in the reconstruction of pre-modern Tungusic languages. This has been a critical addition to the database used by cultural and linguistic historians, who over the past two centuries have developed the theory of the Altaic language family. This Altaic idea was prompted by the realization, beginning in the late eighteenth century, that many languages of Eurasia shared a great number of grammatical characteristics. Many were based upon a fairly simple subject–object–verb word order. Moreover, instead of changing the vowel sounds within words in order to express tense or case as the Indo-European languages did, these Eurasian languages were agglutinative, which is to say that they added syllables to show tense, and inserted particles into the sentences to show case. Such similarities could be observed in languages as far-flung as Finnish, Latvian, and Hungarian in Europe, the many Turkic languages of the Middle East and Central Asia, Mongolian, the Manchurian languages such as Jurchen, Korean, and Japanese, and in some northwestern American languages, particularly the Aleut group. The "Altaic" name was taken for the theory because the Altaic mountains of Central Asia are in the very approximate center of the geocultural spectrum in question.

The Altaic languages appear to fall into subdivisions, primarily the Turkic, Mongolian, and Tungusic groups. In general these categories have some geographical shape, so that the Turkic languages are westerly, the Mongolian in Central and Inner Asia, and the Tungusic languages the most easterly; but this is only a broad generalization. In fact, smatterings of the groups may be found in very complex patterns. For instance, speakers of Mongolian languages are found in Afghanistan and in China, and speakers of Turkic languages, such as the Yakuts, are found in the extremes of Manchuria. These complexities arise from the fact that the peoples associated with the Altaic languages are generally assumed to have originated in the region of Siberia, and spread out in chronologically distinct waves from there in various directions across Eurasia. Each wave of migration buried earlier patterns, but not completely. The earliest known waves were probably of Turkic speakers, who may have included the Xiongnu who battled the Han empire in China, and the Huns and Avars who later invaded Europe. Much later came the Mongolian speakers, including the soldiers of the Mongol empire who conquered and occupied an enormous expanse of Eurasia in the thirteenth and fourteenth centuries.

The Tungusic peoples have a more limited but more dense distribution, in Manchuria, the Aleutian Straits, and northwest

America. Within Manchuria, the group was divided into northern and southern branches. The northern branch included, among those still surviving Evenk, Orochon, and the dialects of the Sakhalin Islands, north of Japan. The southern branch included Jurchen, Gold, and Orok. All the languages preserve a large number of Turkic and Mongolian loanwords, testimony to ancient and continuous contact among Manchuria, Mongolia, and Siberia.

The familial relationships of the language, of course, had very little to do with the history of writing the language. In Nurgaci and in Qing times, Manchu was written with a syllabary. This was a dramatic departure from the way in which medieval Jurchen had been written. But it brought Manchu culture into the sphere of Eurasian cultural influences generally, because there has only been one phonetic invention; Manchu came to represent its easternmost manifestation.

All known phonetic scripts derive from a single origin, the ideographic script of ancient Egypt. Around 1000 BCE, many peoples of the eastern Mediterranean – including the Phoenicians for whom the systems are named – had begun to simplify some features of the complex "hieroglyphics" ("sacred script") of the Egyptians. More important, they associated the written elements with the sounds of the words, and not with the meanings. In these new scripts, a finite number of elements could be used in infinite combination to represent spoken language.

As the Greek and Roman script families were developing in the western Mediterranean, their eastern Mediterranean cousins continued to advance. Aramaic script, in which a portion of the Bible was originally written, predominated in Syria, Lebanon, and ancient Palestine. At an early point, a running script was derived from Aramaic and transmitted westward to northern India. This system, called Devanagari, was used to write the Sanskrit classics as early as the sixth century BCE, and a few centuries later became the primary script of Buddhism. It was carried to Southeast Asia in the early centuries CE and became the foundation of writing in those countries where Indian influence was strong. In the seventh century, it became known in Tibet, and provided the foundation of the script in which Tibetan is still written.

Syriac script, from which Arabic script would be derived in the seventh century, was taken up in the early centuries CE by the Sogdian people of eastern Iran, who were active in the Central

Asian trade and frequently traveled as far as China. The neighbors of the Sogdians, the Turkic Uigurs, adapted the Syriac script for the writing of their own language. They made it distinctively their own by writing the language from top to bottom, which meant that they rotated it by ninety degrees counterclockwise. This seems to have been in imitation of the Chinese script that was prestigious in Central Asia during the height of the influence of the Tang empire (about 650–750 CE). From the Uigurs, the Mongols later adopted the script, and with modifications it was used to write both Mongolian and Manchu until the twentieth century.

Medieval Jurchen, however, had been written in another manner altogether. Through conquest, monumental architecture, and the invention of paper, the early Chinese empires established the Chinese ideographic script as supreme in Eastern Asia. Because the writing was ideographic, it was not necessary to speak Chinese to understand it, and the characters of Chinese could be used to represent the meanings of almost any word in any other language. This allowed communication throughout Eastern Asia among educated people, regardless of their native language. But the system was difficult to learn to read and to write, and so literacy remained limited to an extremely small proportion of the population. Moreover, word order and nuances of meaning did not carry well from one language to another, and there could be many difficulties in translating. The elites of Eastern Asia generally resolved these difficulties by simply learning the grammar and pronunciation of Chinese, and reading the Chinese classics for historical teaching, moral guidance, and entertainment.

From the time of the Tang empire, the peoples of Central and Northern Asia were acquainted with both the phonetic systems of Western Asia and the ideographic system of Eastern Asia. After the fall of the Tang in the very early tenth century, the Kitans who founded the Liao empire, the Minyaks who founded the Tanggut empire, and later the Jurchens who founded the Jin empire all devised writing systems in which ideographic writing derived from Chinese was combined with some phonetic elements. They all show their derivation from Chinese writing, but were also able to represent the grammatical elements of the languages.

The arrangement of the Kitan script was especially striking, because in its use of a square arrangement of the sound elements it seems both to reflect the syllabic Uigur script and to anticipate the structure of the *han'gul* script which was later invented in

Korea. The *han'gul* script is truly phonetic, and uses a small number of abstract symbols to represent the sounds of Korean words. It has often been claimed that *han'gul* script is the only original phonetic script of eastern Asia, but it is more probable that *han'gul* was modeled on Kitan, which was in turn modeled on Uigur, which was derived from the Semitic Syriac scripts of Western Asia. The most important clue, perhaps, to this relationship is the use in *han'gul* of a marker for *aleph* (the unvoiced initial vowel of the Syriac-derived scripts). Ongoing research suggests other possible influences on the origins and developments of *han'gul*, all having connections with the Uigur-derived scripts.[6]

The Kitans had devised a so-called "large-character" script, which used ideographs derived from Chinese but unintelligible to those not specifically educated in Kitan. They also created a "small-character" script, which contained compounded phonetic elements. The Jurchen Jin language was written in a script adopted virtually without alteration from the Kitans, whose Liao empire the Jurchens had destroyed in 1121. The Kitans had spoken a language more closely related to Mongolian, probably, than to any other surviving language. As such it was not identical to Jurchen. But in its most basic grammatical structure – its Altaic features – Kitan resembled Jurchen. By contrast, medieval Chinese was monosyllabic and without case particles.

The Jurchen script survived the downfall of the Jin empire, and had at least some official recognition under the Yuan empire of the Mongols (*c.*1260–1368), who carved *dharāni*, or Buddhist prayers, in the language on major gateways and other monumental displays. In Ming times it was the official mode of communications between the Jurchen functionaries of the fictive "garrison" system in Manchuria and the Chinese court.[7] The Yongning temple, at the military settlement in present-day Heilongjiang province, was inscribed in Chinese, Mongolian, and the Jurchen script, like the Juyong Pass constructed by the Mongols near Peking – one of several Rosetta stones that have permitted reconstruction of medieval Jurchen.

In later times, Jurchens protested against the use of the medieval script in official communications. The Jianzhou Jurchens from among whom the early Qing state arose, for instance, were part of the eastern Jurchens – those who were in much closer contact with the Korean court than with the Chinese – who had lost this script. The date when they ceased to use it is unclear, but the "Translators' Bureau" of the Ming tributary bureaucracy received a communication from the eastern Jurchens in 1444 that stated, "Nobody out here in the forty garrisons understands Jurchen script, so please write to us in Mongolian [*dada*] from now on."[8] Korean emissaries to the headquarters of the Jianzhou Jurchen chieftains in the late sixteenth century had noted repeatedly that the headmen demanded that communications be neither in Jurchen, which they could not read, nor in the Chinese used by the Koreans, but in Mongolian.

Qing imperial history attributes the great change in this to Nurgaci. It is reported that one day in 1599 he had the idea of using the phonetic Mongolian script to write Jurchen, and instructed two of his *bakši*, or literate men (from Mongolian *baghshi* and ultimately from Chinese *boshi*, earlier pronounced *bakse*, "an erudite"), to devise a suitable system. They demurred at first, protesting that the present method of using Mongolian was ancient and seemed in no need of alteration. This caused Nurgaci to thunder, "The Chinese write their own speech, the Mongols write their own speech. Are you telling me that it is better for us all to continue learning and writing a foreign language than for you to find a way for us to write our own?" The two learneds withdrew and devised a new Jurchen script, the historical marker for the beginning of Manchu.

The shift to the new script was troublesome and there is no evidence that an upsurge in literacy among Jurchens ensued. The Koreans, who knew both old Jurchen and Mongolian, did not know this new thing, and for considerable time foreign communications were handled just as they had been before: Mongolian remained the *lingua franca*. Moreover, the new device, which like all of its Syriac-derived ancestors up to Mongolian was unvocalized, confused many readers who could not easily associate the written word with the spoken, partly due to the impracticability of using Mongolian vowel harmony in deciphering Jurchen words. Not until 1632 did the Jin khan Hung Taiji (later the first emperor of the Qing) sponsor a means of vocalizing the script by the addition of circles and dots, which was thereafter called the "circled and dotted script."[9] This allowed the state, for the first time, to represent the actual sounds of Manchu.

Due partly to the logistical needs of the national archives in the People's Republic of China, partly to a change in professional attitudes among specialists of the Qing, and partly to some ethnic enthusiasms among modern Manchus, the language has undergone something of a revival in the late twentieth century. Written resources have made this possible. There are not only the vast reserves of documents from the Qing period, but also some indication of the changes in popular Manchu during the later Qing. *The Tale of the Nisan Shamaness* reflects spoken Manchu of the early twentieth century, and may be compared to the fragments of drum songs and popular stories performed by bannermen in China in the nineteenth century, many portraying a rhyme scheme and alliteration which the Manchu specialist Giovanni Stary has pronounced "typical of the poetry of many Altaic peoples."[10] There are also new publications, including regional histories of the autonomous counties of Inner Mongolia and Manchuria, which are written in a modern, colloquial style.

The Ethnographer from Seoul: Sin Chung-il among the Jurchens

Connections, sometimes friendly and sometimes hostile, between the Jurchens and Korea were old. People calling themselves Jurchens were settled as far south as Hamhǔng in north central Korea at the beginning of the twelfth century. The Yi court from its inception in the late 1300s had considered some Jurchen headmen as useful allies, and it honored the Jurchen Li Douran (Yi Turan), who had become a loyal attendant of Yi Song-gye, the founder of the Yi dynasty. But the creation of the Yi order in Korea had included intense military campaigns to drive Jurchens northward toward the Yalu River and ultimately beyond it, into present-day Manchuria. Among the Jurchens resisting the Korean advance was one Li Manzhu, whom Yi military forces contained at the Pozhu river north of the Yalu in 1434. In the same year Li's rival – the leader of the Jianzhou (then called Odori) Jurchens, Möngke Temür (a Mongolian name meaning "enduring iron") – and his son Agu were killed fighting other Jurchens in northern Korea. Ostensibly the Jianzhou Jurchens were now at peace with the Yi court. But to the Korean rulers, distinctions between Jianzhou Jurchens and the "wildmen" the Jianzhou claimed to be suppressing were hard to maintain, and their records normally refer to all Jurchens as "wildmen" (*ya'in*).

By the late 1500s relations between the Jianzhou Jurchens and the Yi dynasty had again become very tense. The Jianzhou, now ruled by a putative descendant of Möngke Temür named Nurgaci, were rich and powerful. They not only specialized, as they had for many centuries, in supplying China and Korea with precious natural goods but were also, by the sixteenth century, accomplished agriculturists, who supported a growing population on rich soil growing wheat and millet. They were also possessors of a few industrial secrets, particularly relating to the processing of ginseng and dying of cloth. Their access to Ming trading towns such as Fushun, Kaiyuan, and Tieling in Liaodong, and to Mamp'ojin on the Korean border, was critical to their continued wealth and power. The Jurchen trade was both coveted and feared by China and by Korea, each of which attempted to regulate and tax the trade while heavily arming their frontier outposts. Such tactics were resented by the Jurchens, and in the 1590s both China and Korea attempted, unsuccessfully, to enter into negotiations with Nurgaci that would restrict his commercial privileges and his territorial expansion.

Sin Chung-il's mission to the Jianzhou Jurchens was occasioned by an incident of 1594. Several Jurchens, led by a man named Saishangga, had crossed south of the Yalu and been slain by Korean border troops. It was the latest in a series of killings on both sides of the Yalu, dating back to the notorious murder of the Korean Sin Se-son and the settlers he had led into Jurchen territory in 1528, and there and continued a chain of dramas associated with stolen or killed people and livestock. In 1595 the Jianzhou Jurchens were in possession of at least seventeen Koreans who had been recently captured and were being held for ransom. To attempt to resolve the latest imbroglio, Sin was dispatched by the Korean court to Nurgaci's capital. He and a small party of officials crossed the Yalu (to them, the Amnok) at Mamp'ojin, followed a series of tributaries north and west to the Suksu Valley where Nurgaci was based, at Fe Ala.

The world through which Sin's party journeyed was in the grip of its harsh winter, but was otherwise a hospitable land. Its abundant rivers and forests yielded the products upon which the Jurchens were growing wealthy, and where land had been cleared Sin saw stretches of abundant fallow, sometimes alongside pastures where the prized horses of the Jurchens were guarded. Sin found Jurchen society to be organized into villages, usually of twenty households or less, most of them clustered along the forested riverbanks. Outside the concentrations, distances between settlements could be great. Commoners normally carried cured grain in their traveling packs, and when necessary undertook treks of three or four days' duration. Some villages depended upon fishing, pine-nut and ginseng gathering, or pelt-taking for their livelihoods, and were relocated after several years in order to exploit fresh gathering areas or animal populations. Other villages were agricultural, producing wheat, millet, glutinous millet, and barley. As a rule farm settlements were large, with possibly as many as fifty households, and more stratified than the hunting and gathering villages of the forests. Most households, whether agricultural or gathering, were home to a variety of animals; Sin noted chickens, pigs, geese, ducks, sheep, goats, dogs, and cats roaming the homesteads.

The agricultural villages were overseen by headmen who surrounded themselves with armed retainers, and at least a portion of the field work was done by slaves – Chinese, Koreans, or other Jurchens who had been kidnapped for the purpose. Contention among the villages for fields, water, grazing, and hunting had intensified in the fifteenth century. This was partly due to population growth among the Jurchens. The accumulation of captive farm workers from Korea and Liaodong made possible a sharp increase in agricultural output in the 1500s, along with an apparent increase in the population density of the territories. But by the last decade of the century productivity was falling, possibly because of a downward cycle in annual temperatures that would dampen agricultural output for decades to come. The competition among Jurchen villages was also, however, a result of the pincers effect of Ming and Yi military campaigns; the Ming held the line against further westward expansion, the Yi kept pushing the Jurchens north from Korea. The concentration of immigrants in Manchuria, as well as the growth in resident population, sparked frequent contentions among the villages.

For defense, villages depended upon the utilization of lineage and economic links to create federations (*aiman*). Raids upon settlements during which cattle, farm implements, and weapons were stolen, or people were taken to serve the raiders as slaves, were common. Fields were patroled by armed men while other freemen, women, and slaves labored within. No man left his own village without a bow and arrows, and if possible a sword or large knife, to defend himself against murder or kidnapping. One avoided traveling alone. Friends and relatives accompanied a visitor back to his home settlement in parties, and women traveled in carts, surrounded by cohorts of male relatives and family retainers.

Fortified homesteads and small villages were an ancient tradition in Manchuria. The Chinese histories of the fourth and fifth centuries noted that the Wuji had stockaded settlements. Walled towns were built by the Kitans among the Mohes. The earthen walls of the original Parhae double town at present-day Ussurijsk (formerly Nigorsk, northwest of Vladivostok) were still visible in the nineteenth century. Respecting the wars of unification among the Jurchens before the Jin empire, there is frequent mention in the records of settlements called in Chinese *cheng* or *bao*, "fortified villages," controlled by individual lineages or lineage leaders for the same period.

Jurchens of the sixteenth century sustained the practice energetically. Every home was surrounded by a wooden fence, some of them insubstantial pickets that only announced the poverty of the household within, others stout stockades on stone or earthen foundations. Some large villages had, in addition, rammed-earth fortifications with wooden gates, secured on the inside by huge wooden bars. Such installations bespoke the presence of well-organized *aiman*, united under the protective power and distributive authority of a hegemon, or *beile* (see appendix III).

The *beile* was recognized as the "lord" (*ejen*) of the fields, animals, supplies, goods, and people under his control. He had the exclusive right to designate other headmen within his federation as owners and to grant them estates of fields, animals, and people. It appears that distribution and redistribution of property by the *beile* was an extension of shamanic rights, suggesting either an amalgamation of political and spiritual functions or displacement of the latter by the former. In earliest times, for instance, it was shamans who punished murderers by the removal of their flocks and property, and shamans who condemned evil households to ruin by damning their herds. By Sin's time it appears that the *beile*'s rights of ownership had subsumed some of these shamanic functions. The right was, however, paradoxical, in the sense that it was in practice an obligation. To remain supreme within his federation, a *beile* was required to create other men as owners and often to enhance their holdings. In his own interest he might attempt to adjust the amount of grants to his supporters and their frequency, but he was by custom and by necessity required to give. This was fundamental to his definition as *beile*.

Nearby villages could capitulate to the *beile* or test their strength against him. Should they choose the latter and lose, they would thereafter enjoy his protection from the raids of others, in return for which they would supply the *beile* with a portion of their grain, with people to serve as his slaves, with young men to be his soldiers, and with women for the *beile* or his male relatives or retainers. The *beile* would recognize a headman from the village, and he might, if circumstances were favorable, either marry into the *beile*'s family or have the *beile* marry into his. Such marriage alliances were not exclusive, since every *beile* – and many men of means – had multiple wives, and the number of wives grew with the number of important connections any man had to maintain. The ability of the *beile* to extend his territorial and matrimonial reach grew with each added village. The safety of every village grew with the power of the *beile* to whom it was affiliated.

No *beile* could be personally secure, and often he and his family lived in a fortified compound within the walled village. His status within his own *aiman* was dependent upon his ability to continue to gain and distribute booty, grain, and protection. The most powerful *beile*s attempted to acquire exclusive commercial privileges in their relationships with Ming China and Yi Korea. The hope was not only to gain immediate riches but also to enlist the military aid of the Ming or the Yi in maintaining the *beile*'s own position against local rivals. An influential *beile* enjoyed the advantage of being able to promise no assaults against the border defenses of the Ming or the Yi as long as rewards and titles were forthcoming from the courts. But aid could be dependent upon his supplying the Ming or the Yi with information or supplies useful in their own military ventures. Every *beile* who pursued a relationship with the imperial powers was also a master of spies, a geopolitical strategist, and a tempting target for assassination.

With wider territories and hierarchies of ownership came the *beile*'s privilege to reorganize some patterns within the villages. The *beile* himself and his lords each had designated *tokso*, or agricultural grants. Some fields became wholly worked by slaves and their produce monopolized by the elite of the federation. As that elite enlarged or rankings were altered, populations transferred from the control of one *beile* to another. Individuals who could write any Chinese characters or the Mongolian syllabary were extremely rare, and were usually not affiliated with lineages; they invariably entered the service of the *beile*, and would leave it only if given away or taken by a more powerful *beile*. Lineages sacrificed some of their autonomy, particularly their exclusive right to determine guilt and mete out punishments, which was frequently assumed by the *beile* or his advisors.

A circumspect *beile* frequently destroyed smoke towers in villages too close to enemy territory to chance signals being sent by untrustworthy subjects; Nurgaci himself raided the Chinese territories contiguous to him to knock down the towers so that Ming outlooks would not spy upon him. It was common for *beile*s to monopolize the manufacture of arrows and iron weapons and forbid artisans to work at these enterprises in the free villages. Fletchers' shops and smithies were located within the *beile*'s walls, or sometimes just outside them. Those who wished to purchase weapons had to come to the *beile*'s residence and apply for permission. In times of military mobilization, the *beile* authorized his lieutenants to distribute arrows to the village headmen. By the sixteenth century a war leader, whether a *beile* or a lineage headman (*mukūnda*), could enjoy the command rank "lord of arrows" (*nirui ejen*) – later the Manchu title for a captain of the "companies" within the Eight Banners.

Cultural variety was one of the distinctive features of the landscape Sin crossed. He observed a society in which a remarkable diversity of peoples – immigrants from the Ming territories, Koreans, Jurchens from many regions, some traditional peoples of further Manchuria, and Mongols – were being united under the rule of the family of Nurgaci, and were beginning to play roles that were increasingly specialized and complex. As diverse as the peoples present in Nurgaci's domain were the cultural influences. Chinese, Mongolian, Tibetan, Turkic, and Korean languages, religions, and folk cultures were known in some form, and Nurgaci was beginning to use them to make himself an appealing leader.

Partially or fully pastoral groups, whom Sin called "Tartars" (*daji, dazi*: see chapter 1), roamed the open areas. The latter group included representatives of the northern cultures of the Hūlun confederacy, stretching across northern Liaodong and Jilin, a region in which Mongol and Jurchen elements had combined to create a distinct culture more strongly attached to the northerly Mongol populations than to the southerly groups affiliated with

Nurgaci. Mongol soldiers had been present in Manchuria since it had been conquered by the Yuan empire in the thirteenth century. Many had stayed on in Liaodong as mercenaries in the employ of the Ming, and some of that population had drifted eastward to Manchuria. In contrast to the Jurchens, the Mongols whom Sin saw were still primarily pastoral. They kept their yurts on wagons, as their steppe cousins did, and almost always dressed in furs.

Sin was equally interested in another group of immigrants, men from the Ming province of Liaodong. Shortly after his morning arrival at Fe Ala, Sin was ushered into a parlor in the company of three such men. All had been born in Liaodong, and two were natives of the town of Fushun. It is not clear that Sin could pick these individuals out at sight, for he provides no description of them, as he does of Mongols. They were distinguished for him only by their ability to speak Chinese in addition to Jurchen. Sin was completely dependent upon these Liaodongese followers of Nurgaci for his communications and his care, and he noted with pain that among his handlers only one was literate. "Apart from this man, there is nobody else who is at ease with writing, and nobody is learning."

Sin made special note of the case of Kim Adun of Giyamuhu, who spoke some Korean but kept his distance from the visitor. The year before, when the latest difficulties south of the Yalu had arisen, it had been Kim Adun who led the Jurchen troops south to talk peace. Sin knew something of Kim's background. His father, called by the Jurchens Jeocangga, had originally been from Ming Liaodong, but had spent time in Korea and readily assimilated Korean ways. In recognition of this the Yi court had awarded Jeocangga the name Kim Ki-song, and the stipend of a minor official. Kim Adun himself had been stationed at Nurgaci's successive headquarters eight or nine years by the time Sin saw him at Fe Ala in 1596, "and because his father had submitted to Nurgaci this is his native land, and he will not come away." Indeed Adun was still at Nurgaci's side when the Jin state was formed in 1618.

Nurgaci had several policies for unifying these diverse peoples under his leadership, but the most profound was the system of social, economic, and military organization that would later take the form of the Eight Banners. Historians normally date the appearance of the banners to 1601, the year in which the annals mention the inauguration of the original four banners. However, Sin's observations suggest that in 1595 the banners were already present in some form. He noted that on excursions away from Fe Ala Nurgaci was accompanied by about a hundred mounted men, each armed with bows and arrows and each carrying his own supply of grain. The troops raised banners as they rode, each about twenty inches in length, and the colors Sin noted were important: yellow, white, red, blue, and black. With the exception of black, these were the colors of the divisions of the four original banners. The black flag would be flown by the Chinese-martial units until their reorganization and absorption into the Eight Banners in 1642.

Though Sin noted the variegations in local cultures, he also observed that those who served Nurgaci were strictly required to be uniform in their dress and hairstyles. This meant that they shaved a portion of their scalp, near the front, and kept the remaining hair very long, plaited into a single braid. The shaving of a part of the skull and arrangement of remaining hair in some distinctive fashion was an ancient institution of Manchuria, always serving to indicate the social and political affiliation of the individual. Similarly, the men all dressed in the leather boots, breeches, and tunics (the material determined by the season and the rank of the wearer) that were traditional to the Jurchens. The sartorial policy was, like others of Nurgaci's prescriptions, intended to create a uniformity that would transcend the cultural ambiguities and diversities that were characteristic of the populations he was uniting. Ironically, the Manchu "pigtail," intended by Nurgaci as a mark of inclusion, would in ensuing centuries be reviled by generations of Chinese men as the brand of exclusion, and of subordination to their barbarian conquerors.

3

The Enigma of Nurgaci

In the film *Indiana Jones and the Temple of Doom*, the opening scene depicts a meeting among Asian underworld leaders at a remote Himalayan inn during the 1930s. They are gathered to exchange a great deal of wealth for a small blue vial containing "the essence of Nurgaci." In the excitement provoked by the sight of the vial, pandemonium breaks out, and the story's hero makes his first encounter with his archenemy (and apparent Manchu), Lao Che.[1]

Fascination with Nurgaci[2] has been partly due to the fact that in the Western imagination he is seen as a hero of the traditional cultures of the northeast Asian peoples, in many ways reminiscent of great native American chiefs like Tecumseh, Geronimo, or Sitting Bull. But unlike these military geniuses among doomed peoples, Nurgaci won, and the settled, technologically advanced, "superior" civilization was conquered by the horse-riding, arrow-shooting, shamanistic, "tribal" culture. Beyond these fanciful associations, however, there are other reasons for the enduring interest in Nurgaci. He was the putative founder of one of the world's great empires and a colorful personality in his own right. To the historian, there are intriguing tensions among the representations of Nurgaci in folk literature, in the later ideology of the Qing empire, and in the contemporary documents. Depending upon the point of view, he is a proverbial poor boy made good, or the scion of a special lineage destined to rule, or a ruthless conqueror, or a sagely conciliator.

Myth is not necessarily falsehood or fantasy. It is a way of folding interpretations inside one another to create a coherent and if possible persuasive narrative of the origins of cultural authority or political power. The myths of Nurgaci served such purposes. Yet to the historian, Nurgaci need not remain lost in a fog of time and legend. He was in fact rather well documented in his lifetime, and not only by those who inherited his mantle. Indeed through the records of the Korean court officials and private individuals, through the writings of Chinese officials in Liaodong and the Ming annals, and through the early Qing records in the Manchu language, we can assemble one of the most candid portraits of any historical figure.

The Myth of the Avenger

An image of Nurgaci that was central to the historical ideology of the Qing empire was that of the righteous young avenger who rallied and unified the Jurchens in order to seek redress for wrongs committed against his family by Ming officials in Manchuria. In this persona he is the subject of story cycles that still survive in northeastern China. In one version, Nurgaci was not born among the Jurchens at all, but was an orphan boy from the town of Fushun, on the frontier of the Ming empire. The story continues: A powerful Ming general, Li Chengliang, admired the boy's qualities and decided to take him into his home as a servant and protégé. One day, when helping Li bathe, the boy Nurgaci noticed two birthmarks on Li's feet, and asked what their prophetic meaning might be. Li replied that they were the stigmata of a man destined to be a ruler. Nurgaci blurted out that he himself had seven birthmarks on his own feet, and showed them to Li.

That night Li confided to his wife the meaning of the discovery: The boy Nurgaci was the predestined leader of the Jurchens whom Li was now governing in the name of the Ming empire. Li had been given a mission by the Ming court to find and kill this future ruler, who it was feared would lead the Jurchens in revolt. Li rejoiced at the good fortune of finding his prey to be still a relatively defenseless boy, and living under his own roof. He decided to murder Nurgaci.

Li's wife took pity on the boy, and secretly informed him of Li's intentions. Immediately Nurgaci fled the compound, taking with him a horse and a dog that had befriended him during his stay. When Li discovered that his wife had helped Nurgaci escape, he killed her, and then led his troops out to find and execute the fugitive. They burnt the woods through which he fled, and the dog perished in the conflagration. The horse died of exhaustion attempting to carry Nurgaci to safety. When, on foot and surrounded, Nurgaci was nearly spotted by Li's forces, a flock of magpies covered him from view, and he finally arrived at a Jurchen village, where he was quickly adopted. His natural leadership abilities combined with his enmity toward Li to make him in fact the victorious rebel leader of the Jurchens. He established sacred rites honoring Li's martyred wife, made the magpie the patron spirit of his lineage, exempted dogs from being blood sacrifices, and named his empire Qing in honor of the black color (in Chinese, *qing*) of the horse on which he had escaped Li's home.[3]

Though this story is exuberantly fictitious, it is suggestive of several facts that the records confirm. As we have seen in the previous chapter, the connections between the Liaodong territory governed by the Ming and the nearby Jurchen territories where Nurgaci grew up were strong, and complex. Nurgaci was obviously never an orphan on the streets of Fushun, but it is clear that he, together with his father Taksi and grandfather Giocangga, were very frequent visitors to the town, and may indeed have felt at home there. They went to Fushun frequently to trade horses and the products from the Jurchen territories, and also sojourned in Fushun on their way to official visits to Peking. So in a backhanded way this tale pays tribute to the deep familiarity of Nurgaci with Fushun and the Ming province in Liaodong. Moreover, Li Chengliang (1526–1618) was a real person, who had indeed a double-edged relationship to Nurgaci. To understand the ironic representation of Li Chengliang in the folk tale, one must contrast the strong depiction of Nurgaci in Qing imperial historical narrative as a righteous rebel against the Ming with the more contemporary portrait from Chinese and Korean sources, then put the real Li Chengliang in the middle of that contrast.

Li Chengliang's formal rank was military governor of Liaodong from 1570 to 1591, and from 1601 to 1609. Though Qing records often describe him as Chinese, more detailed documents tend to refer to his ancestors as Koreans who had migrated to Liaodong. In fact it is at least equally likely that his distant ancestors were Jurchens from the vicinity of the Yalu river, who at some point assumed the Korean surname of Yi (Li), and later migrated north and west to Liaodong. With the exception of a forced ten-year sojourn in Peking between his periods as governor, Li spent his entire life in Liaodong, and though he enjoyed the rank, pay, and privileges of a Ming military officer, he was in fact the virtual satrap of the province. He raised his own taxes, formed his own alliances (frequently with powerful Jurchen leaders), and distributed wealth and privileges to his family, expecting one of his sons to some day succeed him as ruler of the region.

In the Qing official history written after the conquest of China, Li is depicted as an implacable enemy of Nurgaci's father Taksi and grandfather Giocangga, who according to this version of history were rightful rulers of Manchuria. Not content to control Liaodong province, Li constantly sought to make inroads into the Jurchen territories, and therefore plotted to destroy the power – or the persons – of Giocangga and Taksi. Finally, in 1582, he found his opportunity. He mounted an attack against Atai, who had married into Giocangga's family and was a grandfather of Nurgaci. When Giocangga and Taksi rushed to Atai's fort at Mount Gure to aid him, Li's troops surrounded the stronghold and killed everyone inside.

The imperial narrative continues with a description of how the young Nurgaci – 23 years old at the time – publicly denounced Li for the murders of Giocangga and Taksi, and then began to gather around him the soldiers and the weapons necessary to attack Li's forces in Liaodong to reap revenge. Because Li was a clever and duplicitous man, there were naturally many among the Jurchens who were his secret allies, and so Nurgaci had first to consolidate his base among the Jurchen villages and federations before he was strong enough to confront the Ming directly. When this initial phase was achieved, he turned his attention fully against the Ming forces in Liaodong, and in 1618 – publicly repeating his outrage at the murders of his father and grandfather – he openly declared war on the Ming. By 1621 Liaodong was conquered, and had he not died as a result of wounds suffered in battle in 1626, Nurgaci would have carried his war of revenge all the way to Peking.

Contemporary annals, most of them local records from Liaodong province or annals from the Ming court at Peking, give a starkly different picture both of Li Chengliang and of Nurgaci. It is certain that far from being an implacable foe of Giocangga and Taksi, Li Chengliang was in fact their patron. Giocangga and Taksi, though descended from the great Jurchen leader Möngke Temür (see chapter 2), were not themselves extremely powerful in the Jurchen world of the late 1500s, and they cultivated the favor of Li Chengliang to make themselves wealthy in the Liaodong trade, and also to consolidate their political position among the Jurchens who lived at the Liaodong borders. Nurgaci himself was involved in this alliance with Li Chengliang. The youth, already well over six feet tall and imposing in every way, was regularly seen presenting himself at scuffles and skirmishes to defend Li's authority or reputation. From a young age Nurgaci was included in the rewards Li bestowed upon Giocangga and Taksi, and may even have accompanied Li, Giocangga, and Taksi to Peking at least once to enjoy the hospitality of the Ming emperor.

Once Li's disfavor fell upon Atai, the latter's marriage tie to Giocangga's family seems to have done little to secure their support. It will never be possible to know precisely why Giocangga and Taksi were present at the assault upon Mount Gure, but there is no evidence – and nothing in their known relationship with Li Chengliang – to suggest that they were there to aid Atai against Li. Nor is there evidence explaining their deaths in the battle. They may have been targeted accidentally by Li's troops, or Li may have taken advantage of the occasion to rid himself of allies whose ambitions he considered to have outweighed their usefulness to him. More tantalizingly, it is possible that Nurgaci himself was present at the assault on Mount Gure. His absence, certainly, would demand explanation, since he had hitherto been a visible and vigorous follower of Li, and would have been unlikely to have failed to join his father and grandfather in this campaign to eradicate a man who was both a target of Li's prosecution and a rival to Nurgaci's family for power among the Jurchens.

Contemporary records show that Nurgaci pursued a series of petitions with Li requesting reparations for the deaths of Giocangga and Taksi. Li turned Taksi's body over to Nurgaci for burial (Giocangga had been burned to death), and met with Nurgaci – whom he now recognized as the leader of the Jianzhou Jurchens – several times to hear arguments that the family should be compensated. But Li refused to pay the reparations. Nurgaci professed himself betrayed, and decided to force the issue. In order to impress Li, Nurgaci had first to amass and coordinate all local resources. It took a long time, and the first to feel the heat of Nurgaci's ostensible lust for revenge were the Jurchen villages surrounding his own territory. Beginning with his famous thirteen suits of armor, he and his stalwarts quickly began the campaigns of intimidation, ingratiation, marriage alliance, and the domination of hunting, gathering, farming, mining, and trade that would create the foundation of a state.

By the fall of 1584 Nurgaci had moved toward the west – that is, toward Liaodong and particularly the critical trading town of Fushun. His forces were considerably augmented in the years 1587 and 1588, when many large villages surrendered to him. In the latter year alone he received three groups of five hundred or more each. In 1591 Nurgaci began the inevitable confrontation with the great Hūlun confederacy that would determine whether he or they would dominate Manchuria. He resisted a demand that he return land to a Hūlun group, and in 1593 successfully defended his villages against a concerted attempt by the Hūluns, Mongols, and other Jurchen groups to dislodge him. In 1594 came the pivotal confrontation with a subgroup of the Hūlun. The enemy may have had as many as 30,000 men in the field, who were routed and then followed by Nurgaci's Jianzhou troops until "the corpses filled the ditches and the streams," resulting in more than 4000 dead on the Hūlun side and a gain for the Jianzhou of 3000 horses and 1000 suits of armor. Nurgaci's treatment of his defeated rivals was harsh and decisive, and by 1595 he was the undisputed hegemon of Manchuria.

Curiously, while professing a campaign of vengeance against the Ming, Nurgaci in fact developed a most cooperative relationship with them. In 1586 the authorities in Fushun helped Nurgaci arrest and execute a Jurchen village leader who had resisted Nurgaci's conquests. In 1590 Nurgaci led his own embassy to Peking, and in 1591 he was offering to join the international effort, led by the Ming, to repulse from Korea the invasion of Japanese forces led by Toyotomi Hideyoshi. In return the Ming heaped grand titles and rewards on Nurgaci. The difficult years for him came after 1591, when Li Chengliang was forced into retirement at Peking. The Ming authorities may have been partly seeking to prevent the sort of alliance between Li and Nurgaci that Li had frequently formed with other powerful Jurchen leaders. If so, the policy had the wrong effects. Nurgaci's military machine only grew bigger and stronger in Li's absence. After Li's return in 1601 there was an apparent easing of tensions between the Ming and Nurgaci, even to the point of Ming recognition of a Jurchen boundary in 1608. The border agreement – commemorated by a monument and by a ceremony featuring the sacrifice of a white horse and a black ox – forbade crossing of the border either way, and stipulated that violators would be killed by authorities on the trespassed side. The condition was intended to preserve the Jurchen monopoly on the regional products that commanded a high price in China and Korea, and later would be incorporated into Qing policy toward their homeland. It was after Li's retirement in 1609 that the final break with the Ming came, and Nurgaci began to prepare seriously for an invasion of Liaodong.

The image of Nurgaci as a youthful, determined avenger of the unjust deaths of this father and grandfather owes a bit to rhetoric he developed as he became more powerful among the Jurchens, but much more to his depiction in Qing imperial history well after his death. In 1618, when Nurgaci formally declared war against the Ming empire, he referred first to the deaths of his father and grandfather when making his shamanic oath to heaven. But this reference occurred in the context of a charge of border violations by the Ming authorities, and was followed by six other large charges – altogether known as the "Seven Great Grievances" – that were all related to the fundamental idea that distinct boundaries to the Jurchen territories existed, and that within them the Jurchens ought to be self-governing and free of harassment by Ming forces. Only in later narratives was Nurgaci described as exclusively and unrelentingly determined to avenge his father and grandfather, and particularly to seek out and destroy all Jurchen spies who had aided in the betrayal of Giocangga and Taksi at Mount Gure – retrospectively, the primary explanation for the wars against Jurchens and neighboring peoples which dominated Nurgaci's career between 1582 and 1616.

The Myth of Individual Supremacy

Just as the image of Nurgaci as a rebel and avenger opens doors to the differing sources and their interpretation of early Qing history, so does his image as first emperor of the Qing. Though in his very late life Nurgaci was finally known to his Jurchen followers as a "khan," the annals revised after his death always referred to him as an emperor. In the imperial view, Nurgaci was the "sacred" emperor (*enduringge hūwangdi*), the founder of the Qing dynasty who was worshipped in the religious ceremonies of the imperial family. Yet for most of his life Nurgaci was rated a *beile*, the term for the leader of a Jurchen lineage or federation. The question of whether Nurgaci was ever an emperor in fact is easily resolved, then: He clearly was not. More elusive is the question of whether he intended to rule as an autocrat among the Jurchens, and to encourage a style of government that would have created over- whelming individual power for his direct descendants.

In Mongolian and Manchurian traditions upon which Nurgaci drew, a khan was a keeper of slaves. The conceit was widely known throughout Central and Inner Asia, was ancient, and was very powerful, for in exchange for his total service the slave gained the formidable protection and symbolic (or real) intimacy of the khan. The term of affiliation was simple and level, applying to all regardless of language, custom, or habitat. For all that, it was not a particularly flexible instrument of incorporation, and was ex- tremely limiting to the ruler. Like the *beile* (see chapter 2), the khan had to continue to find and distribute wealth in order to keep his federation stable, and his place within it safe. He had no choice but to conquer, and to plan new conquests to feed the mouths he had acquired in his last.

Khanship was an office of power exercised with the corporate acquiescence and cooperation of tribal or clan leaders. It depended upon fairly regular engagements in war, and originally may have existed solely for the purpose of uniting the confederacies into larger, centralized bodies for more effective attack or defense. In his capacity of conqueror the khan was a granter of booty and slaves to his followers. As such confederacies gained political stability the khans became not only permanent but dynastic, at- tempting to pass the khanship through a single lineage. This does not imply primogeniture, nor did it prevent the internecine strug- gles which the late Joseph F. Fletcher Jr termed "bloody tanistry."[4] Indeed the khans, both Turkic and later Mongolian, were precisely those men who had through intense struggle against their rival candidates demonstrated heaven-favored gifts of intelligence, agil- ity, strength, and eloquence – the complex of qualities the Mon- gols had celebrated as *sečen*, and the Manchus as *sure* – qualities also tested in the medieval judicial combats of Europe. Nurgaci himself, as an intrepid battle leader, enjoyed the use of *sure* in his titles from the early years of his struggle to unite the Jurchens under his control.

Leadership of the Jianzhou confederacies had its origin in the headmanship of the Odori Jurchens, whose leader Möngke Temür (see appendix III) had been recognized both by the Ming and by the Yi. Giocangga, Nurgaci's grandfather, claimed to be a fourth-generation descendent of Möngke Temür, and Giocangga's father Fuman had received the garrison title of "Commandant" (*dudu*) from the Ming court. But within Manchuria, Giocangga was not without rivals. Even in his own Jianzhou federation, he shared power with his older brother Soocangga and Soocangga's son, Utai, as well as with his own son, Taksi.

All were members of the Jurchen lineage whose name in the twelfth century had been represented by the Chinese characters Jiagu, and whose Manchu name one day would be Gioro. The prestige of noble lineages in Jurchen culture gave the Gioro a certain advantage in competing for political leadership, but it was a large lineage and rivalry within it could be strong. Management of the livelihoods of the Jurchen federations was complex, and it was not the practice to place authority over all aspects of life in the hands of a single individual. More often, two senior male members of a leading lineage would manage affairs, and normally in consultation and cooperation with a much larger number of relatives or relatives-by-marriage. Such joint rule was common, but not all brothers were equal. Soocangga and Giocangga were only two of the six sons of Fuman; it appears that their older brother Dorji and younger brothers Desikū, Leodan, and Boolungga were not accorded *beile* status in the federation (though all were headmen of their own lineages, and they were called on account of that "the six headmen," *ninggū da*).

At the time of the deaths of Giocangga and Taksi, rulership of the federation did not immediately devolve upon any single person, for Soocangga and Utai were elder and were experienced at governing. But it was Nurgaci who began to make his own power felt in the early 1580s, and it is likely that Murgaci and Šurgaci, who were both his full brothers, acted as his co-rulers. Nurgaci's tasks as leader of the Jianzhou Jurchens were, because of the new scale of warfare he initiated, even more complex than had been the case for his predecessors. The evidence is that he would have preferred to perpetuate cooperative leadership in the tradition of the region, but that he was repeatedly disappointed. This interpretation is most useful when considering one of the great conundrums of the history of the Nurgaci period: The status, the personality, and the death of Nurgaci's younger brother Šurgaci. The most vivid narrative of a passage in that relationship was supplied by Sin Chung-il.

Three years before Sin Chung-il's arrival, Nurgaci had removed himself, his family, and his followers from his original headquarters at Hūlan Hada to a settlement called Fe Ala, the "Old Hill." Fe Ala was situated in such a way that it was at the westward extreme of the Jurchen territories, virtually at the perimeter of Ming Liaodong. It was only two nights' journey from Fushun, but three or four nights' from other Jurchen settlements of any size. Ula – a subdivision of the Hūlun federation – was eighteen days to a month away to the northeast. The Yalu river (the boundary with Korea) was four days to the south. Thus, Nurgaci was based at the eastern extreme of the Ming territories, whose commercial connections drew the Jurchen elite westward like a force of gravity, and the western extreme of the Jurchen continuum.

On the verge of Nurgaci's territories the party arrived at the land grant of Nurgaci's brother-in-law, a collection of twenty households and rows and rows of horse-pens. On and off, this relative acted as host to Sin's party at Fe Ala, and in this instance his agent saw them conducted further toward Nurgaci's headquarters. The next day the party stopped at a village of forty households. It was a land grant of Nurgaci's younger brother Šurgaci. In a corral, more than twenty horses were gathered. The settlement was surrounded by a strong earthen wall, and fewer than half-a-dozen households stood without. Then came a village that worked Nurgaci's land under the management of one Wang Zhi (a Chinese or Korean name); this was a well-equipped development, on a hilltop surrounded by a wooden stockade, with more than ten arrow workshops, a tower, and over seventy households.

Fe Ala was surrounded, Sin saw as he approached, by uncultivated meadows, except for small fields at the top of the "old hill" itself and the surrounding hills. Outside the walls of the town were clustered households numbering, perhaps, four hundred. The outside wall Sin estimated to be about three and a third miles in circumference. It stood on on a stone foundation about a yard high, and the stockade rose nine feet above that, covered with wattle. Sin remarked on the absence of shooting platforms or observation decks. Only the gate had a surveillance tower rising above it, roofed with thatch. The gate itself was massive and made of wood; when closed it was secured with a giant wooden crossbar. When the outer gates were locked, the inner gates were left open. In the precincts between the outermost wall and the first inner wall Sin estimated that he counted three hundred households. There were a hundred more in the inner town. All of them, Sin remarked, were the families of soldiers. The town was fed by four or five springs, which were shallow and inadequate for the dense population. To augment the water supply gangs day and night carried ice from the Suksu river.

Inside Fe Ala, Sin found the space divided by an interior wall of wood, and inside that another wooden wall. When Sin was at length admitted to the inner sanctum, he found Nurgaci's family, Šurgaci's family, and the leading soldiers of the Jianzhou in residence there. Nurgaci's and Šurgaci's compounds were at the center, Nurgaci's on the north facing south (the superior position), Šurgaci's on the south facing north. They shared a greeting yard and a religious shrine.

Sin was conducted to Nurgaci's compound and, after a long delay, treated to a glimpse of the Jianzhou chief. But no business transpired and Sin spent a chilly night at a house in the outer town. The next morning Sin found that his return to Nurgaci's compound was complicated by the inexplicable inability to acquire a horse to convey him there. Sin instead passed the day distributing gifts to Nurgaci's uncles. On the third day he was obliged to appear at their homes as guest. Having passed muster with the elders of Nurgaci's lineage, Sin was once again conveyed to Nurgaci's compound on lunar New Year's Day, to attend a banquet. Before the meal, Nurgaci instructed one of the interpreters to announce to Sin, "From this day forward, our two countries will be as one, our two families will be as one, forever united and amicable, for all generations, without end." Sin commented afterward to the Yi court, "Thus they attempted to speak with a virtue appropriate to our country."

Sin was impressed by the appearance of the party and its leader. Nurgaci, he noted, was neither fat nor thin, in physique strong and erect, nose straight but large, face long and rather dark. In robes similar to Nurgaci's was Šurgaci, who was heavier than his brother, square-faced, and fair, with silver hoops in his ears. Nurgaci wore a hat of sable fur, with ear flaps (in the Mongol fashion) and a pointed crown, topped by a feather and a small decoration; Šurgaci and the generals all wore similar hats. Nurgaci's robe was stitched with insignia in five colors, and reached to his feet; the lower length was entirely of sable, with rich embroidering at the border. The generals, Sin noted, had robes in which rank differences were indicated by different stitching and degrees of sable appliqué. They and their kinsmen removed their caps in the course of Sin's visit, and he started at their distinctive hair style, with shaven scalps and long queues in the back. Of their facial hair the men spared a small patch on each side of the upper lip, and plucked the rest.

After wine had been distributed, the captive former leader of the Ula confederacy, Bujantai, started to dance. Bujantai together with his older brother and co-ruler Mantai had decided in 1592 to join the effort by the Hūlun confederacy and the Khorchin Mongols to prevent a northward spread of Nurgaci's power. But the forces were defeated by Nurgaci. Bujantai with twenty fully armed men was taken prisoner. Mantai offered Nurgaci a hundred horses for Bujantai's freedom, but he was rejected. By the time of Sin Chung-il's visit, Bujantai was firmly ensconced at Nurgaci's court, and was the head of his own household, with twenty dependents.

One of Nurgaci's sons, probably Cuyen, sitting beside his father, personally accompanied Bujantai on a zither, moving his body in time to the music. When the dance was finished, eight men demonstrated their talents at shooting, wrestling, and acrobatics. As the evening progressed, there were singing and dancing outside the hall, strumming and drumming inside. Sin, standing, drank his wine with the company (he noted distastefully that his cup was made of carved wood), clapping his hands and singing, "in order to enhance the wine's effect."

Speaking through his interpreters, one of Nurgaci's uncles began:

> Our prince and the generals of your country want to join as one country, because then the people who have been taken from your country will be returned. But our prince has not held your country responsible for the murder of Saishangga. What had Saishangga done that you should have killed him? We have very deep feelings about this.

Sin answered,

> The law of my country is: Whosoever among you barbarians trespasses without cause in our country is a felon. For several hundred years your people have been coming under cover of night to steal our cattle and kidnap our people. In the mountains and valleys our people live in terror of being murdered, or taken, without a shred of cause. All barbarians subject to our country must follow this rule: They should honestly render what they owe, and sheathe their

swords. Those who take it upon themselves to violate the borders will be adjudged criminal and punished. In 1588 we had a meeting with you at Mamp'ojin, we exchanged wine and foodstuffs, and we tried to establish an agreement. After that my country has had no wish to harm or kill your troops – apart from those who trespass, and they will be punished.

In the end Sin did not enjoy another interview with either Nurgaci or Šurgaci. He was given a letter (scribed by one of the Fushunese) from Nurgaci to the Yi court, to which was affixed a seal announcing it as the product of the "Commandant" of the Jianzhou Left Garrison – a title once held by his grandfather Fuman, though the transmission to Nurgaci himself was unclear. Sin was advised by another Fushunese, who delivered it to him, that he should be aware that the Jurchens followed the laws of "the Heavenly Court" – that is, Ming China, to which both the Jurchens and the Koreans acknowledged tributary status. Whatever the Jurchens did, the messenger claimed, had to be reported to the Ming. Whatever the Heavenly Court allowed, went. Whatever it did not allow, did not go. Sin listened skeptically to this pious warning. He later reproduced the text of the letter he took back to the Korean court:

This is a letter from Nurgaci, affixed with the seal of the Jianzhou Left Garrison:

Lord of the Jurchen Nation, Jianzhou Garrison Officers and Wildmen Nurgaci announces for edification of the Yi:

The honorable Korean country and our Jurchen nation, we two countries, will advance toward customary good relations, and our two peoples will not habitually raise troops against each other. As we initiate good relations with you, we are protecting more than 290 miles of borders with the Heavenly Court, but the border officials of Liaodong only want to harm us, attack us and gain merit for themselves. I will redeem and send home the seventeen Koreans held captive, to honor your king. I realize that if there should arise some insincerity between our two countries, there is your fort at Lincheng facing our territory. I understand that you will allow our Mongols [*dazi*] to live in that vicinity, to defend our border. If your livestock are lost and our Mongols know of it, they should send them back. You will assign an intermediary from Mamp'ojin to come to my home, and any of your people or animals found there will be sent back. Any of our Mongols who cross into your territory, you will send back to me. Our two family's laws will be observed without exception. In the future, when the officials of the

Heavenly Court harm us, you will represent us and speak out, you will remonstrate with the magistrates of the Heavenly Court, and I will appreciate it.

Sin's mission had been to impress upon the Jianzhou Jurchens the necessity of observing the integrity of the northern Yi border, not to create a political alliance with Nurgaci against the Ming. The Yi court was in fact unedified by Nurgaci's letter, and may have been alarmed by its patently seditious message. Soon after Sin's return to Seoul the court made it illegal for Jurchens to trade any longer at Mamp'ojin. Nurgaci was left to pursue his campaigns against the Ming on his own resources. His quest would lead to the amassing of commercial and military strength that, in 1627, would make his descendants the overlords of Yi Korea.

Presciently, Sin added a warning as a postscript to his report. He reminded his readers of the ongoing conquests and incorporations of populations in northern Korea. He described the Jurchens under Nurgaci as numerous and militarily prepared. He also commented upon what he had previously observed of the ubiquity of Jurchens in Liaodong: "I had not gone three or five steps inside the Great Wall before I began encountering Jurchens." The danger, Sin warned, recalled the error of the founder of the Han empire in China, Liu Bang, in underestimating the forces and talents of the Xiongnu leader Maodun, or the disasters caused in Korea by Wang On's underestimation of the "wild" Jurchens during the Koryŏ period.

Though as an emissary of the Korean court Sin had no reason to accord to the Jianzhou Jurchens the status of a nation, he not only described the institutions and habits of a political order but also reproduced the language by which Nurgaci and his followers represented themselves as an independent regime. Sin in his report referred to Nurgaci by the title "Headman" (*xiu*), which he used also for Šurgaci and the dozens of village headmen he mentions in his account. Though Sin had no occasion to remark upon it, Ming accounts normally referred to Nurgaci by the title granted him, "Commandant." But in the speech of those who were members of Nurgaci's federation Sin reproduced the term "prince" (*wangzi*), which would have translated Jurchen *beile*. Nurgaci himself, however, in his letter to the Yi court conveyed by Sin, referred to himself with respect to the "Jurchen Nation, Jianzhou Garrison Officers and Wildmen" as their "lord" (*zhu*), which clearly represents Jurchen *ejen* – the same word as in Mongolian. In his self-reference Nurgaci adopted the traditional conceit of ownership that underlay political leadership in Northeast Asia. He thus established the monarchical term of self-reference among the Jurchens that would become an expression of the Qing link to the Mongolian Great Khans, and would remain central to the Qing until their destruction in the twentieth century.

Was Nurgaci in the process of building an autocracy among the Jurchens at the time of Sin's visit? Šurgaci's challenge to Nurgaci's position, which would be suggested many times in the historical records of the Qing court, was pointedly remarked by Sin. When a horse could not be found to convey the Korean envoy to Nurgaci, a brace of three suddenly appeared to take him to Šurgaci. Sin declined, however, and noted that he had been warned against encouraging Šurgaci's jealousy. Nevertheless, the day after his visit to Nurgaci, Sin received a message from Šurgaci: "You have gone to see my brother, but I am still waiting." Sin went instead to the home of Nurgaci's uncle and spent the night before leaving Fe Ala. Though Šurgaci could not force recognition from Sin, he nevertheless directed stern messages at him regarding the necessity of properly greeting and rewarding all the uncles and brothers, and not Nurgaci alone. Sin was aware of a profound conflict on the horizon between Nurgaci and Šurgaci.

What Sin observed of Šurgaci's status in 1595 was probably the result of Šurgaci's aggrandizement of his own status at the expense of Murgaci, who was alive but living in complete obscurity by this time. Šurgaci's constant haranguing of Sin was suggestive of a man with a high opinion of his own status, frustrated by his inability to convince others to recognize it. Though Sin as a studiously irreverent outsider referred to Nurgaci and Šurgaci by the same rank, he came to Fe Ala to see Nurgaci, not Šurgaci. He returned with a sealed letter from Nurgaci alone, who designated himself "lord" of the Jurchens. He saw Nurgaci and Šurgaci living in the same compound, but with Nurgaci's house in the superior position, facing south. He saw Nurgaci and Šurgaci dressed in similar clothing at a New Year's banquet, and Šurgaci keeping his cap on when the generals, nobles, and captives removed theirs. But when those same generals, nobles, and captives performed the greeting dance and made their curtsies, it was to Nurgaci. The relative standing of the two brothers was on some occasions even quantifiable: When a Hūlun chieftain surrendered to Nurgaci, his tribute included a hundred horses, of which sixty were given to Nurgaci and forty to Šurgaci.

The ultimate creation of the khanate must be associated not only with the growth of Nurgaci's power and consequent aggrandizement of his personal status, but also with the failure of his attempts to sustain collegial rule within the regime. While Nurgaci might have been willing to affirm the validity of joint rule as a tradition in the region – it had been the practice in Jianzhou before him, and can be demonstrated to have been the rule in Ula and other Manchurian localities in Nurgaci's lifetime – it was another matter to have one colleague conspiring against another, particularly if the one conspired against was the primary of the partners. Šurgaci's attempts to increase his reach, which even wearied Sin Chung-il, brought about a crisis in 1607.

Shortly after Sin Chung-il saw Bujantai dancing at Nurgaci's New Year banquet, the Ula leader was sent back to his people. During Bujantai's stay at Fe Ala, Mantai had succeeded to the status of sole *beile* of the Ula, but not long afterward both Mantai and his son were put to death by other Ula leaders. Nurgaci assumed that Bujantai had learned his place and sent him back to the Ula as *beile*, and also as vassal to Nurgaci himself. Submission of the Ula put their Hūlun neighbors, the Yehe confederacy, in an untenable position, and in 1597 they concluded a truce with Nurgaci.

With his eastern front more or less secure, Nurgaci turned his attention to the Khorchin Mongols who were blocking his progress north and west. In 1606 the Khorchins acknowledged him as their Kündülün Khan, or "Khan of Martial Spirit." It was the first official recognition of Nurgaci as a khan, though it was not yet a title he dared assume among the Jurchens. These years of 1606–8 were the critical ones for the political future of the region. Nurgaci's right to independent management of his territory was recognized both by the Khorchins and by the Ming empire. These were not, however, miraculous years in which state-like institutions appeared or were radically transformed. All Jurchen organization still depended on the banners. In all other political and economic matters, the partnership between Nurgaci and Šurgaci was the only structure that existed, and Nurgaci found it more and more unstable. Part of the reason was that Bujantai had not remained loyal after returning to Ula. He was working to undermine Nurgaci's authority in the east, and Nurgaci suspected that

Bujantai's object was to secretly aid Šurgaci in becoming lord of the Jianzhou, and then to share in the spoils.

In 1607 Nurgaci proposed to remove the population of the village of Fiohoton, near Huncun in the remote Changbaishan region, to Hetu Ala, his new capital built to the west of the old one at Fe Ala. The people of Fiohoton were ostensibly followers of Bujantai, with whom Nurgaci had just opened hostilities. Nurgaci now described the people of Fiohoton as "oppressed" and determined to take them for himself. Šurgaci, disliking to see the resources of his ulterior vassal (and son-in-law twice over) diminished, asked to accompany the expedition, and did all he could to thwart it. But over his objections Nurgaci's sons Cuyen and Daišan went to Fiohoton and accomplished the objective. The result was a sharp rise in the political profiles of Cuyen and Daišan and a rapid imperilment of Šurgaci, who had been a bit too public about his opposition to the campaign. In 1609 Nurgaci ordered the confiscation of Šurgaci's property, including his slaves. The next year two of Šurgaci's sons were found guilty of treason and executed. In 1611, Šurgaci was himself assassinated, evidently on Nurgaci's orders; those of his sons whom Nurgaci favored (Amin and Jirgalang) were taken into Nurgaci's own household.

Evidently Nurgaci's object had been not to destroy co-rulership as an institution, but to rid himself of Šurgaci's ambition to be the superior in the relationship. Nurgaci did not subsequently assume sole rulership in the Jianzhou federation. Instead he rapidly fixed upon his eldest son Cuyen as his next co-ruler. The property confiscated from Šurgaci in the aftermath of the Fiohoton incident had been transferred largely to Cuyen and Daišan already. Removal of Šurgaci left Cuyen as the obvious second man in the order. Cuyen had been recognized as a *beile* in his own right as early as 1598, when he was still a teenager, and shortly after had been honored with a special title for his battle exploits. It appears that at some point Cuyen also assumed that Mongolian title "prince," *taiji*. In 1611 he was given the title *taise*, which later historiography would interpret as "heir-apparent," though what in practice it meant was that Cuyen was Nurgaci's co-ruler. Thus immediately after Šurgaci's death, Cuyen was given the right to manage the economic and political affairs of the regime.

Complaints against Cuyen's governance at once began reaching Nurgaci, who was constantly in the battlefield attempting to suppress holdouts from the Hūlun federation. As they would on other occasions, Nurgaci's other sons and nephews came to him in a group to indict Cuyen's injustices in the distribution of booty; he was slighting Daišan, Manggūldai, Amin, and Hung Taiji, all his primary rivals for power. Nurgaci, in a characteristic response, upbraided Cuyen in front of the others, then left him on his own cognizance. But he was bitterly disappointed. In 1612 Nurgaci left Hetu Ala to pursue his latest (and conclusive) war against Bujantai. During his absence he received reports that Cuyen was plotting against him, and had attempted to hex the entire lineage. Nurgaci ordered Cuyen imprisoned. In 1615, apparently despairing of Cuyen's return to acceptable behavior, Nurgaci killed him.

No *taise* was appointed to succeed Cuyen. Instead, Nurgaci declared himself khan in 1616. As khan Nurgaci was elevated far above his old rank of *beile*, which was now shared by seven of his surviving sons and his nephew Amin. The eight men were distinguished as *hōšoi beile*, the "cardinal" *beile*.[5] They were made lords of the Eight Banners, and were to function as the khan's consultative body.

Nurgaci's impulse toward joint rule – what historians of the period often call "collegial" rule – remained very strong. When eastern and central Liaodong were brought under his control in 1621, he wished again for help in the management of the state, and instituted a revolving co-rulership, which four of his *beiles* – his sons Daišan, Manggūldai, and Hung Taiji, and nephew Amin – each assumed for one month, in cycles. But again Nurgaci's dreams of stable collegial rule were spoiled by indictments and counter-indictments that flew thick in the period between 1621 and 1626. At one point Daišan was severely reprimanded by Nurgaci for nepotism, and on another occasion Hung Taiji was found guilty of accepting bribes from Chinese-martial hoping to gain privileges for themselves. Indeed it appears that Nurgaci was well aware that Hung Taiji was the most ambitious and the most talented of the *beiles*. It was perhaps on that account that he gave Hung Taiji a severe dressing down in front of his peers. He first mocked his son for his arrogance, furiously condemning Hung Taiji for allowing his brothers to see him home after a visit, but never seeing them home when they visited him. Then, declaring that he was punishing Hung Taiji by forcibly removing a portion of his lands, cattle, and slaves, Nurgaci paraded his knowledge of

Hung Taiji's ambitions. "You know that I have established you all as joint rulers with me, but perhaps you will forget my will when I am dead. Are you thinking of sitting on the khan's throne over the heads of your elder brothers?"

In the event, Nurgaci may not have really been able to understand the true degree of Hung Taiji's ambition. It was not the throne of khan, merely, that Hung Taiji coveted. He wished to be an emperor, an institution he would have to invent for himself. But even after creation of the emperorship, and after the later suppression of fundamental powers of the aristocracy, the ideals of collegial rule continued to cling to the political culture of the Aisin Gioro lineage. Regencies – such as that of Dorgon, under which Ming China was conquered, or that of Oboi, who ruled during the minority of the Kangxi emperor, or those that in the nineteenth century set off rounds of intrigue and corruption that helped changed the entire shape of the regime, or that which oversaw the end of the Qing empire in 1912 – were easily and repeatedly created. And regencies themselves were a minor theme in this motif. Equally traditional were strong partnerships among princes that permitted the empire to limp through the disasters of the nineteenth century long after the emperorship itself had lost all means of locomotion.

The Myth of the Great Enterprise

Finally, we must consider the most important and powerful image of Nurgaci in the Qing imperial history, that of conqueror. As suggested in the above discussion of Nurgaci as rebel, the imperial history insists that Nurgaci's real object of war was Ming China, and that battles against Jurchen neighbors were for the intermediate purpose of rooting out traitors and unifying the Jurchens in preparation for war against the Ming. But even if the Ming empire was the single, persisting object of Nurgaci's wars, was it his purpose to assure his rule over the Jurchen territories, to drive the Ming out of Liaodong and back into China proper, or to conquer China, as the Jurchens of the Jin empire had done before him?

As his power grew, Nurgaci continued to shift his capital, and the shift was continually westward. In 1603 he moved to Hetu Ala, the "Level Hill." Water had been a problem at Fe Ala, and

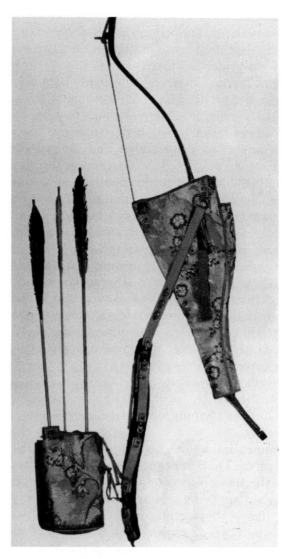

Plate 3 *Like the Mongols before them, the Manchus were accomplished archers, both on foot and on horseback. Long after muskets became the preferred weapons for war and the hunt, bows, arrows, and quivers remained a part of the formal dress of the aristocracy. This set is from the ceremonial armor of the Qianlong emperor (chapter 5). The Manchus also retained as customary adornment the jade thumb rings that were once used by all archers to protect the drawing-hand. (National Palace Museum, Peking)*

Hetu Ala had to recommend it a peculiar conformation, with steep sides and a flat, easily defensible top, for which it was named. Like Fe Ala, Hetu Ala featured concentric formations, where commoners were to be found in the outermost precincts, and Nurgaci's large household of wives, unmarried daughters, young sons, retainers, and bodyguards lived in the innermost. Hetu Ala also featured within the central compound not merely a large and well-appointed parlor of the sort used at Fe Ala, but a grand reception room. On lunar New Year's Day of 1616, it became a throne room, as Nurgaci pronounced himself khan.

The ceremony was well orchestrated and represented not only the conscious assumption of a new status by Nurgaci but also the conscious ordering of those over whom he would claim dominion. He sat on a dais, and behind him were arrayed cardinal *beile*s: His son Daišan, son Manggūldai, son Hung Taiji, nephew Amin, son Degelei, son Yoto, nephew Jirgalang, and son Ajige. The khan and the *beile*s together received the prostrations (*hengkilembi*) of, serially, the Mongol *beise*s, all of whom were sons-in-law (*efu*) of Nurgaci; two lamas from Tibet who had come via the Khorchin Mongol territories; and four officials of Korea. The prostrations were followed by the sacrifice of an ox and a goat. At the conclusion of the ceremony soldiers entertained the party with a demonstration of martial skills.[6] Then began the feast.

Such occasions always involved exchange of goods and people – symbolic in their meaning, but substantial in their value – between the ruler and the ruled. This was partly traditional: The sacrifice of goods through gifting was an old way of expressing sincerity among the Jurchens. And because a "lord" (*ejen*) – which Nurgaci continued to be – was the archetypal owner, the augmentation of his holdings thorough tribute was the purest expression of loyalty. By the same token, all legitimate wealth came from his hand alone, and through personal or symbolic bestowal of wealth on his followers Nurgaci manifested his own role as monarch.

One of the things Nurgaci was empowered to bestow was women – his daughters, nieces, and granddaughters, all of whom functioned as extensions of his ability to benefit those who would severe him. The fact that all the Mongol *beise* presenting themselves at these ceremonies were Nurgaci's sons-in-law was characteristic of the framework of the early state. For Nurgaci the presence of representatives of his subject populations under his figurative roof was a logical extension of his growing dominion.

Plate 4   *Cast bronze cannon had been introduced by the Jesuits into China in the early 1600s. Nurgaci's forces captured some of the artillery during the war against the Ming in Liaodong, and also recruited, by various means, men who knew how to manufacture and deploy the weapons, aiding in the Qing conquest of China in 1644. This particular cannon, 280 kg in weight and propelling shells of 15 kg, was the type used by the Kangxi emperor in his campaigns against Galdan (chapter 4). (National Palace Museum, Peking)*

Normally Nurgaci betrothed one of his daughters, granddaughters, or nieces to a vassal, but often the men of his family were given out in marriage.

For the Qing sovereigns coming after Nurgaci, the imperial harem became a field for the representation of the imperial constituencies. These marriages were not expressions of firm alliance; in fact, the lineages who were closest to Nurgaci, such as the Niohuru, or the Gūwalgiya, were not well represented among Nurgaci's women. On the contrary, the marriages were part of the process of negotiating with hostile lineages and federations. Nurgaci's marriage to Monggo-gege ("Mongol lady," mother of Hung Taiji) of a people of the Hūlun federation, for instance, did not create much good feeling between Nurgaci and them; when she fell ill in 1603 and asked that her mother be allowed to visit her, her people's elders sent two concubines instead, an act that enraged Nurgaci and gave him another excuse for stepping up his war against his in-laws particularly, and the Hūlun generally.

The significance of gifting in the cohesion of the early state created a hierarchy of objects. People were given only to those of rank. Nurgaci's son Tanggūdai, for instance, married a woman of a Mongol confederacy and received from her family a gift of twenty-five horses, twenty-five oxen, a collection of dressed sable pelts, sable hats, gold jewelry, two pairs of earrings, a set of women's court dress, and forty Mongols. Banners and drums, on the other hand, were the exclusive gifts to those chosen to command the military. They could be given only by the court (as in earlier times only the *beile* could distribute arrows), and those with the right to obtain them were carefully noted in the court records. Gold and furs were common currency and could be given to anyone. Since goods – or people treated as goods – were the glue of the khanate, it was necessary that more and more goods be acquired, chiefly through conquest. As the pitch of war rose and an invasion of Liaodong became imminent, *beile*, headmen, commoners, and slaves all looked forward to new opportunities for the gathering of booty, and for the continued returns of new lands and captive workers.

For his part, it is probable that Nurgaci's declaration of war against the Ming was motivated less by the prospect of a dramatic increase in distributable wealth than by fears that the current levels would be constricted. The original articulation of the "Seven Great Grievances" was clearly motivated by Nurgaci's anxieties over the fact that the massive Jurchen federation he had knit together after more than twenty-five years of warfare and bargaining among the independent chiefs of the region was in some danger of unraveling under the pressure of economic setbacks, agricultural sabotage by Ming raiders, and the canny tactics of Chinese officials in exploiting lingering resentments among the eastern Jurchen confederations whom Nurgaci had forced into alliance. For a short time Nurgaci continued to send envoys to Peking to present tribute and beg titles and trading patents; but he later accused the Ming of failing to observe the border agreement, and after 1609 seems to have stopped sending embassies to China altogether.

Ming violation of the alleged Jurchen border was not only worsening the agricultural difficulties of the Later Jin, it was challenging the credibility of the khanate. Nurgaci was ready to press his propaganda, in step with his new war effort in Liaodong, in terms that the Ming might find unanswerable. The Later Jin, he asserted, were the legitimate successors of the Jurchen Jin empire of the twelfth century. They were the same people, living in the same region, with the same language, the same traditions, even the same clans. In his utterances he now called the Ming "the Southern dynasty" (*nan chao*), an imitation of Jurchen Jin practice in referring to the Southern Song, whom they had driven from northern China in 1227.

Quite apart from the historical justification for his argument, the analogy served Nurgaci's ambitions well. As the Jin and Southern Song had once divided China between themselves and coexisted, not peacefully, before both were destroyed by the invading Mongols, so the Later Jin and the Ming could divide the present Chinese territories, with the Ming presumably retreating from Liaodong and surrendering it to the jurisdiction of the Later Jin. Though hardly persuaded by Nurgaci's argument, the Ming proved sensitive to the images he had invoked. They did not deny the historical link of the Later Jin Jurchens to the imperial Jin Jurchens of the twelfth century; on the contrary they desecrated the Jin tombs at Fangshan, near Peking, "to celebrate it."

In order to continue his quest to control borders and trade with both Korea and the Ming empire, Nurgaci had to apply his powers to the reorganization of life among the Jurchens. He utilized, first of all, the deep tradition of household and village self-defense. Every man was expected to purchase his own arms and supply himself with food on the occasion of a campaign, on the assumption that every man was part of a household and every family was experienced in the needs of a man doing battle – typically an ox, grain, jerky, and eighteen taels of silver for ransoming himself should he cross into Korean territory. Nurgaci himself paid nothing to mobilize forces. Men enlisted in the defensive campaigns on the assumption that this was the best way to protect their homes from depredation by Ming forces or their mercenaries, and joined the attack forces speculating on getting a share of the rewards. Households worked together to supply the soldier in hopes of partaking of his booty. They shared together in his misfortunes, too. This went beyond death or injury. Nurgaci's custom required, for instance, that families too poor to provide their soldiers with ransom money would be required to go to Korea themselves to redeem their men if they should fall into the enemy's hands.

Nurgaci is reported to have mustered 10,000 (possibly a rough and conventional figure) men under his command, and was relatively well equipped with horses and armor. The first assault was upon Fushun; from it were taken population and armaments – including the Jesuit-designed cannons maintained by Ming forces there – sufficient to dramatically increase the potency of Nurgaci's challenge. Attempts by the empire to suppress Nurgaci were without effect, despite the fact that he fought a two-front war. He defeated the first Ming expedition at Sarhū, east of Fushun, in the summer of 1619 and in September destroyed the political independence of the Hūlun group of Yehe on his east. In May of 1621 Nurgaci's forces took Shenyang, the Ming provincial capital in Liaodong. He renamed the city Mukden. He built a new residence and administrative center for himself east of Liaodong, but in 1625 moved permanently into Mukden, which would remain the cultural center of the state to be led by his son, Hung Taiji.

The Nurgaci State

The palace complex at Mukden (the modern Chinese city of Shenyang, the provincial capital of Liaoning) is modest by the later standards of the Qing empire, but is clearly the capital of a monarch. Much of the complex was constructed after Nurgaci's death, but the long processional road in the center, culminating in the walled and tile-roofed palace, showed a combination of simple Manchurian esthetic and Chinese elegance. The city-within-a-city pattern, of course, was not exclusively Chinese. It was the one Nurgaci had been comfortable with since his capital towns had been surrounded by wattled walls and rough wooden gates. But Mukden included something that had not been a distinct development of Nurgaci's earlier settlements: The bureaucratic residences and offices that had been built there under the Ming governors, and which the Jin khanate would now need to people on its own, primarily through recruitment of former Ming officials.

The Liaodong campaigns were the last to be motivated by every individual combatant's eagerness to outfit and supply himself in hopes of gaining riches directly from war. Like the Mongolian Great Khans, Nurgaci was learning that he could only enforce his status among his followers if he insisted that all goods were in the first instance his, and that spontaneous appropriation was an offense against the ruler. Looting was forbidden, which required a much greater degree of discipline and professionalization among the troops. Perhaps more important, Liaodong offered opportunities for a political transformation of the Jin khanate that could only be realized if careful planning were applied from the first stages in the taking of Chinese territory.

From the earliest years of his ascent to power, Nurgaci had appreciated the special advantages that came from controlling literate men, when they could be found. They were necessary to his communications with the Ming and Yi courts, and they were necessary to manage the increasing complexity of his organization, since they were they ones who controlled his lists of goods, the records of gifting, and the rosters of those enrolled in the banners. Moreover, if disloyal these men could easily betray him to China or the Korea. Thus from an early point he treated them comparatively well (though frequently deriding them as opportunistic and untrustworthy). Their material needs were amply provided for, and their social status – expressed in his strict rules of uniformity in dress and hairstyle – was equal to that of the Jurchens. As news spread back to the liminal territories of China and Korea that men of any education at all could enjoy comparatively elevated status under Nurgaci, new recruits trickled in. There was, however, a second benefit to this policy. The houses, grain stores, livestock, and people given to these immigrants had to come from somewhere, and Nurgaci had found that he could enhance his powers among high-ranking Jurchens (while selectively diminishing theirs) by forcing them to give their own goods over to the newcomers. A new level of redistribution accompanied his growing dominion.

By 1619, as the war in Liaodong raged, Nurgaci may have begun to give some ideological expression to these ideas. Jurchens, Liaodong-based Mongols, and Chinese-speaking farmers of Liaodong were all of value to him, and he intended to integrate all into his polity. He identified the groups on the basis of their customs and skills, not on the basis of ancestors. Those who spoke Jurchen, lived in Jurchen-dominated territories of Manchuria, whether agricultural or gathering, and were familiar with the political traditions of the region, he continued to organize into the Eight Banners. Those who were farmers, or from the Chinese-speaking towns of Liaodong, he assigned to the Chinese-martial units. The khan, in Nurgaci's rather ambiguous utterance, was the father who was "to nourish" (*ujimbi*) the "various peoples" (*geren gurun*) under his rule (see appendix II).

For the first time, Chinese speakers were not a tiny minority in the khanate, but a rapidly growing majority. They were required to show their submission to Nurgaci by having their heads shaven in the Jurchen style, adopting Jurchen dress, and performing the curtsy, all of which were extensions of his long-standing insistence that immigrants should avoid creating invidious distinctions among the khan's population, and should conform to the dress, hairstyle, and behavior of the majority. The strong egalitarianism of Nurgaci's rhetoric in Liaodong was designed both to win the affection of those who were not rich, and also to undermine the power of native elites, as similar rhetoric in Manchuria had enlarged the khan's power at the expense of the traditional social and economic powers of the Jurchen world. "Instead of letting the rich accumulate their grain and letting it rot away, or letting them pile up the goods for no use, one should nourish the begging poor."[7]

The greatest egalitarianism of all was perhaps Nurgaci's experiment with cohabitation as portions of central Liaodong came under his control. The soldiers needed to be quartered somewhere, and Nurgaci ordered that Jurchens and Chinese should share the same houses, work the same fields, and eat at the same table. As comforting as this might have sounded to the khan who nourished all the various peoples, it was popular neither with the Chinese, who found themselves with unwanted house-guests, nor with the Jurchens, who had expected to eject the vanquished from their homes and to take what they liked for themselves. Jurchen abuses of the cohabitation policy were frequently reported, and were swiftly punished. Like pillage, the reported extortions and thefts were viewed both as violations of the khan's sole right to distribute property and as subversions of the khan's wish to facilitate the Liaodong conquest by treating capitulating Chinese well. The Chinese also were reported to be abusing the cohabitation policies, primarily by taking advantage of their closeness to the Jurchens to murder them, often with poison. Paranoia spread among the Jurchens, who soon developed a mortal fear of eating and drinking, and there were no measures to make them absolutely secure. The cohabitation policy finally ended in 1625 after it was blamed for a series of rebellions by the Chinese.

In the aftermath, the state had to provide not only for separate housing and maintenance of the Jurchens, but also for the clear legal distinctions in Jurchen and Chinese status. In practice this was a distinction between military and civil functions. Chinese military leaders continued to surrender to Nurgaci, to the end of his life, and all were created Chinese-martial by the state, awarded significant lots of people, livestock, and land, and in many cases ennobled by the khanate. Chinese civil officials, however, continued in the functions that they had fulfilled for at least forty years in Manchuria, before the conquest of Liaodong: Functional servants of the khan and the *beile*s, scribes, advisors, and intermediaries with the Chinese and Koreans.

The year after he was forced to abandon his cohabitative policies Nurgaci suffered his first and only serious military defeat. He was determined to press his campaigns westward, perhaps eventually as far as the Great Wall. The Ming stronghold at Ningyuan was a critical target. The canny Ming official Yuan Chonghuan was in command, however, and on a day in late February the Jin forces were routed. Nurgaci himself was wounded, and retired to Mukden to nurse his body and his pride. Neither rallied, and on September 30, 1626, he died.

Because the conquest of Liaodong prepared the way for the creation of the Qing empire, we are often inclined to associate it with the unlimited energies, hopes, and ambitions that "birth" implies. But for Nurgaci, things must have looked rather different. By the time he secured his hold over most of Liaodong in 1621, he was nearly 62 years old, and had spent the latter two-thirds of his life in constant battle, often against members of his own family. He had expanded his rule from a small group of villages to all of Manchuria, including the large Ming frontier province of Liaodong. Yet there is no point at which either the shape of his campaigns or his proclaimed reasons for them departs much from the consistent goal of protecting and enhancing the economic basis of the wealth his lineage had nurtured for generations. Nurgaci's state had been a regional regime, founded upon the enforcement of monopolistic economic rights and control of the wealth proceeding from them. In order to achieve these ends, he would have had to rule Liaodong, and to wring recognition of his regional hegemony from China and Korea. He achieved these ends, but there is no evidence that he was determined to do much more.

4

The Qing Expansion

All his life Hung Taiji had excited the fears of his father, brothers and cousins, who were disturbed by his combination of deep talent and unfettered ambition. After Nurgaci's death Hung Taiji was indeed elected khan from among the *beile*s, the inevitable outcome of years of his manipulation of his kinsmen. He first turned his fury upon the Ming official Yuan Chonghuan, who had frustrated Nurgaci at Ningyuan and indirectly caused his death. When he assumed the khanship at Mukden on New Year's Day, 1627, Hung Taiji dispatched a letter to Yuan:

> The reason why our two nations have raised arms against each other was originally because the officials quartered in Liaodong considered their emperor to be as high and mighty as Heaven itself. They considered themselves to be as those who live in Heaven, while the khan of another nation merely created by Heaven was unworthy of any degree of independent standing. Not able to bear the insults and contempt, we have taken our case to Heaven, raising troops and beginning war with you. Since Heaven is in fact just, and heeds not the magnitude of the nations but only the righteousness of the issue, It has considered us in the right.[1]

Nurgaci had not been able to dislodge Yuan and his Ming forces from western Liaodong, but Hung Taiji decided to let the Ming court do it for him. His letter proposed a truce with Yuan; Hung Taiji had recently decided to engage in a military confrontation with Korea to force Yi acknowledgment of his suzerainty, and had no wish to continue a two-front war. Yuan found the scenario convincing, and informed the Ming court that he had successfully stopped the Jin forces east of the Great Wall. When Hung Taiji's troops attacked Ningyuan barely two months later, Yuan's cred-

Plate 5 *Borjigid-shi, later known as Xiaozhuang Wen (1613–87). A descendant of Genghis Khan, she was a junior wife of Hung Taiji, mother of his youngest son Fulin, and a factor in her son's selection as the Shunzhi emperor. She remained a formidable political force through the Shunzhi era, and during the first quarter-century of the reign of her grandson, the Kangxi emperor. Though never permitted to preside at court, Xiaozhuang Wen initiated the Qing institution of female influence from "behind the screen" that was later used by many senior court women, including the Empress Dowager Cixi (chapter 6). She is a reminder both of the continuing importance of the legacy of Genghis for the Aisin Gioro lineage, and of the prominent role played by women in many of the regencies of the Qing period.*

ibility in Peking was damaged. Another apparent truce ensued, but in the summer of 1629 Hung Taiji personally led the Eight Banners around Yuan Chonghuan, through Mongolia, and into north China. With little obstruction from Ming forces, Hung Taiji's armies rounded up massive herds of people and livestock to be driven back with him to Liaodong and the khan even found some time for sightseeing, visiting and prostrating himself before the tombs of the Jin emperors at Fangshan on the outskirts of Peking. Yuan Chonghuan, in the meantime, was arrested in Peking on suspicion of being a secret ally of Hung Taiji. Thanks as much to the determined persecution of Yuan by the eunuch faction as by the finesse of Hung Taiji, Yuan was found guilty of the charges and hacked to pieces in one of the Peking market squares. Hung Taiji reinstated his campaigns in western Liaodong.

But he did not amass his resources to make an attack against the Great Wall. He had found Mongolia a less uphill route, and had begun to fixate on the powerful khan of the Chakhar Mongols, Lighdan. The Chakhars were the descendants of the Yuan remnants who had returned to Mongolia after the fall of their empire in China in 1368. For more than a century they were known as the Northern Yuan, and at their court continued the rituals, centered on the secretive Mahākāla lamaist cult, that supposedly linked them to the Mongol Great Khans. They were also said to be in possession of the seal of the Great Khans. Certainly Lighdan aspired to unified rule over Mongolia, and had stirred persisting chaos in western Mongolia as his Chakhar warriors drove other Mongols westward, out of the pastures and valleys of the eastern regions. Hung Taiji had used Tibetan lamas in his installation ceremony in 1627, and aspired to the universal emperorship that Lighdan claimed to have inherited (see chapter 5). If he could defeat Lighdan, he would rid Mongolia of an unpopular bully, enlist the Chakhars in his own state, and gain the definitive trappings of a lamaist emperor. After years of struggle, Lighdan was finally overthrown and displaced by Hung Taiji in 1634.

By the time of the defeat of Lighdan, Hung Taiji had won another significant victory in Mukden. As his father had predicted, he had indeed leaped over the heads of his older brothers to assume the khanship in 1627, but it remained to him to dismantle the beams of collegial rule that Nurgaci had left in place. In 1629 Hung Taiji abolished the revolving co-rulership, and between 1630 and 1633 had squeezed Manggūldai and Amin out of the circle of power. He seized their banners, and together with his these formed the "Three Superior Banners" within the Eight Banners that would remain the patrimony of the Aisin Gioro lineage. Daišan, for his part, became silent. Even human sacrifice was newly regulated by Hung Taiji to enforce individual rule: In Nurgaci's time and earlier, wives of a dead man were expected to kill themselves during his burial (and Hung Taiji had insisted that Nurgaci's surviving main wife do just this); the political consequences for survivors were strong, since senior court women could become very influential, and junior princes who lost their mothers in this way rarely rose to the political stratosphere afterward. Hung Taiji insisted in 1634 that only the main wife was required to sacrifice herself; others had the option (in his own case, two of his wives were persuaded by his surviving brothers to join him in death). By the end of 1634, then, Hung Taiji used law, political maneuvering, and the relegislation of female virtue to become the single, personal ruler of the state based in Mukden.

A state it certainly was. There had been a third great change in the early years of Hung Taiji's khanship, and that was the adaptation of the ruins of the Ming bureaucracy in Mukden to the purposes of the growing state. Laws of military occupation, taxes, and the massive documentation now necessary for the management of the affairs of the Eight Banners required a genuine civil administrative apparatus. There was no choice but to rely upon Chinese bureaucrats and examination candidates, though they were personally despised and distrusted by the Jin ruler, who thought that the plots continually exposed among the local literati for rising up against their Jurchen overlords were only the manifestation of the inherently ungrateful, xenophobic, self-seeking nature of the Chinese elites. He employed them in the smallest numbers he could, and at the same time prepared the ground for an educated, all-purpose ruling elite composed of Jurchens, Mongols, and descendants of the Chinese-martial who had been with Nurgaci from his beginnings.

The Birth of the Empire

In the years 1635 and 1636 Hung Taiji publicly transformed the khanate into an empire. He abolished the name Jurchen and renamed that portion of the bannermen as Manchus. He established an official history of the Aisin Gioro lineage as being in themselves emblematic of Manchu history, having roots deep in eastern Manchuria, sharing ancestry with the fishing and gathering peoples of the upper Amur (whom he was busily conquering and impressing into the Eight Banners), with the Mongols, and with Korea (which had given him notional dominion for years, but in 1638 would come under his military occupation). In 1636 he declared himself an emperor, not a khan, and renamed his empire Qing.

Hung Taiji was just over 60, in 1643, when he died after a brief illness of unknown cause. His armies were already set for a move into China. His ninth son, the 5-year-old Fulin (1638–61), succeeded him, ruling as the Shunzhi emperor, and his younger brother Dorgon (1612–50) was appointed regent, though Fulin's mother, later known as Xiaozhuang Wen (1613–87), functioned as a co-regent and would remain influential at court for the rest of her long life. Dorgon's army, in anticipation of an attack upon China, were amassed in western Liaodong, on the east side of the Shanhai Pass through the Great Wall. On the other side of the wall, turmoil reigned. The Ming empire, long plagued by economic and social troubles, was being buffeted by two massive popular rebellions that it could not hope to survive: That begun in the 1630s by Li Zicheng in Shaanxi province, and that of Zhang Xianzhong, which in the same period had spread from Shaanzi to Sichuan. The two rebels were in a race to see which could topple the Ming first and declare a new dynasty. Li won: On April 25, 1644, his troops entered and secured Peking. The last Ming emperor to rule from the Forbidden City hanged himself from a tree on the slope of Prospect Hill.

Wu Sangui (1612–78), a distinguished Ming general and Liaodong native, was commanding a large army when he learned of the fall of Peking to Li Zicheng. He stationed his considerable forces at the Shanhai Pass, virtually across the wall from Dorgon. But his favorite concubine and his father were hostages in Peking, and Wu may have been considering disbanding his army and capitulating to the rebel regime. Dorgon made him a better offer, suggesting that they combine their forces and liberate Peking from the rebels. At the end of May, the combined Ming and Qing armies started for the Chinese capital. On June 4 Li evacuated, and on June 6 Dorgon's Qing armies occupied the city. Preparations were made to bring the child emperor Fulin to Peking, and on October 30 he was enthroned in the Forbidden City.

The conquest of Peking was only the first step in the long and uncertain process of the conquest of China. The central Chinese provinces of Zhejiang, Jiangsu, Anhui, and Sichuan were set upon by the invading forces in 1645 and 1646. The conquest there was difficult and very bloody, since the invading forces met well-organized and sometimes very determined local resistance. Cities such as Yangzhou were the scenes of grotesque slaughter – it was reported that 800,000 corpses were cremated together when the siege was ended – that would become an indelible image of Manchu brutality in Chinese national memory. Yet in the invading forces Manchus were now a dwindling minority. After the conquest of western Liaodong in the last years of Hung Taiji's life, Chinese-martial had come to handily outnumber Manchus and Mongols in the Eight Banners. As the conquest of China proceeded, a new army – the Green Standard – was organized entirely from Ming deserters, and any of its regional divisions numbered more men than all the Manchus in the national forces combined. The conquest of China proceeded as it had begun with Dorgon and Wu Sangui: as an allied enterprise in which Manchus were and remained a numerical minority.

The south of China and its adjacent territories took four decades to secure. Taiwan was annexed as Qing forces attempted to root out loyalist resisters who used it as a base from which to harry the shores of southeast China in the 1680s. The border stretches of Mongolia and the Yunnan–Guizhou fastnesses were stabilized only in the late seventeenth and middle eighteenth centuries, respectively. Tibet was invaded in 1720, its capital of Lhasa was occupied in 1750, and the territory was generally under firm (if fleeting) Qing control by the end of the century. Turkestan, the acquisition of which nearly doubled the expanse of the empire, was conquered in stages during the middle eighteenth century. Though the land-based commercial structure of Central Asia had by this time deteriorated beyond recovery, the empire gained access to the superior horses of Afghanistan and to new sources of coal, iron, gold, and silver, and, more important, was eventually able to neutralize the military danger of the Mongols, which had so seriously afflicted the Ming.

The Conquest Elite

Like the Yuan empire of the Mongols in China, the Qing distinguished between its imperial constituency and its conquered population. On terms of intimacy with the court were the Manchus, the Mongols, and the Chinese-martial bannermen who had formed the core of the conquest state in Manchuria and spearheaded the conquest of China. They were eventually joined by a comparatively small number of Albazinian, often called "Russian," bannermen and of Muslim bannermen from Turkestan.

Though Manchus were a minority in the conquest forces, their role was obviously critical, and the process of the conquest permanently changed life for those Manchus participating in the invasion. When the conquest was secure it was the bannermen who were installed in closed garrison communities where their activities were, at least in the regulations, strictly limited. Until the occupation of Turkestan that portion of the banner population directly involved in the conquest (probably of the order of 120,000–150,000) had been as mobile as the front itself, shifting in units from the ancestral lands in Manchuria to Peking, from Peking to the provinces of China, then on to Tibet or Turkestan.

When possible the bannermen were settled on land confiscated from the Ming nobility, but this was insufficient to supply their needs. Between 1664 and 1669 the process of land seizure was intense. Within a 170-mile radius of Peking alone more than seventy sites were appropriated for the housing, stables and pastures, farmlands, and cemeteries of the bannermen. The total seizure in this period was well in excess of 2 million acres in China proper. Nor did the process of seizure and enclosure end with the seventeenth century. Garrisons continued to be established until the late 1730s, 106 in all (not counting Turkestan and Tibet, which were under separate military administrations).

The political and economic consequences of establishing the bannermen as an occupation force were quickly felt. The progressive bureaucratization of the banners by the central government sharply diminished the discretionary power of the *beile*s over their banners, and by the end of the seventeenth century their role was primarily ritual. The state had become the true proprietors of the banners, and by their means had deprived rivals of the means of military challenge. Court intrigues continued, of course, and were occasionally deadly. But the sort of civil wars that had riven the Yuan empire of the Mongols were obviated. At the same time, hereditary headmen of the *mukūn* were also losing their traditional powers to make decisions to bureaucrats, who by the end of the seventeenth century appointed and sacked the headmen according to the imperial agenda.

Before the conquest, bannermen in Manchuria had been agricultural producers, and their land grants had been taxed. Even in Liaodong, Hung Taiji's policy had been to support the bannermen only when they were mobilized in his campaigns. Otherwise they were supposed to work the fields, rivers, and forests to support themselves. For the population who remained in Manchuria, these practices continued. But in China, bannermen were no longer producers: They were salaried, and lived off the proceeds – distributed by the garrison officers – of the land grants.

It was impossible for the new regime to provide for the real needs, let alone the ambitions, of the occupation force. During the first century after the conquest, the garrison populations grew, but the land given them by the court to support their soldiers was in many instances sold off by garrison officers for personal gain. Stipends, paid monthly in silver, were very modestly increased, but could not cover the decline in per capita support caused by the rising population and shrinking banner lands. In any case, a majority of the populations within the garrisons did not receive stipends, but lived as the dependents of those men between the ages of 15 and 60 who were eligible for, and lucky enough to actually secure, the payments. By the 1680s some garrison commanders were expressing worries that their bannermen would turn to outright banditry, or rise in rebellion, if something were not done. At about the same time, an officer of one of the Peking garrisons reported,

> Weapons are insufficient to supply all the available men, but the subjects may not become officials, or farmers, or workers, or merchants, or soldiers in the regular armies, or commoners, but must remain clustered within less than a hundred miles of the capital. On account of this their livelihoods decline day by day, with no means of alleviation. Those who are not appointed active-service bannermen have no means at all of livelihood.[2]

Fulin's successor, the Kangxi emperor Xuanye (r. 1662–1722), attempted to ameliorate the growing social crisis of the garrisons by increasing the number of stipends available nationally, from about 80,000 to 120,000. Xuanye's successor, the Yongzheng emperor Yinzhen (r. 1723–35), attempted a marginal improvement by creating "youth" appointments – tiny subsidies intended to underwrite a boy's education. The court also attempted to erase the mass indebtedness of the bannermen. The Kangxi emperor budgeted more than half a million ounces (taels) of silver a year to pay off loans to the bannermen. This policy was continued sporadically and on a more modest scale under the Yongzheng emperor, who preferred a new program of reassigning bannermen from the garrisons of China to government farms in Manchuria. Like Emperor Shizong of the Jin (see chapter 2), he considered that the character as well as the economic condition of the soldiers would improve once they were back in the bracing air of Manchuria. Unfortunately 90 percent of those removed under the emperor's program ran away from the farms, probably to return to China proper and make their living as thieves, beggars, or enforcers for the criminal underground.

Imperial distress over the condition of the bannermen of the 1700s was the miserable end to what had been a grand plan, under the Kangxi emperor, to create an all-purpose conquest elite, not unlike the *osmanli* class under the Ottoman sultans. According to this vision Manchus, Mongols, and Chinese-martial were to be both rugged, resourceful soldiers and liberally-educated erudites. They would govern and stabilize the newly-conquered territories, move between military and civil appointments as necessary, and exhort the leagues of banner commoners to follow the path of personal discipline and cultivation.

The origins of this ideal had lain with Hung Taiji, whose distrust of conquered Chinese officials had made him impatient to produce a class of literate bannermen who could perform the civil tasks of government. The first emperor had established examinations in both Manchu and Chinese for bannermen, and personally insisted that historical works, as well books on philosophy and mathematics, be in the curriculum. The first examinations were held in 1638, but from the beginning there was little success. Bannermen had the same difficulties that poor Chinese had always had in preparing for the examinations: No time and no money for the time-consuming, risky study. They did have, however, a more appealing avenue to advancement: Service on the battlefield, which brought quicker and better rewards. Later emperors had to deal with a situation in which opportunities for battlefield merit were declining steeply, but bureaucratic appointments remained difficult to secure. Most bannermen after the conquest had time to be educated, but no means: Only rudimentary schools existed in the garrisons, sustained by the charity of garrison officers or even local Chinese well-wishers, but wholly inadequate to provide the advanced literacy and rote learning that would qualify a man to compete in the examinations.

The Kangxi emperor, whose carefully-crafted public profile was that of an exemplar in combining both military and civil brilliance, was uncompromising in his demand that the bannermen should follow his model. "The Manchus take riding and archery as their root, and this was originally no obstacle to book learning. Those bannermen examined as county and provincial candidates should also be required to show proficiency in riding and archery." The book learning in question was Chinese classical studies. Though there were deviations from the policy during the Kangxi and Yongzheng reigns, it is worth nothing that as late as the 1750s the Qianlong emperor was still assuming that Manchu was the first language of most Manchus, and that the major advance to be wrought through education was improvements in the bannermen's grasp of Chinese.

But garrison officers had been informing the court since the 1670s that bannermen were taking up the local dialects of the regions of China where they were settling, and that upcoming generations not only were illiterate in Manchu but did not understand the spoken language very well. Some of the implications of this cultural change were grave: The military depended and would continue to depend upon Manchu for secure communications between the court and the field. Schools were established at which members of the Aisin Gioro lineage, leading families of the aristocracy, and high-ranking banner officers would be given comprehensive educations, including the Manchu language. But for the mass of common bannermen there was no education policy, and would not be before the end of the eighteenth century. The state devised no universal, effective means of elementary education for the banner populations – a failure that is possibly akin to the absence of state-sponsored elementary educational institutions in the civil sector, but also is characteristic of many aspects of garrison financing, which by policy was always too little too late. Instead of creating a school system, the state created and supervised the examination system, on the apparent principle that control of standards through the medium of the examinations obviated control of the institutions of education (and responsibility for their maintenance).

Whatever potential functions the examinations for bannermen may have served for the conquest state in terms of identifying and cultivating talent, their administration was also affected by social and political developments. The court never stated an intention of supporting a growing banner population forever. On the contrary, it seems to have utilized the examinations as a means of attracting a certain proportion of men (and their families) out of the garrisons and out of the military altogether, to become self-supporting as civil officials. In accord with this aim, incentives were often applied, though the examinations never became as attractive for the bannermen as the court hoped. Preferential routes for Manchus into the bureaucracy were a reflection of the early state strategy to gradually diminish the dependent banner population.

The conquest state, its resources stretched to the limit, was never able to underwrite a program for the cultivation and selection of an amalgamated elite. The result was that for decades the empire remained dependent upon the Chinese-martial to govern the newly-conquered provinces, particularly in central and southern China. These were primarily men of Liaodong, since the very old immigrant families – those who had lived at Fe Ala at the time of Sin Chung-il's visit – had been absorbed into the Manchu banners. The Chinese-martial of Liaodong were Chinese speaking, and the elite among them were literate. As bannermen, their loyalty was supposed to be secure, though it was carefully husbanded by the ostensibly even-handed treatment of the banner populations in the middle 1600s. The most extreme dependence upon this population occurred in south China, where the Qing conquest remained superficial, and the occupied provinces were put virtually under the personal rule of three powerful Liaodong families. Eventually, this dependence upon the Chinese-martial for administration of conquered territories was regarded with suspicion by the Kangxi emperor. At the level of the garrison populations, the declining standard of living and the rarity of managerial positions created such competition that the court gradually came to feel that it had to intervene to provide greater leverage for Manchu bannermen. A dramatic demonstration of this policy occurred during the later decades of the Kangxi reign.

Since the initiation of the examinations for bannermen under Hung Taiji in 1643, a quota system had been put in place in an attempt to keep examination success equitable. The scheme changed from time to time, but generally adhered to a 5 : 5 : 2 ratio, meaning that for every five successful candidates from the Manchus, there would also be five from the Chinese-martial and two from the Mongols. In the immediate post-conquest period the Chinese-martial bannermen may have represented as much as 40 percent of the military population, and in the decades immediately following the conquest of north China may have ballooned to as large a proportion as 70 percent. But as Chinese-martial enrolments grew during the early Kangxi period, Chinese-martial were gradually displaced among successful examination partici-pants. This happened principally through the simple device of reversing the Chinese-martial and Mongol quotas. Where in the early Kangxi period the Manchu and Chinese-martial quotas were identical and Mongol quotas about half, by the end of the Kangxi period Manchu and Mongol quotas were identical and Chinese-martial quotas had been lowered to about half. In the late 1600s, these quotas pertained to a population in which the ratio of Manchu to Mongol to Chinese-martial might have been as skewed as 2 : 1 : 7.

In 1669, the fissure in the conquest elite was made overt. For the first time a primary distinction was made between Manchus and Mongols, on the one hand, and Chinese-martial on the other: A single quota was thereafter to apply to Manchus and Mongols, and a separate one to Chinese-martial. In comparison to the evident population of the Chinese-martial, this ratio was a pro-found disadvantage to them. A similar change in quotas applied to the distribution of paying positions within the garrisons. Chinese-martial and Mongol ratios were reversed. Since there were rarely enough Mongols to fill all their mandated positions, Manchus were often given the leftovers. On the other hand, Chinese-martial could rarely find employment in the garrisons after Kangxi times, and increasingly applied for permission to – in the words that became formulaic in banner documents – "leave the banners and become commoners."

As will be shown below, this progressive alienation of the Chinese-martial from the garrisons, the middle ranks of the mili-tary command, and the civilian hierarchy began before and contin-ued after a cataclysmic confrontation with the Chinese-martial families who had been given licence to rule south China in the early decades of the conquest. This disowning of all but a very small remaining portion of the Chinese-martial by the state was a definitive passage not only in their family histories (for most would ever afterwards consider themselves "Chinese") but also for the Manchus, whom the state felt it must now more closely identify in order to organize and distribute its resources.

Consolidation under the Kangxi Emperor

Like the Shunzhi emperor Fulin, the Kangxi emperor Xuanye began his emperorship under a regency, but unlike his father displayed a precocious talent for politics and went on to one of the most brilliant reigns that any ruler in the world can claim. His selection as emperor, at the age of 8, was probably connected to the fear of smallpox. Soon after the arrival of the Manchus in Peking, they encountered the disease and died of it in comparatively high numbers. They pushed the native Peking population out of the walled inner precincts of the city and reserved them for bannermen, hoping to lessen the effects of the disease by lessening their exposure. They also systematically submitted themselves to the Chinese practice of variolation (controlled exposure), but evidence from the imperial genealogies suggests heavy losses among the Aisin Gioro, and probably the Manchus at large, in the 1660s. One of the victims was the Shunzhi emperor himself, at whose bedside the boy Xuanye – who had survived the infection and for the rest of his life had the scars to prove it – was chosen as successor in the knowledge that he would be immune.

The Kangxi emperor was remarkable for his stamina throughout his life, but was even more noted for astounding intellect and acumen. The Chinese historian Liu Danian once compared him, at length, to the roughly contemporary Peter the Great. Liu noted that, like Peter, Xuanye was able to construct a convincing public image as one sympathetic to the people, and thus generate legitimacy for his regime among the literati in particular; that he was enlightened and creative in his attempts to promote economic growth; and that he reached out to Europe for new ideas.

In the Kangxi emperor's youth, the opinion among the Manchu elite was that his father had been far too enthusiastic about the Chinese elite and their culture. The Shunzhi emperor's interest in

Plate 6   *The young Kangxi emperor, probably not long after destroying his regency and assuming personal rule. He wears traditional Manchu cap, robe, and riding boots, but is shown in the pose of a Chinese scholar, surrounded by the conventional paraphernalia of reading and writing. The painting is a reminder not only of the emperor's genuine interest in and unusual aptitude for literature, but of his energetic campaigns to win the sympathy and support of the Chinese elite for the conquest regime of the Qing.*

Chinese poetry and literature (which he started late, and was never very good at) was considered effete, and his virtual retirement from public life in order to concentrate upon Buddhist study was seen as close to dereliction of duty. The Manchu aristocrat Oboi,

Plate 7   *The sixty-year reign of the Kangxi emperor permitted him
extraordinary personal influence in the growth and stabilization of
the Qing. His tremendous intellect, political instinct, and physical
stamina are generally credited with making the Qing one of the
greatest of the early modern empires. The emperor was ruthless,
and as he aged was forced to be perpetually suspicious of his sons,
many of whom were scheming to become emperor after his death,
and may even have wearied of his long life. In hopes of calming the
situation the emperor named a favorite son as heir apparent, but in
1713 was forced to acknowledge the pretender as hopelessly corrupt and sentence him to be confined for life. The princes were
thereafter more circumspect, but the emperor died knowing that his
household had become a nest of factionalism, betrayal, and corruption. He is shown here is full court dress, and in the pose commonly
used in portraits for posthumous veneration.*

who was influential in the regencies of both the Shunzhi and Kangxi emperors, had advocated the strict limiting of the political influence of the Chinese.

To be sure, there was no point at which Xuanye wished to change the Qing polity from Manchu into Chinese; on the contrary, he worked assiduously to keep the Qing emperorship from becoming captive to Chinese interests. On the other hand, he had both an attraction to the foundations of Chinese culture and an acute appreciation of the political value of persuading Chinese elites of the justice of the conquest regime. His own education, densely compressed into the early years of his childhood, had made him fluent in speaking, a passable calligrapher, and an excellent writer in Chinese. He was attentive in the lectures that emperors regularly received from their Confucian tutors, and did all he could to persuade Chinese scholars that he was their personal patron. Projects to restore libraries destroyed in the Li and Zhang rebellions, as well as the conquest, were sponsored by his court. To repair the Manchu image in the regions where the violence of the conquest had been concentrated in southern and central coastal China, he undertook a series of "southern tours" with members of his family, in which he was hosted by locals, listened raptly to the details of local history, and celebrated the beauties of the landscape. Most acute, however, was his attempt to co-opt those Ming loyalists who believed they could express their fidelity to the late dynasty by living as self-proclaimed "hermits," refusing all form of government service. The emperor sponsored a special examination to attempt to draw out the recluses, and with great fanfare invited them to join a Qing-mandated project that no Ming loyalist could reasonably refuse – the writing of Ming history. No miracles resulted from these initiatives, but the chill between the conquest state and the former Ming elite began to thaw, and continued to do so under the count's steady attempts to flatter, employ, and selectively elevate Chinese literati.

Like Peter the Great, the Kangxi emperor was not content to address himself to the lofty minority among the population. The economy of the early Qing years was in a shambles. The bloody rebellions of the late Ming had reduced the population in Sichuan and Hunan, both central agricultural regions, and the conquest had devastated some of the most densely populated cities of the central coast. Refugees from the fighting were continuing to avoid the wasted regions, and the state in the Kangxi period had to create new incentives to draw the populations back to the deserted areas. Cheap land helped, as did generous government expenditures for the reconstruction of road and irrigation systems. Transit taxes were kept low to ease the flow of goods towards the town and cities, and market regulations in the critical regions were relaxed. Not only did the economy revive, but the population expanded at a strong rate by the end of the seventeenth century. To avoid crushing the enlarged population under the head tax, the quotas were frozen in 1711. The emperor worked hard to earn a reputation among common people as a monarch exhibiting the Confucian virtue of "benevolence" (*ren*), and he probably deserved it. To avoid strangling the economy or alienating the population with weighty taxes, his regime managed its policing and its campaigns of expansion on thin budgets. Though many of his visions, such as the creation of an all-competent ruling elite, were sacrificed on this alter of frugality, the empire was put upon a firm foundation in China.

Also like Peter the Great, the Kangxi emperor was not averse to learning from all peoples he chanced upon, including Europeans. But the "Europe" to which he had access was not the world of the Enlightenment that inspired Peter, but that of the Counter-Reformation. Francis Xavier had made an early foray from his base in Goa in 1552, but died on a small island near Canton. He was buried there, but when disinterred by the faithful two years later his body was described as undecayed and returned to Goa for reburial. Xavier inspired other Jesuits to set their sights on China, and Matteo Ricci (1552–1610) had stunned the Ming court with his ability to master both the Chinese language and mores. The Manchus had themselves been benefited in the conquest by Jesuit contributions, particularly in the forms of cannon captured in Liaodong and of detailed maps that guided them to unknown territories in central and southern China. Indeed in the later part of his reign Xuanye would sponsor a Jesuit-guided project to produce a unified scale map of the entire Qing empire.

In the early Kangxi years the emperor considered adopting the European calendar in the empire, since his review of the Jesuits' calculations had proved to him that theirs was the more accurate means of marking the year (Ricci, together with Li Zhizao and Xu Guangqi, had translated Euclid into Chinese the century before, and the text was introduced to the emperor by the Jesuits of his time). An intense backlash from Chinese officials, who considered the calendar a pillar of state rectitude, ensued. Xuanye was forced to consider that the goodwill of the Chinese literati outweighed the considerable charms of the Jesuits, and dropped the project. But for the remainder of the century Confucians watched him closely, looking for signs that the emperor was being seduced into any of the many seditious ideas that the Jesuits were likely to spawn.

They were probably right to be wary. Many of the Jesuits in China at this time – Jean Baptiste Régis, Pierre Jartoux, Thomas Pereira, Jean-François Gerbillon, and others – learned Manchu as well as Chinese, and would engage in colloquies with the emperor on astronomy, mathematics, and philosophy. In 1692 the emperor survived a bout of malaria after being administered quinine by Pereira and Gerbillon, and thereafter he inquired eagerly into their knowledge of medicine. The result was a complete anatomical text, with drawings adapted from European manuals but the commentary entirely in Manchu. Like much of the information channeled to the Qing by the Jesuits, this was not stale news, but the latest thing – in this case, based upon Thomas Bartholin's *Anatomia* of 1684, which the emperor probably came to know earlier and better than many European doctors. He also granted the Jesuits a plot of land inside the Forbidden City, where they erected the church later called the Beitang ("northern church," one of four at each of the cardinal directions). And he vigorously defended his Jesuits against charges from Rome that they had descended to heresy by attempting to reconcile Confucian ancestor-worship with Catholicism.

In 1690 the Kangxi emperor wrote to the Vatican a letter simultaneously produced in Chinese, Manchu, and Latin advising Pope Innocentius XII to be more relative in his spiritual judgments. When a papal legate arrived in 1705 to enforce the pope's will that Confucian influence be purged from the practices of the Jesuits in China, the emperor had him locked up in Macao, where he later died. Subsequent visits by papal commissioners were also brushed off by the emperor, who grew colder toward the prospect of new Jesuit arrivals. He keenly felt, after that time, that they could not serve both the pope and the Qing emperor, and was not wholly inclined to trust that they would be able to resist the power of the church.

The Kangxi emperor's general mistrust was learned early. When at the age of 14 in 1667 he had announced his intention to assume power from his regency, he found that the aristocrat Oboi was subverting his authority. The teenage emperor quickly assembled a political coalition – including his grandmother, the redoubtable Xiaozhuang Wen – that permitted him to arrest Oboi (who died in prison) and command the severe punishment or execution of Oboi's collaborators, including at least one member of the imperial lineage. The emperor's reputation for decisiveness and perspicacity was perhaps insufficiently appreciated in the southern part of China, where the Chinese-martial rulers of the three occupation zones (*fan*) – often called in English the "Three Feudatories" – unwisely played to his mistrust of those too comfortable with power that was not their own.

The occupation regimens of the south had been established as an expediency of conquest. As they stood in 1673, the Three Feudatories were the survivors of the larger number of military governorships (*zongdu*) established throughout China in the first decade of conquest. During the Shunzhi (1644–61) years, the appointments were reshuffled so that surrendering Ming Chinese who had been temporarily appointed to the posts were supplanted by Chinese-martial. In this way, natives of the pre-conquest Qing order in Liaodong were given control over consolidating the conquest in China. The Shunzhi court rested more easily knowing that the occupation was not in the hands of Ming deserters, and the political effects of using men who were speakers of Chinese in these posts may have been considerable.

The Feudatories were given extraordinary powers to conquer, police, and tax the southern regions of Yunnan, Guizhou, Guangdong, Guangxi, and Fujian. All were under the control of Chinese-martial who had joined the Qing in the later, westward campaigns of Hung Taiji. Geng Jingzhong had inherited control of his feudatory in Fujian province from his father Jimao, whose own father Zhongming had joined the Hung Taiji cause in 1633. Shang Kexi had come to Hung Taiji shortly after, and in 1672 was still controlling Guangdong province in the name of the Qing court. But the most powerful of these southern warlords was Wu Sangui, who had led the Qing forces into Peking in 1644, later had his son marry a sister of the Shunzhi emperor, and in the process of the Qing conquest of the south assumed the role of satrap of Yunnan and Guizhou. He seemed to consider the position permanent.

Wu drew his extraordinary civil and military powers in the southwest from completion of his mission to destroy Ming resistance in Yunnan and Burma in 1661, when the Ming pretender there was executed. In reward Wu was made an imperial prince. His mission in the southwest accomplished, Wu showed no signs of remitting his special political or economic rights. In fact his activities resembled the early campaigns of Nurgaci to monopolize control over economic resource (in Wu's case, salt, gold, copper, ginseng, and rhubarb) and to dominate local political relations (in Wu's case, the bureaucracies of Yunnan and neighboring provinces, as well as Tibetan settlements east of Lhasa). The Board of Revenue complained to the court of the enormous subsidies provided to Wu's troops, and the court hinted that Wu might, in view of his advanced age (he was in his middle 50s), retire. In 1667 Wu did offer to retire, but an orchestrated clamor from the bureaucrats of his domains moved the Qing court (then under the Kangxi regents) to reject his offer. Uneasiness over Wu's growing power and anxiety over his subsidies – which had to be covered by funds drained from other provinces – continued at Peking, and was growing stronger as the Kangxi emperor assumed rule.

When, in 1673, Shang Kexi was forced out of his position as ruler of Guangdong and Guangxi by his son Shang Zhixin, Kexi requested that the court allow him to abdicate in favor of his son. Now 19 years old, the emperor did not intend to tolerate the continued compromise of consolidated Qing rule of the south, nor did he intend to drain the imperial coffers to pacify the satraps themselves. Worse, Shang Kexi now proposed to make his feudatory into a hereditary kingdom. Over the apprehensions of many of his court advisors, the emperor abolished the Shang feudatory and ordered its armies dismantled.

Wu Sangui understood the meaning of the court's action. In late December of 1673 he seceded, declared Yunnan to be the state of Zhou, and went on the offensive in Guizhou and Hunan. He proposed to the Kangxi emperor that they should agree to put China into Wu's hands, and the Manchus should return to Liaodong. Xuanye promptly had Wu's son executed. Sangui, now having no reason to hold back, attempted to march north toward Peking, but the Eight Banners had already been positioned to stop him moving north of the Yangzi.

The campaigns of Wu Sangui thereafter did not in themselves threaten the Qing, but his uprising shattered the delicate and superficial structure of the military occupation in south China. Within three years his cause was supported by his fellow Chinese-martial Shang Zhixin and Geng Jingzhong. By 1679 the Qing forces had broken the will of the other feudatories and their supporters. Wu Sangui, stockaded in the fastnesses of Yunnan, died in that year. He was succeeded as emperor of the Zhou dynasty by his grandson Wu Shifan, who finally ended the civil war by committing suicide in 1681.

The Three Feudatories War was the crucible in which the Qing fate in China was determined: To survive on a shaky foundation of affiliated autonomous regimes, or to build centralized rule in the south from the ground up. Wu Sangui, in his rather eerie imitation of the career of Nurgaci, demonstrated the logic of allowing military leaders to aggrandize themselves in exchange for occasional service to the regime. It was the same logic that had led to the evisceration of Ming ability to rule Manchuria and the eventual victory of the Qing, and the Kangxi emperor intended to guard severely against the concentration of power independent of the emperorship, whether in the provinces, in the bureaucracy, or in the imperial lineage. Previously the court had primarily been wary of the ambitions of the Manchu nobility. Now, it discovered that equally serious threats could be posed by the elites of the Chinese-martial. The response of the emperor was to smash the military governorships with which they had been entrusted, while systematically diminishing their roles in the civil bureaucracies and in the Eight Banners.

New Conquerors and Old: The Manchus and the Mongols

Ming China had known of deep rivalries between eastern and western Mongolia, and attempted to exploit them in order to prevent a recrudescence of Mongol power. But twice there emerged prolonged and effective efforts to recentralize power in Mongolia, and in each instance the Ming were threatened. In the 1440s the western Mongol leader Esen reunited the two halves of Mongolia; a hapless Ming campaign to stop his advance at Tumu in Turkestan resulted in the death of the leading Ming eunuchs and the abduction by Esen of the Zhengtong emperor (who was returned to China seven years later). The danger subsided with the disintegration of Esen's power some years later, but returned when, in the middle 1500s, Altan Khan strengthened the regime of the eastern Mongols and for a time threatened the Ming capital of

Plate 8   *In the Qing period, imperial architecture generally carried inscriptions in at least three languages – Chinese, Manchu, and Mongolian (as shown here, from left to right). This is a gate inscription from the Forbidden City. The emperors themselves were adept in all three languages until the late nineteenth century, and expected the aristocracy to be so as well. Manchu and Mongolian were written in similar but not identical scripts, both derived via a Uigur script from the Semitic ones of the ancient Middle East. (National Palace Museum, Peking)*

Peking, in the process bringing the third Dalai Lama (but the first to be recognized as such) from Tibet to act as a unifying and legitimating presence. Though Altan's power, too, lessened in ensuing years, he contributed to the establishment in eastern Mongolia of a stable, complex, and prestigious tradition of rulership in the region. Under Lighdan khan, that regime would in the early 1600s be the greatest challenge to Nurgaci and Hung Taiji in their ambition to wrest control of the commercially and agriculturally important area, Liaodong, from the Ming.

At the time of the coalescence of the Qing state in Manchuria under Nurgaci at the beginning of the seventeenth century, systematic Mongolian influence was integral to the region. Mongolian political influence, particularly in language, was pervasive; Mongolian names were widely adopted by the Jurchens (who were soon to be Manchus); the Mongolian written language had become the standard means of communication in Manchuria as well as between Manchurian rulers and Korea; Mongolian horses, saddles, clothes, musical instruments, and other goods were regularly traded in the markets of the region. Chakhars and Khorchins had come into Manchuria in waves, driven sometimes by drought or famine, sometimes by political disorders, and had attached themselves as soldiers to the Ming garrisons of Liaodong; many had gone further east, to settle among the Jurchens.

The early Qing empire did all it could to co-opt the terms of loyalty that had become institutionalized among Mongol descendant peoples of Inner Asia. Hung Taiji used his conquest of the Chakhars to claim dominion over their kinsmen who had migrated to Liaodong and settled in the Chinese garrisons, claiming that they and the imperial lineage of the Manchus were "one people." Indeed those Mongols who were incorporated into the state before the conquest of China in 1644 were brought into the Qing military apparatus, the Eight Banners, as "Mongol bannermen" (*menggu baqi*), on terms in all ways comparable to those of the Manchu bannermen with whom they served. It was and remained the Mongol Eight Banners, which subsumed the Chakhar and Kharachin populations, that was the Qing link to the Northern Yuan and its continuation of the imperial rights of the Genghis–Khubilai line. Through the Chakhars – that is, through the Mongol Eight Banners – the Qing could construe themselves as heirs of the Mongol Great Khans, and thus considered themselves given the right of dominion over the eternal followers of Genghis on the steppe.

Mongols of Mongolia, however, incorporated after the conquest of China were taxonomized and administered very differently. It is no contradiction to say that as the Qing court worked to preserve the prestige of Mongol culture and achievement with which it identified itself, it also undermined the economic and political autonomy of the Mongol confederacies. The earliest, and what remained the primary, instrument for Qing control of the Mongol confederacies was the Court of Colonial Affairs (literally "department for the governance of outlying provinces," *tulergi golo be dasara jurgan, li-fan yuan*). Like all organs for the management of borders, the Court of Colonial Affairs did not use Chinese as its primary language of business. Its ancestor had been the Mongolian Bureau (*monggo yamun*) of the Hung Taiji era, which after 1638 became the Court of Colonial Affairs and expanded its jurisdiction to Turkic, Tibetan, and in some cases Russian matters. Its president was by law a Manchu or Mongol.

After the conquest of China, the Qing correctly feared that Mongol leaders would attempt to enlist Russian aid in their power struggles and bring a Romanov military presence into Mongolia permanently. In the earliest years of the Qing regime in China, these fears were excited by the energetic leader Khungtaiji, who in centralizing and expanding his power base in western Mongolia frequently appealed to the Romanovs, requesting firearms, cash, and advisors. Like the Mongol unifier Altan Khan, Khungtaiji also used Tibetan religion to consolidate his authority, even sending his talented son Galdan to Tibet to be educated for service as a lama.

Galdan (1632 or 1644–97) returned to Mongolia in the late 1670s to avenge the murder of his brother, and in the ensuing years he prosecuted a war of unification among neighboring Mongol groups that strongly resembled Nurgaci's early career (also as a putative avenger) among the Jurchens. Some of the Mongol groups Galdan battled were based not in Mongolia proper but in Turkestan, and Galdan invaded the area in 1678. He conquered several of the major caravan cities, including Kashgar, Yarkand, Hami, Yili, and Turfan, and brought the Muslim populations there under his control.

In 1677 the Kangxi emperor was informed that there was trouble on the western frontier, and that the Muslims of Turkestan were requesting relief. At the time the Qing was in the middle of the war against the Three Feudatories, and the Kangxi emperor elected not to get involved. But as soon as the war against the Three Feudatories was concluded, the emperor sent messengers to the leaders of the Mongol federations, foremost among them

Galdan, informing them that he had defeated the Three Feudatories and was now at liberty to interest himself in the affairs of Mongolia, Turkestan, and Tibet. Instead of war, the emperor proposed all-party talks, including Galdan, the Dalai Lama, and the khans of Inner Mongolia. In 1686 the talks were convened, with representatives of the Dalai Lama and Galdan visiting Inner Mongolia to discuss the disposition of eastern Turkestan. But Galdan disavowed the resolution of the talks, claiming that the eastern Mongols had deliberately insulted the representative of the Dalai Lama. He immediately amassed troops to invade eastern Mongolia, much of whose population fled by the tens of thousands into Qing territory, seeking protection. The Kangxi emperor, assuming responsibility for his part in the failed peace process, sheltered the refugees.

The new difficulties threatened to upset the Qing's ongoing negotiations with the Russians for a border treaty. Russia had been an ally of Galdan's father, and the Kangxi emperor feared that they would arm or aid Galdan at this critical juncture. But the Romanov empire was equally eager to conclude the treaty with the Qing, and indicated that they would leave Galdan to his own devices. One last time, the emperor tried for a peace conference. This time he was frustrated by an inability to secure approval from the Dalai Lama. As it happened the Dalai Lama was dead, but this fact was being concealed by the Tibetan official Sangye Gyatso, who joined Galdan in a demand that the Mongol leaders under Qing protection be surrendered to Galdan before the beginning of talks. Before this was resolved, Galdan was met with a surprise challenge from within. His nephew, Tsewang Araptan, drove him into Outer Mongolia in 1690. Desperate to regain influence and decent grazing lands, Galdan's decimated forces again attempted an invasion of Inner Mongolia, but this time Qing troops stationed there drove him off.

The Kangxi emperor had in the meantime solidified his position with Russia in the Treaty of Nerchinsk, and determined to hasten an end to the Galdan saga one way or another. He tried a two-pronged approach. He offered amnesty to Galdan, and rewards for surrender. At the same time, he began outfitting a new military expedition, arming his vanguard with muskets and cannon. The khans of Inner Mongolia formally accepted the Kangxi emperor as their supreme khan at Dolonnor in 1691, but Galdan was determined to resist Qing rule forever. In 1694, a drought in Outer

Mongolia and Turkestan forced him to attempt another incursion into Inner Mongolia. A massive campaign of the Eight Banners, with the emperor himself in command of a battalion of 80,000 men, turned Galdan back in 1696. The Qing forces pursued him as far as Jao Modo, where Galdan's supporters, including his wife and many of his children, were mowed down; survivors defected to Tsewang Araptan. Galdan escaped and for a time lingered in the vicinity of Hami in Turkestan, where his 14-year-old son was being held captive by the Muslim ruler.

The emperor, realizing that Galdan was all but finished, did not relent. In 1697, Galdan received news that the Qing were organizing a new campaign against him. Betrayed, surrounded, and hopeless, he poisoned himself. His nephew Danjira had his body cremated and took the ashes to Tibet. Shortly afterward, Danjira himself took up the offers from the Qing that Galdan had so often rejected. By 1705 he had been appointed the governor (*jasak*) of those western Mongols who had submitted to the empire. The Qing organized conquered Mongolia into "banners" (Chinese *qi*, Mongolian *khōshun*, Manchu *gūsă*), but they were in no way comparable to the Mongol Eight Banners, nor were they intended to be understood that way. "Banners" were in this case just a way of disrupting federated structures with the imposition of new administrative lines whose divisions mimicked those of the Eight Banners; but these were in reality territorial rather than demographic units (not unlike the way the "garrisons" of Manchuria had functioned under the Ming).

The Kangxi emperor remained wary of strategic combinations between Tibet and the unconquered Mongols of Central Asia. The lamas had been influential in persuading the khans of Inner Mongolia to join the Qing, rather than the Russians, at the Dolonnor Conference. Now that Inner Mongolia was secured, the emperor heeded the requests of the secular king of Tibet, Lhabzang Khan, that his own bid for a restoration of his power be supported. The result was the coup of 1705, backed by Qing troops. Sangye Gyatso was removed as regent, and replaced by Lhabzang Khan, who quickly deposed the fifth Dalai Lama and installed the sixth. When the new Dalai Lama died en route to Peking for his recognition ceremony, Lhabzang Khan tried to install his own son as the new Dalai Lama, which led to widespread disorders in Tibet and Mongolia. Tsewang Araptan, who had succeeded Galdan as leader of the western Mongols, invaded Lhasa in 1717 and deposed

Lhabzang. The Qing intervened, and in 1718 occupied Lhasa, after which they installed the seventh Dalai Lama themselves.

This first Qing attempt at military occupation of Tibet was not a success. Tsewang Araptan's forces destroyed the Qing regiment posted to Lhasa. The Kangxi emperor mobilized the submitted Mongols of Qinghai and Inner Mongolia against Tsewang Araptan in Tibet, realizing that the stability both of Mongolia and of southwest China was at stake. In 1720 regiments of Qinghai and Sichuan retook Lhasa. A permanent Eight Banners garrison was established, as well as the Manchu commissioners (*ambans*), who were basically political informants to the emperor. The kingship was abolished, and Tibet was thus stripped of claims to secular political independence.

The restructuring of Mongolia demanded not only the creation of new jurisdictions but also the integration of the noble class of the steppe, through the normal means of marriage alliances and incorporation of the steppe Mongols into the imperial aristocracy. Thus the khans who had submitted at Dolonnor were allowed to remain as hereditary administrative officials after their surrender to the Kangxi emperor and were incorporated into the imperial lineage through marriage alliances. In 1706 a new khan, the Sayin Noyon, was created and at the same stroke married into the imperial lineage. Tsereng (d. 1750), the Sayin Noyon Khan, became in fact the symbol of steppe submission to the empire, and enjoyed the singular honor of having his tablet worshipped in the imperial lineage temple.

Titanic Competitors: The Qing and the Romanov Empires

The Qing campaigns of conquest had never been exclusively westerly in orientation. In Hung Taiji's time the Qing campaigned to militarily secure and commercially dominate the Amur region, as the eastern terminus of the empire and the newly-identified "ancestral" source of Qing legitimacy. During the reign of the Shunzhi emperor, Qing military presence in the Amur region was increased, but very modestly: The demands of the conquest of China on the military apparatus were high, and Qing troops throughout Manchuria remained thinly applied. The primary assertion of Qing dominion in Sanxing (Ilantumen) and Ninguta was the tendency to banish offending military officers and bureaucrats, whether civilian or banner, to these regions. In 1653 a civil admin-istration, based at Mukden and extending eastward to the Amur, was constructed, and the small garrison at Ninguta was regular-ized. Though part of the object was to create a firm wall against Russian intrusion, the process also impressed or attracted a larger number of northern peoples – most numerous among them the Sibos – into the Qing military, where they were organized into special units of the Eight Banners as "New Manchus."

In the course of its conquest of northern Manchuria, the Qing empire came into increasing conflict with the Romanov empire in Russia. In the 1500s Russia had already begun to dominate Sibe-ria, which became important for its furs, timber products, and rich mineral deposits. A century later the Romanovs and Qing came into direct competition for the Amur river. Rising military tensions were resolved by treaties in the late seventeenth and eighteenth centuries, and domination of the Northeast Asian peoples was split between Russia and China. The treaties permitted Russia access to the Pacific coast, from which were launched the explora-tions of North America in the early eighteenth century that made the peoples of Alaska subjects of the Russian tsar, and nominally adherents of the Russian Orthodox Church, before the year 1800.

Russian conquest of Siberia began with the expedition of the Yermak Timofeyevich in 1581–2. Siberian furs and minerals be-came a major source of wealth for the Russian empire. From the early seventeenth century Siberia was also used as a penal colony for criminals and political prisoners. By the 1650s, the Amur valley had been claimed for the Romanov empire by a series of explorers (the best known being Yerofei Khabarov and Onufri Stepanov). Many villages along the Amur were rendering tribute (*yasak, jasak*) to Russian officers representing the Russian court. In 1654 a clash occurred between bannermen stationed at Ninguta and Russian soldiers based at Fort Kumarsky (on the north bank of the Amur), and the next year the banner troops tried unsuccess-fully to capture Kumarsky. In order to deprive the Russians of the goods rendered by the Amur peoples, the Qing court ordered forced resettlement of the Evenks and Dagurs westward to the Nani river valley. But increasing Russian presence in the Amur continued to alarm the Qing. In 1661, as the young Shunzhi emperor lay in the final stages of his fatal smallpox, the governor of Mukden province submitted a panicked assessment of the condition of Qing rule in their homelands, including Liaodong: The migration to China of the Eight Banners, in combination with the restrictions on immigration from China, had left Manchuria underpopulated, its cities falling into ruins, its fields untended, its perimeters without adequate defenses. For the remaining residents there was little but poverty and aimlessness, and the entire region was vulnerable to conquest by Russians or Mongols.

It was the Kangxi regent, Oboi, who first determined to rectify the situation in Manchuria in the middle 1660s. China had been nearly stabilized, and banner families who wished to return to Manchuria were permitted to make application. The garrison at Ninguta was enlarged. A new line of fortifications was constructed around Liaodong (now marginally broadened to the east to include the site of Hetu Ala), and a new military command site, complete with workshops for the construction of war-junks to be used on the Amur, was built at Kirin.

It was the struggle against growing Russian control of the Amur river valley that inspired the Qing court to identify a "Manchuria" (*Manzhouguo, Manju i gurun*) and to claim it as its native place. Along with the military measures came the first elements in the ideological co-optation of Manchurian history that would reach high pitch in the next century. In 1677 the Kangxi emperor commissioned the Manchu Umuna to lead an expedition to Changbaishan. The emperor explained to Umuna that no one knew the "exact spot" of the origin of the Aisin Gioro lineage; Umuna's mission was to find it, and to sacrifice to its gods on behalf of the imperial family. The mission was difficult, not least because the lineage had no exact origin and few spots associated with its history were actually in the vicinity of Changbaishan. Nevertheless Umuna pressed bravely on into a literal wasteland (by its name, a place of perpetual winter) of thousands of square miles of unexplored territory. He well understood the unvoiced purpose of the mission: To establish a Qing familiarity with and ancestral claim to the region and its geographical features that would be useful in delimiting boundaries with Korea (to the south of Changbaishan) and Russia (to its east). After some misadventures Umuna and his mission miraculously achieved the top of Changbaishan, and accurately described its crater lake and the five promontories around it. They found also the source of the Songari river, and provided the Qing court with a detailed description of the region's topography.

The struggle between Russia and the Qing empire for control of Manchuria was finally concluded in the Treaties of Nerchinsk (1689) and Kiakhta (1727), which defined a geographical relationship between Russia and China that is still a cause for dispute. The diplomacy behind the first treaty had been especially tenuous at the political level and arduous at the physical. From Ming times, the exchange of a letter between the Chinese and Russian courts could take literally the better part of a century, since nobody at either end understood the other's language and occasions for face-to-face contact were rare. The Qing, unlike the Ming, were keenly interested in languages, and were not embarrassed to learn those of their neighbors. In practice, however, it was difficult. Qing troops on the Russian frontiers in Manchuria were instructed to snatch stray individuals in Russian service, and their harvest was respectable; but most were Central Asians or Tungus themselves, and if they knew any Russian were certainly illiterate. Over the course of the middle 1680s the Qing border officials had enticed an entire company of Cossacks (the "Albazinians") to surrender and join the banners, but nobody qualified to teach Russian was netted. The Kangxi emperor, however, hit upon the idea of using his Jesuits, with their Latin, as intermediaries with the Romanov court, assuming that Christians in Moscow understood the language. Finally, in 1689, both emperors approved the treaty – in Russian, Manchu, Chinese, and Latin – defining the border between them in Manchuria, identifying trading points, and establishing tariffs. Xuanye moved quickly to establish a Russian-language school in Peking, with a live Russian instructor, later slightly fortified by the arrival of a permanent mission of Orthodox churchmen. The school was never a resounding success, but did its part in easing the communications to the extent that the subsequent Treaty of Kiakhta in 1727 (which added some trading posts) could be translated from Russian into Manchu directly.

World Trade and the Qing Court

The early Qing empire knew Europe not only through its Jesuits, but also through some contact with the sea trading empires that had been fellow-travelers with the Jesuits from the sixteenth century. Earliest came the Portuguese, who after 1500 dominated the Moluccas and Java, where spices were grown, and the trade routes around India. The Spanish were also interested in the trade, and established a small base on Taiwan. Soon after 1600, however, the Portuguese and Spanish were dislodged by the Dutch, whose East India Company was chartered by the monarchy of the Netherlands to manage all commerce in the Indian and Pacific Oceans. In order to secure their influence in Eastern Asia and to discredit their rivals, the Dutch East India company willingly complied with both Chinese and Japanese demands in the style of communications with their rulers. They kowtowed to the Ming and then the Qing emperors in China, and managed to retain exclusive permission to remain on the Japanese island of Deshima, off Nagasaki, after Japan had been formally closed to all foreign contact in the early seventeenth century.

Outside of Japan, however, the Dutch East India Company had a strong rival in the British East India Company (BEIC), chartered by Elizabeth I in 1600. Originally the British company had hoped to take the spice trade away from the Dutch, but gave up the plan after the murders of English merchants in Java, and instead concentrated on India. Gradually the BEIC was given powers to coin money and to make and enforce laws, as if it were itself a government. The British crown gave the BEIC the right to control Bombay (previously a Portuguese colony), and the BEIC began to expand its base of political, as well as economic, control in parts of India. By dominating the trade in goods from India, including cotton, silk, and the minerals needed for gunpowder, the BEIC made enormous profits for its British investors, particularly between 1660 and 1700. The company became so powerful that the Mughal rulers of northern India granted the BEIC the right to control Bengal and Bihar provinces in the middle eighteenth century, and the company rapidly evolved into a quasi-government.

By the time of the Qing conquest of China, a European trade in Ming exports – particularly porcelain and silk – was already under way. As we shall see in the next chapter, a large and, for some parties, threatening trade in tea would develop in the eighteenth century. The courts of the Kangxi and Yongzheng emperors were reconciled to the presence of Dutch traders on their shores. The Dutch had sent embassies to the court, performed the kowtow, and were entered in the record of respectful tributary states. Otherwise they were not a bother to the court, and kept themselves to contact with their Chinese agents along the southern coasts. The sale of luxury goods to Europe, particularly when they were ordered from the Qing imperial factories, was a modest addition to the state's revenues, and was not regarded as a troubling matter. Strenuous meditation upon the containment of European trade and contact was a matter for later Qing rulers, who did not enjoy the inviting, success-strewn horizons that surrounded the empire in 1700.

Until the eighteenth century, the Qing empire was a conquest regime, whose resources were centered on invasion and occupation. Under the Kangxi emperor and the Yongzheng emperor (1721–35) this process was nearly completed. They effected an economic and demographic recovery in China, repairing roads and waterworks, lowering transit taxes, mandating comparatively low rents and interest rates, and creating economic incentives for resettlement of areas that had been devastated in the peasant rebellions of the late Ming period. After the end of the seventeenth century the western Mongols, who had been such a threat to the Ming, were neutralized as a military and political challenge, and by the middle eighteenth century western Mongolia, Central Asia, and Tibet were all under Qing control. With the re-establishment of unity in eastern Eurasia, the overland routes of communication from Samarkand to Korea were revived, though their economic and cultural influence was a shadow of what it had been under the Mongols in the thirteenth century.

From the time of the conquest of Peking in 1644 the Qing had been overt patrons of Chinese literati and bureaucratic culture. They quickly learned to express themselves in what was considered "Confucian" idiom, exerted themselves to restore and enhance the literary resources of the society, and from the middle seventeenth to the middle eighteenth century worked ceaselessly to flatter and co-opt the bureaucratic elite. They were so convincing in this role that until recently – when research materials in Manchu became available – it was a widely held assumption in Chinese studies that the Qing court had been thoroughly "sinicized" and alienated from its own roots. It is more accurate to say, however, that the emperors became not Chinese, but accomplished speakers of Chinese in addition to other symbolic languages.

The early Qing emperors assumed dominance over the cultures of eastern Asia, but patronized only a small number. The reason for their selectivity is obvious. They incorporated into their own self-representation those cultures that enhanced the emperorship and, by extension, the empire. From the Mongols they drew their claims to inheritance of the world empire and a number of the religious pillars of their legitimacy. From the Manchu bannermen they drew the military strength and skill to lead the conquests, and the court maintained access to the ancient political traditions of Manchuria. From the Chinese they drew the bureaucratic skill and moral code of Confucianism that legitimated their rule in China, as well as their moral leadership in Korea and Vietnam. From the Tibetans they drew their supernatural empowerment as universal Buddhist rulers. From the Muslims they drew the additional military strength to conquer and control Central Asia. From the Jesuits they drew not only abstract insights into mathematics and medicine, but also the practical rudiments of what William McNeill has called the "gunpowder empires," permitting domination over the nomadic armies of Mongolia and Turkestan.

There were, however, large numbers of non-Chinese peoples within the confines of China who gained no recognition and no patronage under the Qing. The Yi, Zhuang, Miao, Tong, Lolo, and Shan were among those peoples, some of whom had indigenous roots in the country, who were inhabiting China at the time of the conquest. For centuries – sometimes for millennia – before the coming of the Qing, these peoples had been struggling to survive in the marshy, mountainous, or otherwise difficult regions to which they had been driven by the encroaching Chinese populations, and were subjected to nearly continuous pressure from successive Chinese regimes to migrate or to acculturate.

The Qing posture toward these internal minorities was a combination of conquest and accommodation. Under the Yongzheng emperor the administration of southwest China, where such peoples were concentrated, was reconstructed in such a way as to allow native leaders to participate in a system of modified home rule. But these "leaders" were carefully chosen by the Qing from a class of acculturated and cooperative candidates. There was, in fact, continual unrest in the aboriginal territories of the southwest, culminating in the destructive wars that would contribute to the bankrupting of the state at the end of the eighteenth century.

Moreover, representation, under the Qing imperial system, was not enfranchisement. On the contrary, representation was a form of control, and was coordinated with policies designed to diminish the real power of Chinese, Mongolian, Manchu, Tibetan, and

Muslim elites while enhancing the power and ideological sway of the emperorship. Thus as the court assumed an increasingly positive stance toward the cultural and spiritual management of the Manchus, it gradually dismantled the foundations of princely and noble power among them. As it enshrined the history and culture of the Mongols, it worked to fragment and displace their traditional leadership. As it paid compliment to the culture and history of the Muslims, it cultivated the goodwill of willing headmen, or *khojas*, and violently dispossessed those of less friendly inclination. As it honored the religious traditions of Tibet, it worked to degrade the power of the Dalai Lama – the leader acknowledged by the Tibetans and the Mongols – and from Kangxi times encouraged gradual usurpation of power by the Panchen Lamas, the putative regents of Dalai Lamas.

The extraordinary combination of expansion and stability in the early empire is clearly due to a number of factors. No neighboring state of sufficient magnitude stopped the expansion cold, yet there was enough resistance to keep the conquest authorities vigilant and resourceful. Here, the personal qualities of the Kangxi emperor were critical, and may be the largest explanation for the creation of such a firm imperial base. His inborn genius was tempered by an almost unerring sense of who could be enlisted as an ally, and who had to be destroyed. Whichever the case, he never delayed in action longer than was necessary to make a secure assessment of the situation. Both within China and without, his combination of charm and coercion won him the critical portion of the Manchu aristocrats, Chinese bureaucrats, Chinese commoners, and Mongols necessary to keep his empire growing. Nor is there much to indicate that he was ever spoiled by success. In his own habits and in the stringencies he forced on the state, there was no waste. Perhaps most important, he was, like his grandfather Hung Taiji, a student of history, and believed that those who do not learn from the successes of the past are condemned to allow others to repeat them. Neither in Mongolia under Galdan, nor in Yunnan under Wu Sangui, did he ever permit the coordination of regional enthusiasms that had allowed Nurgaci to crack open the Ming empire's shell.

5

The Gilded Age of Qianlong

As conquerors, the early Qing emperors had been wary of seditious literature. The Kangxi emperor had done what he could to charm the Chinese elites, but it was inevitable that among them would be a certain number who would not reconcile to the new regime, whose hearts would not leap at its glorious domination of the Asian continent, who might even try to preach against the empire, or against the Manchus. Because of the peculiar allusive qualities of classical Chinese, a single word, if expertly employed, could communicate rebellion to a receptive eye. The imperial censors were always on the lookout. Truly seditious literature was rarely to be found in the open, and offenders could sometimes be identified only after their deaths. This was what happened in 1730, when exposure of treason led to an eventual revolt by an emperor against the philosophy of his ancestors.

In 1730 the Yongzheng emperor was on the throne, and he was notified by local officials in central China that a plot against the empire had been discovered. A small group of scholars had been arrested and sent to Peking for interrogation. The leader appeared to be one Zeng Jing, a native of Hunan who, in spite of humble beginnings, had achieved a signficant level of education. At some point he had heard of a dead scholar of Zhejiang, Lü Liuliang, who had written a secret treatise exposing the unworthiness of the Manchus to rule. Zeng had become eager to acquire a copy of these writings, and through the exertions of friends had finally done so. Transported by the logic and power of the writing, he had determined to approach his local governor, who was a descendant of the medieval Chinese patriotic hero Yue Fei, to discourse upon the deficits of the Manchus and to persuade the governor to lead a great uprising against the Qing. The governor had promptly clapped Zeng Jing in irons and sent him to Peking, probably predicting the worst for the prisoner.

If so, he was surprised. The Yongzheng emperor, after reviewing the writings of Lü Liuliang and hearing the tale of Zeng Jing's misadventures, was not galvanized by fear of a nativist uprising. The person really at fault, he explained, was Lü Liuliang, who had died in 1683; nevertheless it would be just as well for the corpses of Lü and his son to be dug up and desecrated, his living son executed, and his grandchildren banished or enslaved, all of which was arranged. As for Zeng Jing, his upbringing in Hunan had been a difficult one of dispiriting poverty punctuated by floods, earthquakes, and other natural disasters. It was no wonder that Zeng was easily disoriented by flashy rhetoricians of the sort that Lü had been. More important, Lü's arguments were easily disproved. He claimed that, because the ancestors of the Manchus had been described in Chinese texts as early as the Zhou kingdoms of classical times as barbarians, therefore the Manchus themselves must still be barbarous in character. This was contrary to all the teachings of Confucius, who had emphasized the power of the truth in humans to transform them into moral beings, even into sages. The Manchus, the emperor pointed out, had been transformed in just this way by their centuries of exposure to civilization. They were benevolent, just rulers, and the success of the empire was the manifestation of heaven's will, just as the early Confucian philosopher Mencius had prescribed.

There would be no difficulty in refuting Lü's arguments, using not only the letter but the spirit of the Confucian texts. The emperor decreed that his interrogation of Zeng Jing should be recorded and published. Zeng's recital of Lü's mean, ill-informed ideas would appear in small, unimposing print. Looming over them would be the emperor's patient, authoritative rebuttals. A small essay of recantation by Zeng Jing would follow, and the whole collection would conclude with a learned essay by two court scholars on the hermeneutical errors committed by Lü. The completed text would be required reading for examination candidates. Zeng Jing should be not only released, but given employment as a minor official in his home province, showing the bounty of the emperor, and keeping Zeng's troubled mind occupied on useful things.

The 20-year-old imperial prince, Hongli, watched this whole perfomance with intense dissatisfaction. His father could not be faulted for his fidelity to the political philosophy established by earlier Qing emperors, not for his understanding of the philosophy of Confucius and Mencius. Nevertheless there was something degrading in the emperor's apparent willingness to assert that the worth of the Manchus came only from the degree to which their original nature had been scoured away by Confucian "transformation," and painted over with borrowed rectitude. Even if the posture was assumed for political reasons only, was it really necessary that the emperors of the great Qing empire continue to humble themselves before the image of Confucius, still placidly denying the culture of their own ancestors in order to curry favor with those whom they had conquered?

For years this matter lay upon Hongli's mind. On October 7, 1735, the Yongzheng emperor died, and arrangements were made to install Hongli as the Qianlong emperor in a few weeks. But the emperor-to-be had business that could not wait for his enthronement. He immediately ordered a reopening of the Zeng Jing case. Copies of the work his father commissioned on the basis of Zeng Jing's interrogation were to be rounded up and destroyed, a shockingly unfilial act that the new emperor justified on the basis of supposed misstatements in the work about the private business of the Aisin Gioro lineage.[1] And finally there was the matter of Zeng Jing himself, who had been living as a sort of local celebrity in Hunan, his humble circumstances transformed by government grants as well as local largesse. Everyone, the young emperor intoned, must take responsibility for his actions, no matter how distracting his personal circumstances. Zeng Jing and one of his confreres in the Lü incident were dragged back to Peking, retried, and sentenced to one of the empire's more severe punishments: death by slicing (*lingchi*), which in addition to its immediate torments anguished the victim's ancestral spirits, as they were piecemeal deprived of the earthly body they had provided their descendant.

This revised ending to the Zeng Jing case still did not satisfy Hongli, who as the new Qianlong (1736–95) emperor proceeded to an overt representation of himself as a universal ruler that amounted to an ideological revolution. During his long reign, literary inquisitions, the patronage of new writing on history and culture, monumental building and landscaping projects, and the intense cultivation of a new imperial person made him the embodiment of an age of universal Qing rule. Imperial ostentation reached its height, and for a time not only Asia but Europe as well was mesmerized by the image of the omniscient, omnicompetent, omnipathetic emperor of the Chinese. Never, as long as the Qianlong emperor lived, did the Qing emperor pretend to have been transformed by anything greater than himself. It was, on the contrary, he who did the transforming, from his cosmic point around which all things revolved.

The New Imperial Style

The Qianlong emperor's conception of himself as a universal ruler, one commanding an undelimited moral domain, was not invented out of nothing. At root its elements, and much of its vocabulary, came from Buddhist ideals of the "wheel-turning king" (*čakravartin*), an earthly ruler who by his conquests in the name of the Buddha would move the world toward the next stage in universal salvation. The historical wheel-turning king was Ašoka, who ruled northern India in the third century BCE. The Qianlong emperor certainly identified with Ašoka, and believed that in the course of his own reign he caused the unearthing and collection of relics from the time of Ašoka, and in some historical sense had reconstructed the earthly domain of the original Buddhist king.

But there was a more immediate connection of the Qing emperors to beliefs concerning Buddhist kingship. In Nurgaci's time, missionaries of the Sa-skya pa sect of Tibetan Buddhism were influential among the Chakhar and Kharachin Mongolas. Nurgaci may have cultivated the goodwill of these missionaries, since their brand of lamaism promised heavenly favor – and earthly legitimacy – to the monarch who became their patron. Representatives of the sect were present in the procession that proclaimed Hung Taiji khan in 1627. When Hung Taiji finally defeated Lighdan and assumed rulership over the Chakhar Mongols, he also assumed the role of patron of the cult of Mahākāla, the spirit guide of the dead, who was believed to have effected the reincarnation of Buddhist imperial consciousness in an unbroken chain from the conquering emperor Li Shimin of the Tang (r. 926–47) through Genghis Khan, Khubilai Khan, and Lighdan. The progression now included the

Qing emperors, and the cult was practiced in secret both at Mukden and in Peking.

It was not in the emperor's nature to keep a secret this big. Qianlong univeralism was founded on a complex of religious and political ideals that bound together Tibet and Mongolia. Since the time of Nurgaci it had been clear that legitimate rule over the Mongols depended upon patronizing Tibetan lamas, whom Altan Khan had established as the spiritual guides of the Mongols. Indeed by the late seventeenth century reincarnation of the lamas could be found among the Mongols themselves, consolidating the ideological identification of Tibet and Mongolia. During the Qianlong era, Tibet in particular functioned as an ideological resource, while at the same time being subject to the strategic interventions of imperial forces that will be discussed below.

The Qing began patronizing Mahākāla – the lamaist imperial cult created in eastern Mongolia – from the time of their wars against Lighdan. From 1634, when Lighdan's regime was destroyed, the Qing monarchs were invested as incarnations of past imperial consciousnesses. Tibetan cult objects were introduced into the Aisin Gioro temple in Mukden well before the conquest of north China, and patronage of Yellow sect temples and monasteries is documented from 1639.

Earlier Qing emperors had generally satisfied themselves with hosting the lamas, engaging in the appropriate ritual relationship, and presenting themselves as the earthly successors of Genghis Khan. For the Qianlong emperor, this was insufficient. He intended to make his imperial capital at Peking the spiritual capital of the lamaist realm. He initiated a massive project which not only rendered the Tibetan Tripitaka into Mongolian and Manchu but also produced original commentaries on Tibetan scriptures by Mongol and Manchu scholars. Tibetan Buddhism was enshrined in various temples closely linked with the imperial family, the most prominent being the great palace of Eternal Harmony (*Yonghe gong*) – the Qianlong emperor's birthplace – which during the late eighteenth and early nineteenth centuries housed several hundred Tibetan, Mongol, and Manchu monks and served as a teaching center of the Sa-skya pa sect. At Peking, the supreme religious leaders of the Mongolian territories were appointed, and child Dalai Lamas were raised and educated, and later maintained their administrative offices. Even the Potala residence of the Dalai Lamas at Lhasa was replicated at the summer palace at Rehe. "Ti-

Plate 9   *On ceremonial occasions the emperors and officers of the Eight Banners dressed in padded silk armor. This suit of the Qianlong emperor's is in the imperial yellow that he was uniquely entitled to wear, and his helmet is inscribed with* dhārāni, *or protecting incantations, in Sanskrit, marking him as a* čakravartin. (National Palace Museum, Peking)

Plate 10 *The Qianlong emperor's tomb at the Eastern Mauso-leum (Dongling) complex at Malanyu is a further testament to his self-image as a* čakravartin. *Designed and built in his own lifetime, the outer chambers are covered in Sanskrit* dharāni, *and the ceiling of the inner chamber is adorned with the wheel of the law. The grave goods, the burial clothes, and the body itself were all destroyed when the tomb was raided by the troops of a local warlord in 1928. (Hu Chui)*

bet," in the ideological system of the Qing, was transformed into an ideal, though an ideal of tremendous importance.

Over the course of the Qianlong reign, visual and metaphorical allusions to the *čakravartin*ism of the Qing emperors were increasingly overt. They were often associated with the idea of the emperor as a bodhisattva, or living enlightened being, a device of spiritual legitimation that Chinese emperors had used for many centuries. In silk banners of the Tibetan type (*thangka*) and in portraits of himself as a Buddhist monk Hongli alluded to the centrality of Buddhism to his own beliefs and to the culture of the Aisin Gioro lineage. His lamaist councillors were prominent and influential, and more than previous Qing emperors he interested himself overtly in the affairs of Tibet. But perhaps more convincing and touching was his last testament on the subject: His tomb, designed in his lifetime, featured the symbol of the *čakravartin* – a wheel whose spokes open petal-like in identification with the lotus symbol of Buddhist meditation – on the ceiling of the crypt, directly over the catafalque upon which his coffin would be placed. The walls approaching the catafalque are carved with the protective prayers in Sanskrit for the *čakravartin*. At his death his body was wrapped, as with all the Qing rulers, including the Empress Dowager Cixi (see chapter 6), in a silk shroud covered with similar prayers (*dhāraṇi*).

On the foundation of *čakravartin*ism, the Qianlong emperor was able to construct his moral authority over all cultures. He was, in the well-known phrase applied to Chinese rulers, the Pole Star: The point around which everything else moves, and by its own immobility gives meaning to all movement. In practice, to patronize all cultures Hongli had to encourage them to be standardized – or more precisely, stereotyped. This is the essence of the cultural brilliance of his period: The imitation, stylization, and replication of cultural icons became the means by which he achieved his literal universal representation of culture. The purpose behind these practices was to enhance the imperial authority over the cultures in question, not to develop objective, descriptive knowledge of the peoples themselves.

A monumental expression of the universal integration of historical particulars – the role of the emperor, or the *čakravartin*, as Hongli characterized himself – was found in polylingualism. Architecture and literature equally could be put to monumental uses. Like the Mongolian khans before him, who had expressed their universalism in displays such as that which survive at Juyong Pass and elsewhere (see chapter 2), the Qianlong emperor used both. Sometimes the monuments with which he invoked and intended to embody the cultural authority of distinct traditions was literal, as when he had the residences of the Dalai and Panchen Lamas reproduced at this summer park at Chengde (Rehe), or a rough replica of the Trianon constructed at the Yuanming summer palace. Whether on his monuments in Manchu, Mongolian, Tibetan, and Chinese (and, after the conquest of Turkestan, Uigur), or in the pages of the enormous multilingual dictionaries published repeatedly during his reign, the display of his cosmopolitanism was awesome in itself, but always pointed back to the emperor, as the center at which all cultures converged.

The persistence, sophistication, and extravagance with which the Qianlong court pursued its role as universal cultural patron produced the indelible image of the period as the height of the power of the Qing – indeed, it could be and has been argued, as the period unrivalled by any in Chinese imperial history for sheer magnificence. The emperor himself was lionized in Europe as an oriental philosopher-king trampling the forces of superstition and self-seeking in his society. Yet beneath the facade of inexhaustible wealth and achievement, the resources of the empire in fact were being rapidly exhausted. The Qianlong emperor would abdicate before he died, the only emperor in Qing history to do so. He left a society of rapidly declining per capita income, mired in a series of inconclusive and financially ruinous regional wars, with a bureaucracy shattered by entrenched factionalism. His own prestige was sadly squandered by his doting for the last twenty years of his life on the handsome, talented, but profoundly corrupt Manchu Heshen, whom it was rumored the emperor believed to be the reincarnation of a beloved concubine Hongli had lost in his youth. At Hongli's death in 1799 Heshen was arrested by the next emperor, his illicit wealth (reported to be in excess of what remained in the imperial treasury) was confiscated, and he was ordered to hang himself with a silken rope.

Tibet and Mongolia under Qing Dominion

"Tibet," as suggested above, was transformed into an ideal under the Qing, though an ideal of tremendous importance. But it was also a geo-political sector of fundamental importance in the maintenance of Qing dominion, and intimately associated with progressive Qing control over Mongolia. After the Qing occupation of North China, the Qing attempted to pursue a direct relationship with the Dalai Lamas, and in 1651 the regents for the Shunzhi emperor were successful in formalizing a ruler–lama relationship. In return, the Dalai Lama enjoyed the role of spiritual teacher to the universal empire, and ensured his position against challenges from a rival sect in Lhasa. From that point forward Tibet was a fountain not only of political legitimacy, but of strategic supremacy.

The event that first provoked the strategic concerns of the Qing was that which had prompted their alienation from the Liaodong

Chinese-martial population: The War of the Three Feudatories (see chapter 4). While developing his power base in the southwest, Wu Sangui had attempted to cultivate Tibetan favor by creating regular trade with Lhasa along the Kham–Yunnan road. When Wu rose in rebellion against the Qing in 1673, he appealed to the Dalai Lama, who refused to endorse Qing suppression of Wu's state of Zhou. This hampered attempts of the Kangxi emperor to mobilize Mongol troops to block Wu's northward advance, and in rejecting the Dalai Lama's recommendation of a truce the young emperor placed his relations with Tibet, as well as with the Eight Banners, in jeopardy.

The Three Feudatories were at length suppressed, and though relations with Tibetan clerics were repaired, the Kangxi emperor remained wary of strategic combinations between Tibet and the unconquered Mongols of Central Asia. His concerns had proved justified when the western Mongol leader Galdan enlisted ambitious factions in Tibet to support his cause, and in order to prosecute the war against Galdan the Qing were led to their first stable military occupation of Tibet in 1720. In 1757 the western Mongols were finally defeated, which lessened the immediate strategic interests of the Qing in Tibet. But for good measure, the Qianlong emperor decreed that no more reincarnations of the living Buddha would be found among the Mongols; only Tibetans would henceforth be living Buddhas.

Qing control of the symbolic significance of Tibet was enhanced through creation of the Panchen Lamas as regents of the Dalai Lamas. In this way the Qing court lessened the opportunities for one lamaist sect or another to become a vessel of Tibetan regional sentiment. The court claimed on the Panchen Lama's behalf that he was the worldly ruler of most of Tibet and the spiritual leader of the Buddhist world, outranking the Dalai Lama. Meanwhile, of the Dalai Lamas, only one between the fifth and the twelfth Dalai Lama lived past the age of 23. It is more than probable that the Qing preferred working through the regents to dealing with the spiritually-empowered and Mongol-oriented Dalai Lamas themselves.

The last Qing attempt to mobilize military force in Tibet came in the very late Qianlong reign, in 1792. This concluded a four-year war against invading Gurkhas from Nepal. With the Gurkhas defeated, Qing troops proceeded to invade Nepal. The Gurkhas become tributaries of the Qing, but thereafter Qing military might in Tibet atrophied (as it did elsewhere) and by 1855 the Gurkhas were able defeat the Tibetans, without Qing intervention, at Lhasa.

The Qing court was canny in its attempts to manipulate the office of Dalai Lama for its own purposes. This was largely the motivation behind the institution of the famous "golden urn," sent to Tibet in 1793 by the Qianlong court for the purpose of selecting future Dalai lamas by lot. The proposal was for the most part politely ignored in Lhasa, except for a period during the middle nineteenth century – far beyond the period of the Qing being able to impose their will in Tibet – when the Tibetan leadership wished to symbolize their attachment to the Qing in order to ward off intrusions from Nepal and, via Nepal, the British East India Company.

The Mahākāla cult, with its combined Tibetan and Mongolian references, had been fundamental to the universalist vision of the Qianlong emperor, but it was intertwined with another Tibeto-Mongolian object of worship, Geser Khan. In the Tibetan folk beliefs that were later imported to Mongolia, Geser had been known as Geser of Ling – a general reference to the eastern part of Tibet. This appears, however, to have been a late imposition, since Geser was earlier recognized as the founder of a non-Buddhist people from the western regions, known as Khrom. This is evidently a reference to Rūm – that is, Asia Minor and Anatolia in particular, as it was known in the time of the Seljuk Turks. The Seljuks, whose culture was certainly known as far as Tibet in the eleventh century, had themselves adapted the cult of "Geser of Rūm," a hero of the Sassanians in Persia. His name was clearly inspired by the title *caesar* – which the Seljuks in their time introduced to portions of Central Asia, though no trace of this clung to the understanding of "Geser" in Tibet, Mongolia, or China under the Qing, where he was the supreme god of conquest.

The Qing court appropriated the cult of Geser (now a khan), identifying him with the Chinese god of war, Guandi. Among the Mongols Geser was also the embodiment of the spirit of Garuda, the king of birds, a helpful association since Nurgaci himself was a companion of the magpie (see chapter 3), now the totem creature of the Aisin Gioro lineage. Since the Aisin Gioro already identified Guandi with Nurgaci, Geser was now the bridge to subsuming all these conquest personalities under the Buddha manifestation Vaisrana, who oversees the conquest of "all four corners" of the material world by true knowledge. Geser was also a *deva*, a state-protecting deity of the sort known in eastern Eurasia since the time of the Later Han empire. Finally he was a "son of heaven" and, more, an "incarnation of the *tngri* [gods] who rule all those who live on earth." Geser had the great power of seamlessly integrating Eurasian folk history, Buddhist iconography, and the conquest narrative of the Qing imperial lineage into one cultic address. For the Qianlong emperor, Geser had one last metaphorical charm. He was – like the Pole Star, or the Bodhisattva Manjusri – a point upon which all revolved and was suspended: he was described in incantations as the "supporting beam of the dwelling-house," a graceful confluence of the *čakravartin*ism of Hongli and his reign name itself, since the words *qianlong* can be interpreted to mean "the pillar of heaven."

Like Tibet, then, Mongolia had its critical symbolic importance for the Qing, primarily because it provided their link to the legacy of the Great Khans. But like Tibet, Mongolia had also a strategic importance for the Qing. In communications with his military planning council, the Qianlong emperor pointed out in 1756 – when the empire was in the process of quashing the last of the great rebellions among the Mongol princes – that the western Mongols must have four khans recognized among them, "in order to keep their forces divided. Each has to be concerned about his own welfare, and submit to the empire for protection from the others." The four divisions were only a fraction of the total number of independent entities that the Qing recognized in Mongolia and Turkestan as "dependent tribes" (*fanbu*), of which there are a high total of thirty-eight. In a corollary of the Qing policy of fragmenting Mongol federations and tribal units into progressively smaller portions, the names and divisions multiplied. Many of these peoples were not considered Mongols (though most of them were speakers of Mongolian) by the Qing court, which reserved the term either for those incorporated into the Eight Banners before the conquest, or for those who surrendered to the Kangxi emperor at Dolonnor.[2]

As patrons of Tibetan lamaism, incarnations of Ašoka and Geser, and heirs of Genghis Khan, the Qing could find Mongols who would acknowledge their supremacy, even welcome it. Thus Lomi, the mid-eighteenth-century poet and Kharachin nobleman who was himself a descendant of Genghis, wrote in his history of the family, "Can we say that it is not a great good fortune for us descendants of Genghis that we have continued to have the grace of the Holy Lord Genghis constantly bestowed on us? In my opinion, the fact that our Mongol nation, when about to collapse, was restored again, and when on the point of falling apart was reborn, is in truth entirely due to the amazing mercy of the Holy Emperor Kangxi."[3]

Not all Mongol nobles shared so enthusiastically in the self-appointment of the Qing emperors to rule Mongolia. As, in the 1740s and 1750s, the policies of the Qianlong emperor for the reorganization of Mongolia proceeded briskly, dissenters realized that they would quickly be encircled. The Qing had consolidated a second border treaty (Kiakhta, 1727) with the Romanovs that had stopped the flow of weapons, advisors, and supplies from Russia. Tibet was under Qing military domination, the Dalai Lamas themselves were virtual prisoners of the Qing court, and the remaining western Mongol-related peoples were now concentrated in Turkestan.

Amursana, a western Mongol who had already submitted to the Qing court and accepted a military commission, was briefed on the emperor's intention of creating four small and mutually suspicious khanships in the west. He was ordered to head up a mission against holdouts in Turkestan, around Yili, and easily achieved his goal. But on thinking the matter over, he concluded that it would be more desirable to have a single, united Mongol federation, and that all things considered he would be the best choice of khan. He informed the court of his proposed change of plans, and proceeded to organize his own khanate in Turkestan.

Forces from among the Eight Banners quickly set out for Turkestan, but other khans of Mongolia attempted to head west to join Amursana's rebellion. They were inspired by the call of Galdan's grandson Galdantseren, who had a different view from Lomi's of the relationship of the Qing emperors to the legacy of Genghis.

> Considering that [the Mongol] aristocrats are the heirs of Genghis Khan, it is contemptible that you should be the subjects of anybody else. I have advised the Qing emperor to restore [Inner Mongolia] as it was before. But now he says he wants to organize us [western Mongols] into banners and companies, and give us titles. I am going to resist this by force of arms.[4]

As it happened the Qing forces reached Turkestan before other khans could join the uprising. Amursana escaped to the Kazakhs, and eventually fled to Siberia, where he died of smallpox. Not only

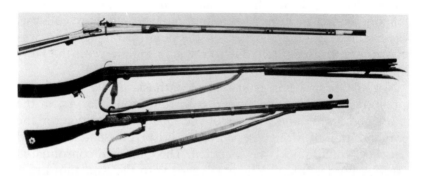

Plate 11   *The Qing imported a small number of muskets in the
eighteenth century. Those distributed to the troops for use in the
wars against the native peoples in southwest China were still in use
– though sometimes only as clubs – by the Eight Banners at the time
of the Opium War (chapter 6). These guns were from the private
collection of the Qianlong emperor, who used them for hunting, as
illustrated in plate 12. (National Palace Museum, Peking)*

was the reorganization of Mongolia completed in ensuing decades,
but Turkestan was incorporated into the empire under a separate
government of military occupation, and in the next century would
become the Qing province of Xinjiang.

The Formalization of the Manchu Heritage

Manchuria and the Manchus were, like Mongolia and Tibet, of
special ideological and strategic interest to the Qianlong count. As
a consequence they were subjected to the burden of peculiar
pressures from the court for cultural conformity to a new ideal.
The emperor's enthusiasm for rigid, stereotyped cultural types was
focused intensely upon the Manchus. It was, after all, their essen-
tial qualities and honor he had intended to champion in recalling
and killing Zeng Jing, the symbol of the "transformation" arguments of the earlier emperors. If Manchus were not ashamed to be
themselves, the Eight Banners would regain their marshal virtues.
The conquests of the Aisin Gioro would be vindicated.

The Qianlong emperor commissioned, as part of his great literary projects, a new comprehensive history of the Manchus. He
prefaced it with his own disquisition on the imperial history of

Plate 12 *The Kangxi and Qianlong emperors were both strong advocates for the bannermen retaining their martial skills as well as gaining civil ones. Drawing on the model of the Jurchen Jin emperor Shizong, they made the hunt the ground for reinvigorating traditional Manchu values. Both used guns as well as bows and arrows in their hunts. In this painting by Giuseppe Castiglione, the Qianlong emperor is shown taking aim at a deer with what appears to be the middle gun from the collection in plate 11. (National Palace Museum, Peking)*

Manchuria, which he regarded as glorious in its own right, not a frontier imitation of Chinese civilization. According to his reading of Jin history, the ancestors of the Jin imperial clan had lived among the Mohe confederation, within the territory of the ancient Sushens of Zhou times where were found the White Mountain (Changbaishan) and the Black River (the Amur). Not only was this the very scene of the rise of the Manchus (in his view), but the ancient Sushens had flattened backs to their skulls like the Manchus – not, as the ancient Chinese histories had ludicrously surmised, because they used stones to flatten their infants' skulls, but because they obviously used the same distinctive cradle's as the Manchus and their cultural cousins. Thus both geography and culture proved the unbroken ancestral claim of the Manchus to the region, its peoples, and its cultures.

The emperor complained that during the Ming period in particular, "propagandists of the most scandalous inclinations picked over every word, every line, every paragraph, with no object other than to defame." Perhaps, he suggested, the Chinese thought that the Manchus would now attempt to excise from the histories of their ancestors all references to barbaric practices. Far from it. Even the ancient sages among the Chinese had been proud to be called barbarians, and it was not different for the antecedent peoples of the Manchus. The Qing had no fear of reproducing in their new libraries the descriptions of their ancestors.

As good as his word, the emperor had his scholars not only reproduce but excerpt and highlight passages providing unflattering descriptions of Manchurian peoples. The *History of the Northern Wei* dynasty contained, for example, a rather long account of the Wuji. They were described as the fiercest of Manchurian peoples, dressed in dog skins, frequently drunk, and accustomed to wash their faces with urine and to use the corpses of their parents to attract sables, whose pelts were a basic element in Wuji trade with the Chinese. The Heishui Mohe were described in the Tang imperial history as an uncultured people of terrifying fierceness, possessed of a poison for arrow tips so potent that "whatever is struck is dead where it stands." The drunkenness of the Jin Jurchens was reported in Song period records to be unbroken; acquisition and consumption of the powerful *gaoliang* liquor for which the region was famous appeared to be a driving force in Jurchen culture. The physical conditions of their life could hardly have been cruder, and the people – in this account quarrelsome, avaricious, and often unconscious – could hardly have been more unpromising. But it should not be forgotten, the emperor mused, that while the Qing were rooted in these warlike peoples, they were also rooted in the ancient kingdoms of the Korean peninsula, whose achievements in ceramics and metallurgy had fostered a local, independent civilization, and in the Parhae kings, who had their own script, court rituals, bureaucracy, and multiple capitals.

The Qianlong emperor wished Manchus not only to read and understand their own history, but to share his idyllic vision of the topography, the wildlife, and the bracing climate of their ancestral and spiritual home, the Changbai region. Using the report of the Manchu explorer of the Kangxi era, Umuna, Hongli worked with his scribes to compose the "Ode to Mukden" in Manchu, extolling the Changbaishan region and recalling the myths of Aisin Gioro origins there. Such idealism was not limited to the emperor himself. Sungyun, a Mongol and official of the Court of Colonial Affairs, had written extensively on Tibet and Mongolia before turning his attention to the banner communities of Urga. His "notes" on banner life there, written entirely in Manchu, probably first appeared in manuscript in 1791. So far from describing the actual life of real Manchus in the garrison (which by that time would have made bleak reading), the work is actually a string of homilies and uplifting moral tales, most drawn from Chinese history. It was the sort of literature that the Qianlong emperor would enthusiastically have ordered his Manchus to read, but it appeared too late to snare the emperor's attention, and after the emperor's death friends of Sungyun's put the inspirational work into private circulation.

The court publications, all seamlessly integrated with the imperial catalogues of "classic" works, were designed partly to reinforce and partly to justify other programs, to be discussed below, intended to restore the martial orientation and effectiveness of the Manchus, while drawing their attention away from the civil society of China in which they actually lived. In response to the Qianlong demands for extreme rigidity in national behavior, most Manchus voted with their feet: shirking garrison duties, avoiding the new educational programs, and in increasing instances fleeing the provinces to which they were assigned. But the stringency with which Hongli conceived of ethnic identity applied also to criteria of gender. Indeed since the time of the Kangxi emperor, Qing society had consciously turned away from the late Ming tolerance of blurred gender lines and – in Qing eyes – effeminate male dress and behavior. By the end of the eighteenth century, Qing literature had begun to show many traces of dissent from the intolerances of the early court. One of the most famous instances of this occurs in the novel *Dream of the Red Chamber* (*Honglou meng*), often acclaimed as China's greatest novel. It is not a coincidence that it was written by a Chinese-martial bannerman whose family had a strong connection with the Qing court, reaching to Hung Taiji times.

The author, Cao Xueqin (also known as Cao Zhan, d. 1763), came from a family who had served as household retainers of the Aisin Gioro in the time of the Kangxi emperor, and been appointed managers of the imperial silk factory in Nanjing. In earlier generations the family had known every privilege of wealth, education, and imperial society. But in 1728 the family came into the disfavor of the Yongzheng emperor, through circumstances that have never been fully explained. Their lands and wealth were confiscated, and the large extended family moved into cramped quarters in Peking. Cao Xueqin himself retained personal connections with some members of the imperial lineage. Despite his poverty, Cao could not or would not work, and so spent his ample time writing the chapters of the amazing novel that was unfinished when he died, published in fragments in the ensuing century, and not known as a full work until modern times.

The novel opens with a long Buddhist metaphor for incarnation, but soon takes up the story of Baoyu, a boy growing up in the portion of his family mansion (the "red chamber") that is primarily reserved for women and girls. Time, the pressure of society, and family expectations all demand that Baoyu grow up and assume the responsibilities of marriage and the examination system, but he resists. His terror of going out into the world, beyond the comfortable studios and gardens where he plays as a boy, is so deep that he actually sees his personality as split into two: a conforming, adult, definitively male "Baoyu" who survives, and another Baoyu who is a perpetual child who must remain in the gardens, in company with the images and creatures of his imagination, and with his equally undefined (and therefore immortal) companions. Baoyu's predicament reflects elite discomfort with the transition from military to civil society, from a protected environment to increasing uncertainties, from prosperity to decline. It is noteworthy that his opposite in the novel is Daiyu, an educated girl of the household who defies the society's demands for female behavior. She suffers the fate of most educated heroines in fiction: She dies an early death. Baoyu mourns her, but also envies her: By death she had escaped the process of sexual definition, for him a living death.

Apart from the realm of literature, there were greater difficulties in meeting the demands of the Qianlong emperor's ideals. The pre-conquest ideal of the Manchu language as a comprehensive state language and of the bannermen as comprehensive state functionaries appears to have continued to shape imperial educational policies after the conquest. Circumstances ultimately forced the abandonment of such a design, but the lingering three-point emphasis upon the Manchu, Mongolian, and Chinese languages remained the hallmark of the educational and administrative policies relating to the bannermen until the very late eighteenth century. As the universalism of the Qianlong emperor's style began to change the shape of intellectual preparation and inquiry, the court directed greater attention to the status of Manchu among the Manchu population (still a difficult and in some ways contradictory idea at the time). Reports to the court that bannermen were neglecting both their education in Manchu language and their cultivation of military skills appear to have prompted the frequent admonitions from the emperor that bannermen should remedy their defects and avoid becoming "lost" in Chinese culture. The resulting specialization of banner identity and banner education created the foundation for the reprofessionalized military of the late nineteenth century and the emergence of technical, vocation, and professionalized education in the languages, sciences, and military arts.

In order to cope with the rising populations and declining state support, garrison commanders had granted rights to residence outside the garrison to an increasing number of officers, who often purchased lands or businesses near the garrison, and to enlisted men, who often went into trades or menial jobs to make ends meet. On a large scale, Manchus were integrating themselves with the local populations. The Qianlong emperor found this a security risk, since there could be difficulties in ordering the bannermen who normally worked as noodle vendors, sedan-chair carriers, carpenters, or ferry-men to catch up weapons and move against their neighbors or employers should the need arise. But it also offended his sense of universalism and the need for Manchu integrity.

The Kangxi emperor had rewarded households whose sons or fathers did well in the examinations. In contrast, the Qianlong emperor, when he learned that his bannermen were already by and large adept at Chinese, promptly abandoned this policy. After 1765 he advised bannermen that they need no longer disturb him with notifications of their households' success in the examinations unless the candidates had also distinguished themselves at riding and shooting. And those who could not speak their ancestral language should look to it. "Speaking Manchu is the Old Way of the Manchus," Hongli admonished four officials of the Court of Colonial Affairs who had been unable to keep up their end of an audience in the winter of 1762.

Though the Kangxi emperor had established himself as a grand exemplar to the bannermen and frequently demonstrated his literary and military skills before them for their improvement, the Qianlong emperor had a very different message for his bannermen. He, the Qing emperor, was a paragon of multi-literacy, the esthete of all cultures, and the universal emperor. They were not. They were to apply themselves to their language, their religion, and riding and shooting. "Whether you have studied classical literature is a matter of no concern to me." He was especially fierce in his demands upon members of the Aisin Gioro lineage, who could be fined heavily if found deficient in spoken or written Manchu, or in martial skills. Funding for the higher schools for imperial kinsmen was increased, but it is not, perhaps, surprising that an increasing number of aristocrats sought ways to avoid the schools – and the testing grounds – altogether rather than run the risk of being found deficient in their studies.

Educational policies for bannermen generally continued to be reformed to promote both the speaking and writing of Manchu as a primary objective. In 1791, the Qianlong emperor outlined his plan for establishment of standard banner officer schools in all garrisons. The greatest change was in the provincial garrisons. The curriculum, which was not intended to be distinguished for inno-vation, was based upon the program of the National Academy and the Eight Banners Officers' Schools in Beijing: Manchu, Chinese, astronomy (*tianwen*), and mathematics (*suanxue*), with frequent and rigorous testing in riding and shooting. The charters were imbedded in Hongli's continuing demands that written Manchu be revived among the bannermen. "Every single man has a responsibility to study written Manchu," the emperor had continued his endless and largely unheeded sermon. "This is the root of his mission!"

The reform of higher education within the garrisons was quickly seen to be useless without a corresponding emphasis upon the cultivation of boys. The perceived cultural and social condition of the garrison populations is revealed in the edict, in 1800 (a year after the Qianlong emperor's death), demanding that garrison officers identify talented boys to receive intensive instruction from their company corporals in Manchu, riding and shooting, and a very small number of administrative arts. At the same time, the state affirmed its intentions never to return to the unfocussed, comprehensive education policies of earlier times. "Of the Manchus' roots, riding and shooting is the first. If the bannermen concentrate on and are allowed to be successfully examined on the Confucian classics, they will despise the bow and the horse, and that will not enhance our military preparedness; on the contrary they will contravene the very purpose for which the nation established garrisons."

The structural defects of the system described above were evident well before the Qianlong period. Attempts to enforce systematic education were made only at the capital, and only affected a very tiny portion of the adult males of the banner population. Banner males of eligible age must, at any one of these times, have numbered hundreds of thousands, of whom not more than a thousand were being educated in the Peking higher schools. Moreover, the proportional emphasis put upon educating members of the Aisin Gioro lineage was overwhelming; it appears that in the middle eighteenth century this group represented half of all bannermen attending the higher schools in Peking. More compromising, perhaps, was the profound ambiguity in the design of bannermen's education in the earlier dynastic era. The role of governors once envisioned for the bannermen had faded very early in the Qing period, under insurmountable pressures to meet continuing military challenges and to give way in civil affairs to the well-entrenched Chinese bureaucratic class.

The abandonment of the Shunzhi–Kangxi idea of bannermen as universal functionaries as well adapted to the upper rungs of bureaucratic service as to the command of an elite cavalry corps, in favor of a rigid regime of cultural purification, physical reinvigoration, and spiritual reintegration, had implications for beyond what the Qianlong court foresaw. What later emperors were advocating, in essence, was a vocational, even professional, course of study for the bannermen, in which adeptness in Manchu – as the language of the military sector – was fundamental, and in which the more liberal, more obviously civil educational elements had little or no place. The significance of this did not emerge until the military and educational reforms of the period after the Opium War.

There was some realization at the court that merely requiring specialized education for the bannermen would not in itself be effective. The small and thinly spread imperial government was an easy thing to circumvent, which was one of the reasons the penalties for circumvention had to be so high. In order to get bannermen's minds focussed on their renewed martial mission, the state desired to alleviate their economic woes. In the early Qianlong period four outlays of about a million ounces of silver each were ordered for the redemption of banner lands that had been sold to local Chinese. Within a few years the lands had all been sold again by the banner officers. After being redeemed by the state at top prices, the lands had been sold again (very possibly to the same Chinese who had owner them before) at distress prices to pay off new debts. The imperial government had actually invented a new species of land speculation. These policies were abandoned after the middle eighteenth century, and Hongli determined to move large numbers of Peking bannermen back to Manchuria. Virtually all returned to Peking or its environs within a short time, and of necessity lived outside the law. In 1763, the military administration recognized that the greatest impediment to survival for the bannermen was the walls that were supposed to segregate them from the rest of society. In that year, bannermen were permitted universally to apply for permission to seek private employment and live outside the garrison, while keeping their registration – and identity – as bannermen.

Glory and Decay in the Universal Empire

The Chinese literate class, aspiring to examination success and bureaucratic employment, was in a paradoxical position under the

Plate 13　*Castiglione and Attiret are credited with this panoramic painting of the great ceremonial yurt in the summer retreat at Rehe where the Qianlong emperor received the submission of the western Mongols in 1754. This was also the site of the emperor's reception of the Macartney mission in 1793 – in fact young George Staunton claimed that it was at this very point that the British delegation joined the throngs on either side of the yurt's forecourt in the kowtow to welcome the emperor. (National Palace Museum, Peking)*

Qianlong emperor. The early emperors had all been enthusiastic in crafting a governmental apparatus that featured an efficient personal bureaucracy, including secret communications in Manchu, which permitted them continual oversight of the central government and of a surprising number of provinces. At the same time, they were willing to put in fourteen- and sixteen-hour days. Like his predecessors, the Qianlong emperor was an indefatigable worker, but his energies went into an unusual number of literary activities. He was supposed to have written over 40,000 poems, in Manchu and in Chinese, and he claimed to have read feverishly. As part of his oversized literary persona, he was the sponsor of a project, often called the emperor's "Four Treasuries," whose aim was to review all existing literature for rectitude and beauty, and to reproduce all worthy writing in fresh editions that would be housed in new libraries at selected points in the empire.

For aspiring officials, the prospects for employment were brighter than usual, but fulfilling all the emperor's wishes could be nerve-wracking. Prosperous families, always seeking to be of service and get recognition for it, either offered their personal libraries to the emperor or invited imperial commissioners to come and inspect their libraries for desirable texts. Some families made an irrecoverable material sacrifice. Others laid themselves open to political peril, since the search for worthwhile literature was also an inquisition of sorts, a search for seditious or licentious material. If such were found, the consequences could be very serious, and, as suggested above, some seditious messages announced themselves only to supremely suspicious minds. Not surprisingly, the Qianlong era was interrupted by a series of literary trials, most ending in the demotion of the convicted and the requirement that he write, publish, and distribute elaborate self-indictments – which only increased the staggering volume of publication of the age.

The unprecedented opportunities created for the review of existing literature, the writing of commentaries on its origins and meaning, and numerous reports on whether works should be reproduced, kept in limited circulation, banned, or destroyed all reinforced the tendency of eighteenth-century literati to use elaborate hermeneutical techniques called "evidentiary research" (*kaozheng*) in these projects. "Evidentiary research" had developed in the sixteenth century from the efforts of private scholars, and had already produced a few shocking literary discoveries – one being that a work, *The Book of Documents*, accepted for a millennium and a half as an authentic ancient text that had had a critical influence on Confucius himself, was actually a forgery of the Han period. Hongli was eager that such techniques should be applied to the texts he wished to reproduce in order to weed out corruptions that had crept in over the centuries. He also demanded much wider education in Manchu and Mongolian, reasoning the same skills could be applied to the Liao (Kitan), Jin (Jurchen), and Yuan (Mongol) imperial histories. The cumulative, and evidently intended, effect was to eradicate the former Ming dynasty's curatorial authority over the histories of past dynasties in China and its ethnographic authority over the peoples of Northern and Inner Asia. With modern methods, Hongli was sure, the true history of the Manchus could be reconstructed.

For bureaucrats of less literary inclination, government life in the middle of the eighteenth century was showing the strains of the empire's settling foundation. For the first time, strong factions, sometimes breaking down along the lines of bannermen on one side and Chinese on the other, were crystallizing, and the struggles among them to have their followers recognized in the examinations, promoted, and enriched were sometimes calamitous. Earlier Qing emperors had bitterly denounced the tendency of officials to form factions. They had forbidden eunuchs to participate in government because they had been convinced that the crippling factionalism of the late Ming had been primarily due to the eunuchs' liking of cronyism and corruption; certainly, the Qing emperors did not intend to allow whole men to engage in the same vices. The Qianlong emperor was opposed to factionalism also, but often was distracted by his many cultural missions, and at the same time partly convinced that by leaning to one side or the other he could use the factions to maintain his own political leverage. For the early decades of his reign he used this tool effectively, but by the 1760s there were strong signs that the complexity of the bureaucracy, the enormous size of the empire, and the staggering range of the emperor's own interests were gradually stifling his ability to maintain control. Heshen, had he not arrived, would have had to be invented, so eager was the emperor for a trusted and capable colleague to manage affairs while he carried on with his artistic pursuits (many of which included carving laudatory poems on Tang-period architecture or Zhou-period jades). The fact that Heshen and his suspected corruption quickly became a lightning rod for new indictments, trials, and punishments was, to the emperor, only proof of the necessity of having him around.

Though the Qianlong government was large and extravagant by the standards of his father and grandfather, it still displayed the characteristic Qing frugality when compared to the Ming. The empire in the middle eighteenth century was twice the size of the Ming, but it carried on with the same number of county magistrates. This was not necessarily good news for those who felt themselves in need of government leadership in education, the regulation of commerce, or the inhibition of crime. Magistrates themselves, underfunded and understaffed, generally found that the smoothest course was to form a working relationship with local bosses, whether they were respectable gentry, ingenious merchants, or forthright thugs. In the middle seventeenth century, the

Plate 14 *At the summer retreat at Rehe the emperors had representations of the institutions and architectural patterns of sectors of
the imperial domain. Here, the palace of the Dalai Lama at Lhasa
– the Potala – is partly reproduced, with the mountains of Inner
Mongolia behind.*

government attempted several major reorganizations of provincial
administrations, the general pattern of which was to encourage
local landlords to take the lead in establishing charitable schools,
community grain reserves, and militias. In few cases did these
reforms encourage the upwelling of local morale and organization
that the court envisioned. More often, the privatization of government functions opened the way to tax farming, hired enforcers
who soon turned to extortion, or helpless magistrates facing irate
and unruly populations. These incipient disorders did not result
merely from government unwillingness to expend resources at the
local level after about the middle of the eighteenth century. They
were also aggravated by the immense population growth that
occurred after the stabilization of Qing control of China. Instead
of the wars, rebellions, epidemics, and agricultural disasters that
afflicted the late Ming, the early Qing enjoyed peace and a return
of prosperity.

An additional stimulus was the foreign crops commonly used in the Qing period to supplement or replace traditional crops. For instance, in regions of northern China, years of planting wheat and barley had exhausted the soil, but at a relatively superficial level. In these regions, the introduction of corn from America temporarily revived agricultural productivity, because the roots of corn grow much further into the soil to seek their nutrients. Field crops were sown in neat rows, by a mechanical seeder, at a time when most of Europe still used the broadcast method, which wasted much of the seed. Because of the efficiency of Chinese planting, the fact that population growth had driven the per capita area of arable ground to one-third of what it had been a century before had not yet created general poverty. In regions of central and southern China, the use of crops from Africa such as sweet potatoes made possible the opening of new agricultural land that had not been suitable for the cultivation of rice or wheat. With these stimulants, and in the absence of major inhibiting factors such as war or disease, the early Qing population doubled, from about 150 million in 1650 to a minimum of 300 million in 1800.

What woodlands were left in China proper at the beginning of the 1700s were rapidly diminishing by the end of the eighteenth century. Houses could thereafter be built of brick, but deforestation was added to soil exhaustion as a cause of more and more erosion. As erosion advanced, flooding became a danger. This happened at a time when, because of government corruption and general inefficiency, there was less ability to prevent flooding or recover from its effects. Waterworks – dams, dikes, and the dredging of silted-up river channels – were not maintained, and though local elites could sometimes make up the deficit, they were soon unable to carry the burden either. By the end of the eighteenth century even the Grand Canal – the artificial waterway that for a thousand years had connected the Yellow and Yangzi rivers – was virtually unusable, its towns starved for commerce.

The result was localized misery in many parts of interior China by the year 1800. Environmental deterioration and the decline of agriculture produced a large moving population. They sought seasonal work in the better agricultural areas, or worked as barge pullers, charcoal burners, or nightsoil carriers, or in other low-status trades. Many drifted to the cities to make their way by begging, prostitution, or theft. In central China and the southwest, where indigenous peoples had been driven off their traditional lands and farmers had been impoverished by serious flooding

Plate 15   *Castiglione and Attiret were among the Jesuits who helped design this summer palace for the Qianlong emperor on the model of the Trianon in the Yuanming gardens near Peking. In 1747 the central fountain – its pool surrounded by the twelve animal signs of the Chinese zodiac – was added by Michel Benoist. The palace, along with all the architecture of the Yuanming gardens, was reduced to rubble by British and French forces who invaded Peking in 1860. (National Palace Museum, Peking)*

from the Xiang and other rivers, rebellions became endemic. There was spectacular evidence of this in southwest China, where the introduction of new crops allowed Chinese farmers to begin to work lands that had been the traditional home of indigenous, non-agricultural people, generally referred to as the Miao and Yao.

When these peoples rose in rebellion, local officials and military bureaucrats were unable to completely restore peace. The unending Jinchuan Wars, as they came to be called, created profound misery for local inhabitants, whether Chinese or indigenous. It did not help the situation that in the 1780s and 1790s the Qianlong emperor was showing the effects of age, and was more disinclined than ever to look closely into the affairs of Heshen's network, which supplied the court with rosy reports of progress in the wars

in the southwest, while pocketing the resulting military appropria-
tions. By 1796 a series of persistent rural revolts in central China
had been linked by the White Lotus sect of millenarian Buddhism,
which wished to restore stability and prosperity in China by
driving the Manchu conquerors out. The rebellions were still
raging when the Qianlong emperor died in 1799.

The Fall of the Philosopher-King

In the eighteenth century, Europe – to the extent that this can be
generalized about – had a high opinion of the emperors of China.
The empire was, among other things, the source of things highly
prized by the middle and upper classes of Europe: tea, rhubarb,
silk, cloisonné, wallpaper, decorative fans, porcelain, and
bentwood furniture. Techniques of variolation known to the Chinese for over a millennium had inspired the invention of the
smallpox vaccine in Europe, and the methods of the Qing imperial
porcelain factories had given Josiah Wedgwood the idea of "in-
venting" the assembly line.

There also arose an image of the Chinese emperors as paragons
of political virtue. Notions of "oriental despotism" had, after
Montesquieu, begun to specify themselves around the sultans of
the Ottoman empire. The Chinese monarchs, on the other hand,
were vaguely understood to be rational, even benevolent rulers.
They had the advantage of being far enough away that almost any
ideal could be imposed upon them, a role which the Qianlong
emperor would have been only too delighted to be awarded. In
1762 Oliver Goldsmith used the conceit of spies of the enlightened
emperor of China reporting on the idiocy of European society.
Voltaire wrote at length on the rationalism and even scientific
orientation of Confucianism, in sum contriving to describe it as
the prescription for the cultivation of rulers so balanced, so
selfless, and so unswerving in their pursuit of justice that any
greedy, parasitical aristocrats or hypocritical priests would be
ground beneath the imperial heel like so much cheap glass. He
highly recommended their deistic but anti-clerical approach to his
readers.

But Voltaire did not have to be vague and hypothetical about
the existence of philosopher-kings among the Chinese, for there is
reason to believe that he actually read at least part of an epic poem

Plate 16 *Like many emperors of the Aisin Gioro lineage who venerated elder women in the family, the Qianlong emperor was famous for his devotion to his mother. This detail from a silk scroll painting of the enormous banquet held in the Forbidden City to celebrate the empress dowager's birthday shows the Qianlong emperor himself bringing drink to his mother, who as the guest of honor is seated at the dais. (National Palace Museum, Peking)*

composed by the then-present ruler, and infused to a fine point with the virtues of benevolence, learning, patience, and sagacity that appeared to be so wanting in European rulers of the same era. This work, the "Ode to Mukden," Voltaire supposed, had been translated by the Jesuit Amyot from the original composition of the Qianlong emperor of the Qing.

By the time of the Qianlong emperor, Qing trust in the Jesuits as selfless servants, come from afar to serve the emperors, had evaporated. Many Jesuits stayed as advisors, doctors, and court designers and painters. Giuseppe Castiglione (1688–1777) and Jean-Denis Attiret (1702–68), for instance, worked with other Jesuits and with dozens of Chinese court painters to create a new form of Chinese watercolor, using light and dimension in wholly unprecedented ways. The school was both mannered and stylized, at once meeting the eighteenth-century Qing taste for stereotyping and presenting the Qianlong emperor and his entourage as vivid, palpable individuals. Though Castiglione was instrumental in changing the ways that Qing emperors presented themselves and their environment to their contemporaries and to later genera- tions, he was not, as Jesuits had been in the seventeenth century, an important advisor to the emperor.

Indeed religious activity by the Jesuits made the eighteenth- century court uncomfortable; certainly the Aisin Gioro lineage cults, of which Manchu was the primary vehicle, had been well concealed from unauthorized Chinese perusal, and curiosity on the part of Jesuits was not welcome. Later foreigners continued to exploit the grasp that Manchu offered of official communications in China, and by the early nineteenth century Protestant mission- aries began to use Manchu to proselytize among the bannermen. Alarmed that knowledge of Manchu was spreading among Euro- peans, the Qianlong emperor's son and successor, the Jiaqing emperor, in 1805 prohibited the teaching of Manchu to foreigners, during a series of anti-Christian proclamations.

The prohibition was not honored. Foreigners continued to study Manchu, and it is now impossible to trace the development of scholarship on Asia in the West without according a primary place to knowledge of Manchu and curatorship of Manchu mate- rials. Seventeenth- and eighteenth-century Jesuits, who continually sent Manchu materials out of Peking, created the core of what are now the "oriental" manuscript collections in France and Italy, just as late eighteenth- and early nineteenth-century traders from Britain and the German territories created their respective collections. By the early nineteenth century, the great Chinese classics had all been translated into Manchu. Most were available in bilingual editions, and Europeans used Manchu as a bridge for the study of classical Chinese. By the middle of the century, the New Testament would be translated into Manchu and distributed to several major cities.

Père Joseph-Marie Amyot (also Amiot, 1718–94) passed through Macao and reached China in 1750, then lived in Peking until his death. Manchu was his primary means of communicating with the court, and he has left several important (though not flawless) works for the study of eighteenth-century culture. Among them were a rendition of the "Ode to Mukden" and an untitled transcription of a shamanic prayer which Amyot heard offered during the Jinchuan wars. Parisian readers were able to peruse Amyot's "Ode to Mukden" in 1770. As it happened, Amyot was a translator with a point of view. His "Ode" bristled with philosophical asides and flights of patently Christian fancy that owed nothing to the brushes of Qianlong's scribes. Later scholars excoriated Amyot's treatment of the ode, pointing to whole passages that had evidently sprung from the brain of the translator, completed unaided by the letter or spirit of the original. But denunciation of the work and the extravagant ideas of the Qing that it had produced in Europe came a generation too late. The idyllic landscapes of Manchuria, the virgin birth of the Aisin Gioro forebear, and the enlightened Christian soul of the Qianlong emperor (and perhaps his surprisingly good grasp of French) had already made an indelible impression upon those who read it.

The speed with which the European opinion of the emperor was reversed, and the episode that caused it, have been sources of wonder for the past two hundred years. In essence, a dispute between the British government and the British East India Company (BEIC) was transmogrified into a dispute between the British and the Qing empires, and the rupture led by degrees to the grinding away of all semblance of political unity, international honor, or economic stability for China.

Like all their contemporary governments of Eastern Asia, the Ming and Qing empires attempted to closely regulate commercial activity. This was done partly because of their wish that agriculture should remain the most important and best-protected source

Plate 17 *The Qianlong emperor with two of his wives and nine of his children, in an apparently casual pose as they let off fire-crackers on the eve of the lunar New Year. The painting shows the realistic perspective and detail introduced to court painting by Castiglione and other European painters. It is not, however, the naturalistic representation it appears – each child's figure is actually a model that is repeated in a series of paintings done about this time, and the emperor's pose and actions are in accord with a set of New Year's symbols for good fortune in the coming year. (National Palace Museum, Peking)*

of wealth, but it was also consistent with the Confucian philosophy that merchants should always be lower than scholars on the
social and political ladders. In the Qing case, there was as well the
unwavering conviction that monopolies – upon which the Nurgaci
state had been founded and driven to enforce the integrity of its
borders – were the foundation of economic stability. Combined
with increasing concern about banditry and piracy, the philosophy
led the Qing empire to strictly limit the access of foreign merchants
to the Chinese trading cities. This was true whether the merchants
were caravan traders on camels attempting to sell dried dates at
Kashgar in Central Asia, or Japanese merchants trying to sell
lacquerware at Zhapu on the eastern coast of China. It was also
true for European merchants. After 1784 the practices known as
the "Canton system" were fixed: European merchants were permitted to trade only at Guangzhou ("Canton"), they were to be
insured, protected, and vouchsafed by Chinese merchants in the
city, and all tax revenues from the Guangzhou trade were to be
directly rendered to the imperial family through its resident commissioner, known to the Europeans as the "hoppo."

To the Europeans, who imagined this system was unique to
them and whose sea-based empires were built on entirely different
principles, the "Canton system" seemed irrational. Great fortunes
had been made in the tea trade, but the search for a suitable
product to sell to China had still not been successful. After the loss
of the American colonies, Britain in particular feared that its
markets would diminish. British and some American merchants
believed that China was a vast unexploited market, with hundreds
of millions of potential consumers of lamp oil made from whale
blubber; or cotton grown in India or the American south; or guns
manufactured in London or Connecticut. Only the "Canton system" stood in the way.

Tea was first shipped from China to England in 1664. It was
earlier a prized import to Russia, Central Asia, and the Middle
East, all of which knew it by the northern Chinese name of *cha*,
and all of which acquired it by the overland Eurasian routes of
medieval and early modern times. Europe, however, knew the
product from sea routes first exploited by the Portuguese and
Dutch, and thus from its name in Fujian province of coastal China,
te. From the time of its introduction to England in the middle
1600s, tea displaced chocolate and coffee as the favored drink. By
1800, tea accounted for 80 percent of all exports from China to

Europe. The remainder consisted primarily of porcelain, which by the middle 1700s was manufactured in the imperial complexes at Jingdezhen and Dehua to the brightly-colored designs specified by European merchants, then trans-shipped from Canton to Europe by the hundreds of thousands of pieces.

Like many Europeans, the directors of the BEIC believed that China's technological achievements and its gigantic potential markets made it the key to limitless profit. Private fortunes had indeed been made, by British merchants who were members of BEIC, by Chinese merchants who were their bankers, guarantors, interlocutors, and brokers in Canton, and by Dutch, British, and Spanish smugglers who circumvented the BEIC monopoly to bootleg tea into Britain. But George III's government was experiencing a general and disquieting imbalance of trade with China, as British silver went to China to pay for the exported products. By the end of the eighteenth century, the British government had become suspicious of the power and influence of the BEIC, and as part of its attempts to regulate BEIC activities, it attempted to open direct diplomatic relations with China.

In Britain, the imbalance of payments created anxiety and anger over the alleged unfair restrictions that the Qing empire placed upon the import of foreign goods. To make matters worse, the BEIC had managed its worldwide holdings badly, and as it teetered on the edge of bankruptcy its attempts to manipulate the Parliament became more intrusive. In 1773 the British Parliament passed a series of laws designed to curb the political activities of the BEIC and dismantle some of its monopolies. At the same time, in order to allow the BEIC to recoup some of its income, it was granted a market monopoly for the American colonies, where it began to sell inferior tea at high prices. Protests – "tea parties" – later broke out in Boston, Philadelphia, and elsewhere. The crown, hoping to quiet British America and destroy the influence of the BEIC in domestic politics, decided to undercut the company's ability to control access to Asian tea. For that to happen, the trade in China would have to be restructured. In 1792 George Macartney was sent to China, to open diplomatic relations with the Qing empire.

Macartney and his entourage arrived at Canton in 1793 and requested permission for an audience with the emperor, at which they hoped to present a letter from King George III. Things began to go wrong almost immediately. The letter, written in Chinese,

Plate 18 *The painter William Alexander accompanied the Macartney mission as far as Peking, but had to reconstruct this meeting of the Qianlong emperor and the Macartney party from verbal accounts. Here, the emperor rewards the child George Staunton with a silk pouch from his own belt, after listening to the boy say a few polite things in Chinese. (Property of Librairie Artheme Fayard, Paris)*

which Macartney hoped to present to the emperor was found by the Chinese officials to be lacking the necessary words acknowledging the supremacy of the Qing emperor. When Macartney explained that the purpose of his visit was to establish diplomatic equality between the British and Qing rulers, the explanation was rejected. At length Macartney and his entourage were allowed to proceed to Peking and the summer palace at Chengde, because the Chinese officials believed that once there he would perform the "kowtow" (*ketou*, or "head knockings") and acknowledge the supremacy of the Qing emperor.

This was a strict ritual which officials performed not only before the emperor but before any representation of his presence, most often a throne. The ceremony was traditionally Chinese; before

Plate 19 *Macartney and the elder Staunton were each given a* ruyi *("it will be as intended") of this sort by the Qianlong emperor at the time of his visit. It is the baton of imperial authority, given in jade or gold to members of the imperial family, in ivory or precious metals to others as a sign of imperial favor. This one is of gilt lacquer. (National Palace Museum, Peking)*

the creation of the Later Jin state, Jurchens had been accustomed to making a sort of curtsy before their superiors, which continued as a Manchu custom outside the presence of the emperor in Qing times. The kowtow was also sometimes called the "nine kneelings and three bows," which describes the duration of the ceremony, though "knocking" of the head on the ground was clearly expected, and Qing officials sometimes knocked until they drew blood in order to show their sincerity. Qing envoys who greeted Macartney at Tianjin and conducted him inland attempted on several occasions to instruct him in the performance of the ceremony, and each time he refused, explaining that before his own king he would reverently go down on one bended knee, and would gladly do the same for the Qing emperor – going down on two knees was for showing reverence to God alone.

In exasperation Macartney suggested that if the Qing officials would kneel before a portrait of George III, which had been brought as a gift for the Qianlong emperor, he would perform the prescribed rituals before the emperor. But the Qing officials were mystified at his suggestion that they should worship the picture of an unknown person. Though Macartney was granted an audience with the emperor, no negotiations followed. He eventually fell ill, and lay in bed for months hoping for an invitation to the Qing court. Amyot, on his deathbed and hearing of the stubbornness of the British envoy, wrote to warn him that such an invitation would never come. In the end Macartney despaired of being able to accomplish his mission, and returned to London.

Though the Macartney mission is usually noted as an intriguing failure, it had a strong influence over later developments both in Europe and in China. Both the British and the Qing were rigidly insistent upon certain rituals, and it may appear that these concerns were what doomed the Macartney mission. But beyond ritual, the Qing government was concerned to keep the "Canton system" intact, because it worked very well for them at this time. It brought the imperial family money that was needed, created lucrative virtual monopolies for certain merchant families in Canton (who in turn were careful to enrich the officials who allowed them their privileges), and simplified some problems related to the control of contraband. Moreover, it was perfectly true that although the Qing court was fascinated by some of the goods brought by Macartney as gifts (really advertisements) for the court – especially ornamental and amusing timepieces and landscape paintings – neither Europe nor America had a product that was of genuine appeal to the Qing empire. Realizing that the export of tea was a major advantage, the Qing emperor did not feel a need to exert himself to improve the relative trade position of Britain.

Dutch, French, and Russian embassies soon attempted to achieve what Macartney had failed at, and when they failed too, European frustration with China mounted. To the British government, the imbalance in trade between Britain and China was more obvious and more worrisome after the Macartney mission, because the chances of a political solution to the problem appeared to be diminishing. On the other hand, it was recognized that greater familiarity with the Qing empire and its cultures was necessary. Macartney's group had included only one English member who knew Chinese, and that was the child George Staunton, who learned it on the sea voyage.

The lifetime of George Thomas Staunton, who was born in 1781 and died in 1859, framed dramatic and profound change in the relations between China and Europe, and Staunton himself was present at many of the pivotal scenes. The first series occurred when he accompanied his father, George Leonard Staunton, on the Macartney embassy to China in 1793 and 1794. At that time, as outlined above, the Qing empire was regarded as the key to limitless mercantile wealth, and as a well-regulated and technologically advanced society. Macartney had been commissioned to open diplomatic relations with China, and to present as gifts to the Qing throne such goods as Britain hoped to interest the Chinese in importing in large numbers. These included an elaborate carriage, which had to be disassembled and reassembled many times in its hapless journey to China – and back again after it was rejected.

The embassy left Europe with no interpreters, but with four priests (three Chinese and one Manchu) who had been studying in Rome and wished to return home. The two Stauntons, father and son, used Latin to communicate with the priests on the journey to China, and to learn Chinese from them. The elder Staunton failed in this, but 12-year-old George, who had a photographic memory and had already mastered German, French, and Latin, was a very quick study. By the time the party arrived at Tianjin in north China, young Staunton could, in partnership with his companionable Chinese priest, handle both the written and spoken communications of the party adequately.

It is hard to believe that the success of such a grand undertaking by the world's most ambitious empire rested almost entirely on the shoulders of a well-behaved, home-sick boy, and almost as difficult to imagine the pressures upon the child as the complex and rigid ritual demands of the two empires came closer and closer to collision. At first the letters translated by young George from the British King George III to the Qianlong emperor were summarily rejected because of mistakes in grammar or etiquette. His improved letters were accepted, but the Qing emperor, who was holding court at the summer palace at Rehe, refused to grant an audience to the Macartney group unless they would perform the kowtow.

The disputes over the ritual were long, eventually overshadowed the proposed substance of the talks, and ended in mystery – thanks to the diary kept by young George Staunton. Chinese records state that the Macartney mission were instructed in the ritual and performed it when they encountered the emperor at Rehe. Macartney's report, and those of the adult men who accompanied him, all say that the British party knelt on one knee to the emperor. George's diary, however, which is noteworthy for its matter-of-factness and lack of romantic idealizations of either China or the journey, states that when the British joined a crowd of dignitaries greeting the emperor as he approached his great audience tent, "we went down on one knee and Bowed our heads down to the Ground," which could be a description of the kowtow. George, or somebody who read his words later, realized the seriousness of the implication, and the words "to the Ground" are crossed out in his original diary. Unfortunately, the child's diary also strongly suggests that the British party performed the kowtow at least one other time, before an imperial throne at Canton.

Whether or not they performed the kowtow, the British were permitted an interview with the aged Qianlong emperor. Though they found him pleasant, he complained after a time that speaking through interpreters was very tiring for him, and asked whether anybody in the British party could speak Chinese. Young George was brought forward, and "my papa and I went up and made the proper ceremony. The Emperor gave my papa a [*ruyi*, a ritual gift of jade] . . . and took off a little yellow purse hanging by his side and gave it to me. He wanted me to say a few words in Chinese, which I did, to thank him for the present." Again, we will never entirely know the meaning of "the proper ceremony," but an English artist who was not in attendance clearly interpreted this to mean that George bent his knee before the emperor.

The Chinese and British observers alike were stunned at the personal gesture on the part of the emperor toward the child. Some time later, during an opera performance which the British attended with the emperor, a request from the women of the emperor's harem to see a European was met with the presentation of young George before them, another sign (interpreted by the British according to their assumption that all Qing officials were homosexually inclined) of the emperor's special favor toward the child.

After months of frustration, false leads, and illness, the group arrived at Canton, George's first glimpse of southern China, and he was both amazed and disillusioned. The merchants of the BEIC and other European charter companies lived comfortably at Canton, surrounded by Chinese business partners, tradesmen, and servants who commonly spoke some degree of English. Had the British government not wished to bypass the channels of the BEIC, he believed, his own sufferings would have been greatly diminished. For the rest of his life, Staunton remained suspended between his memories of the kindnesses and honor shown him when he was a frail child in China, and consternation at the pale imitators who later claimed, but in his eyes never merited, the mantle of the Qianlong age.

6

The Lingering Death of the Empire

The life of George Staunton continued to frame the deteriorating relationship between the Qing and the British empires. He spent many years of his later youth and young manhood in Canton and in Macao, rising to an executive position in the BEIC, and after returning to Britain in 1818 began a political career that often engaged him in debate on Britain's China policy. But he also was an originator of modern Western scholarship on China. He made the first translation of any work from Chinese into English, an abridged version of the Qing legal code, and in 1805 translated the work of an English physician on inoculation into Chinese, thus completing the cycle of technological transmission that had begun when the Jesuits had learned of variolation from the Chinese. Staunton's work in Britain was parallelled by the growth of early studies of Qing documents in Europe and in Russia, where J.-P. Abel-Rémusat (1788–1832) and Heinrich-Julius von (also Henri-Jules de) Klaproth (1783–1835) developed a small corpus of translations and monographs based upon their studies of Qing documents in Chinese and in Manchu.

In 1816 Staunton was called upon by the British government to accompany William Pitt Amherst on a second attempt at a diplomatic opening with China. Though Staunton approved of the idea of diplomatic relations, and agreed to go along as Amherst's interpreter and chief aid, he adamantly advised against agreeing to perform the kowtow – perhaps because he knew that the Macartney group and other Europeans had tried it and gained nothing by it, or perhaps because he fully believed that the adults he had accompanied to China in 1793 had not performed it, and that agreeing to do it now would only achieve a further lowering of British dignity in the eyes of the Qing empire. In any case, Staunton's skepticism was justified. The Amherst mission was a worse disaster than the Macartney, as the group were bodily bounced from the imperial summer palace at Yuanming yuan (designed and built in European rococo style) when they refused to kowtow.

After his return to Britain and assumption of a political career, Staunton's feelings toward China were ambivalent. He supported the BEIC, and believed that further trade between the two countries would be a positive good. He also continued to promote in Britain greater knowledge of Chinese language and culture, and was a co-founder with Henry Thomas Colebrooke of the Royal Asiatic Society in 1823. He had strong and in his time unique childhood associations with his experiences in China, his favor from the emperor, and particularly his acquaintance with the brilliant and generous Manchu official Songyun (see chapter 5). After entering Parliament Staunton was a strong supporter of the anti-opium lobby, and remained so until his death in 1859. But when in 1839 Staunton came to believe that the Qing empire had presented the British empire with a cause for war, he responded to the raw and unromanticized vision of China he had formed in his early teen years, and argued that "the unprovoked outrages of the Chinese [have] placed right on *our* side."

The Princes of Disorder

Staunton certainly knew, though he clearly did not consider it an excuse, that it was not merely obtuseness and vanity that kept the Qing from cooperating with British demands. It was the successes of the Qing empire in the earlier eighteenth century that created much of the domestic and political chaos of the later period. The Qing conquest had brought stability to central China, which previously had been subjected to decades of rebellion and agricultural shortages. By deliberate policy the Qing state encouraged the recovery of farm lands, the opening of previously uncultivated land, and the restoration and expansion of the road system. The result was dramatic expansion of the agricultural base together with a gigantic leap in population. Enormous numbers of farmers, merchants, and day laborers migrated across China in search of less crowded conditions, and a permanent "floating population" of the unemployed and homeless emerged. By the century's end, population strain on the land had resulted in serious environmental damage in some parts of central and western China: Deforestation, erosion, and soil exhaustion left swollen populations stranded on land that was deteriorating rapidly.

The dissatisfactions of this population were joined by those of minority peoples in central and southwestern China who had been driven off their lands during the boom of the eighteenth century; by Mongols who resented the appropriation of their grazing lands and the displacement of their traditional elites; by village vigilante organizations who had grown used to governing frontier and inadequately policed regions when the underfinanced Qing government had proved powerless; and by the growing numbers of people who mistrusted the government, suspecting that all officials were corrupt. In the nineteenth century, these endemic social problems were aggravated by the growing presence and privilege of foreign merchants and missionaries in the treaty ports. They were a visible reminder of the inability or unwillingness of the Qing court to protect the Chinese people from the intrusions of foreigners. In some parts of China the Qing were hated because they were themselves a foreign conquest regime, and were suspected of having sympathies with the newly-arrived foreigners from Europe. Indeed as the Qianlong emperor lay on his deathbed the White Lotus Rebellion, partly inspired by a mystical ideology that predicted the restoration of the Chinese Ming dynasty and the coming of the Buddha, was raging across central China, and could not be suppressed until 1804.

After the deaths of the Qianlong emperor and of Heshen, the new Jiaqing emperor (1796–1820) had attempted to restore some of the damage to roads, waterworks, and defense works that had deteriorated so badly in the last Qianlong decades. A major hindrance to these improvements was the urgent need to suppress the White Lotus rebels. Many localities had found that the imperial armies or other aid from the central government was either not available or not effective. In response, the gentry had begun to form their own militia units and to organize their own fundraising for the repair of city walls and stocking of grain stores in case of attack. The imperial government acceded to the requests of local governments for tax relief in order to maintain defenses against the rebels. Though the local methods proved effective, government revenues were further squeezed. The exigencies of the White Lotus crisis combined with the general inability of the government to increase its revenue base to stall the reform zeal of the Jiaqing emperor and his officials.

Though Qing officials considered the White Lotus uprising quashed in 1804, the ideology of the movement – which predicted the eviction of the Manchus from China, the end of the secular political order, and the coming of the age of Buddhist salvation – continued to spread, combining with the distress of some localities to enflame more rebellions. One of these, the Eight Trigrams uprising of 1813 in northern China, actually burst through the gates of the Forbidden City. The prince Minning – who would become the Daoguang emperor in 1821 – saw the invaders from his classroom, and rushed to the scene with a pistol. He is reported to have killed two of the rebels before imperial troops recaptured the courtyards.

Incidents such as this inclined the emperors of the early 1800s to attempt a restrengthening of the Eight Banners. They approved of the policy established during the Qianlong years of reviving the study of Manchu among banner officers, in particular; as a secure means of communication, Manchu would continue to have its uses well into the middle of the 1800s. And the Qianlong emperor's insistence upon martial skills was also considered valuable, though the ideals of Manchu pureness with which he attempted to inspire the bannermen to these achievements were obviously not working. Material incentives were needed, but these were what the court distinctly lacked the ability to provide. As the gentry of the civilian sector turned to local resources and initiative to make up for lack of state support, so did banner garrison commanders throughout the Chinese provinces try new schemes using varying degrees of thrift, sharp book-keeping, and plain violation of regulations. In some localities, the commanders refused outlays for paper and ink, which quickly hobbled many of the bureaucratic tasks necessary for running the communities. In others, budgets for the acquisition of weapons and horses were slashed, virtually ending any hopes of using the bannermen in combat. In extremity, some commanders sold off the last of the lands in their possession.

For its part, the state hoped to salve the banner budgetary crisis by continuing to remove the banner populations from China to Manchuria (which was a general failure), and by greatly reducing the number of relatively costly officer stipends, while slightly increasing the less costly stipends for enlisted men. The result was chaos by design, as the growing banner populations had their leadership decimated. By the 1820s, the banners within China were barely considered part of the miltary complement of the empire. They were primarily a social problem, as the Daoguang emperor thought constantly how to keep them from clogging the streets as beggars, alarming the population as bandits, or infecting society as opium distributors and addicts.

Opium and Foreign Privilege

For more than a century, British officials had been dissatisfied with the enormous trade deficit between Britain and China that had resulted from the British demand for tea and the Qing failure to facilitate the importation to China of any product (see chapter 5). In the early 1700s, a few European merchants and their Chinese partners were importing small quantities of opium, and in 1729 the first Qing law making such activities illegal was passed. It has been estimated that at the time as few as 200 chests were being brought to China, and neither Britain nor the Qing considered it a great issue. By 1800, however, smuggling had increased the quantity to as many as 4000 chests a year. British merchants had discovered an extremely lucrative trade, and a large Chinese commerce had arisen around the distribution of the drugs brought ashore by foreigners. Most devastating to Chinese society, however, was the dramatic increase in the early 1800s of use of and addiction to the drug. British importers were now competing with Americans, and a price war in the early 1820s raised demand so sharply that by the 1830s as many as 30,000 chests were being imported, and addiction had spread to all levels of society, with a large number of very high-ranking officials affected.

Officials had expressed their concerns to the court for years about the spread of opium use, but it was not until 1831 that systematic investigation revealed that addiction was widespread not only among the populations of those parts of China easily communicating with the coasts and major rivers systems, but also among the Qing elite. Banner officers, the highest civil officials, and members of the imperial lineage were found to be involved in use of the drug. The Daoguang emperor claimed to be beside himself with outrage. The economy was being drained of silver to pay for the contraband at as high a rate as the specie had flowed in fifty years before. Elites were pawning their fortunes, poor people were selling their children. Among court officials and literati in the provinces, a debate ensued over how to handle the problem. One group advised the emperor to legalize the trade and tax it, to ease the government financial crisis and possibly make opium expensive enough that addiction would at least return to its level before the price war of the 1820s. Others argued that such a policy would do nothing to ease the social maladies that opium addiction had engendered.

One particularly clear voice among this group was the provincial governor Lin Zexu. He advised that it would be useless to focus punishments on those who used the drug. Addicts should be consigned to programs for a graduated recovery and retraining for useful employment. At the same time, those importing and distributing the drug should bear the brunt of government sanctions. The Chinese merchants receiving the drug and moving it through the cities and countrysides should be told to desist, and if they did not do so they should pay with their lives. The foreign merchants bringing opium to Canton and to illegal depots along the southern coasts should be stopped.

Lin's persuasiveness and his unusual reputation for honesty and consistency caused the emperor to order him to resign his governorship and go to Canton as a special commissioner to stop the opium trade. To the consternation of the Canton merchants and the foreign traders, Lin actually made surprising progress. As the international merchant community tried at each step to divert, deceive, or bribe Lin, he steadfastly stalked the primary merchants, and eventually put the entire foreign community in confinement until they would agree to surrender the opium already landed at Canton and give written promises that they would import no more. But when the British Captain Charles Elliott, his marines, and a detachment of the Royal Navy arrived, Lin's unswerving campaign against the opium traders slipped across the threshold to the first exchanges in war.

A faction at court immediately recommended that Lin be recalled, and that the Qing court temporize with Britain. The leader of that group, the Manchu Mujangga, argued that the empire was unprepared for war, and that the strength of the British forces could not be readily assessed; better to back down and attempt another course than to stick doggedly to Lin's single-minded crusade. The emperor wavered, but decided to back Lin. Events soon gave a fatal tinge to this decision, and within a year Lin was sacked and sent into internal exile at the urging of Mujangga.

The Opium War of 1839–42 exposed the fact that the traditional imperial forces were hopelessly obsolete. The war was fought mostly from the sea. British ships landed troops who pillaged the cities at selected spots and then returned to their ships and sailed to a new destination. The Qing had no national navy at all, and until they were able to engage the British in prolonged fighting on land, they were unable to defend themselves against the attacks. Even in the land engagements, Qing resources proved spectacularly inadequate. While the British could move their forces quickly along the coasts and land them at strategic sites, Qing troops moved primarily by walking. Moving reinforcements from central to eastern China took more than three months.

Once the defense forces arrived, they were not only exhausted but virtually unarmed. The few muskets the empire had imported during the 1700s were now used by the bannermen against the British invaders. Not only were the weapons unreliable, but they were matchlocks that required the soldiers to ignite the load of gunpowder in them by hand. Firing the weapons was dangerous, and the canister of gunpowder each musketeer was required to carry on his belt was likely to explode if a fire broke out in the vicinity – a frequent occurrence when encountering the artillery of the British. A majority of the bannermen fought with swords, knives, spears, and clubs.

For their part, the soldiers under British command – many of whom were Indians – carried self-firing rifles, far quicker, safer, and more accurate than the antique matchlocks some Qing soldiers carried. The long-distance artillery of the British was flexible and very deadly in the cities and villages of eastern China. Finally, the Qing commanders expected that the British gunboats would be too low in the water to penetrate the Chinese rivers, and that evacuating the coasts would be enough to protect the country from the British threat. But new gunboats, like the *Nemesis*, were shallow-drafting, and moved without impediment up the Yangzi river. When the invaders approached the revered former Ming capital of Nanjing, the Qing decided to negotiate an end to the war, and in 1842 the terms of the Treaty of Nanking were concluded.

The treaty was only the first in a series that, through the 1840s, erected a scaffold from which Qing coastal sovereignty and much of its internal control were eventually hanged. While local officials in Canton delayed implementing the treaty provisions, the court cast about for scapegoats, and found an easy target in the bannermen of the southern and central provinces who had encountered the British forces. Officers were accused of treason and cowardice, and often subjected to the ultimate punishments. Bannermen were scolded for their general unworthiness, and denied extra funds to bury and commemorate their dead. Worse, the growing coldness of the court toward the garrison communities led to a set of economic and political measures designed to fray and gradually sever the ties between the court and the bannermen. In the 1840s and 1850s rice stipends were delayed, then cancelled. Lands granted to the garrisons were sometimes sold by the court itself, which not only kept the proceeds of sale but collected tax on the land thereafter. The bannermen, who since the conquest had not always borne their trials in silence, were overt in their protests: Riots increased in frequency in the 1850s, first in Manchuria, then in southern China, and finally in the tenuously-occupied garrisons in Xinjiang.

The malaise of the 1850s was due not only to unresolved tensions over the Treaty of Nanking and constant threats from Western powers of new wars to enforce the agreements, but also to the profound bankruptcy of the court, and the realization that the empire had no real line of defense against the growing clamor of the West for privileges and land. Even the officials and aristocrats of Peking had begun to feel the bands tighten, as the court demanded that treasury officials make up accounting deficits from their own funds, and some were notified that if the indemnities from the Opium War were paid to Britain, they would be required by the state to make a significant personal contribution. In 1850, with public morale on a steep downward pitch, the popular Daoguang emperor, Minning, died. His personal frugality and sense of duty had been ineffective in restoring the empire's soundness, and he died having forbidden the encomia normally heaped upon a dead emperor from being granted to him.

The Taiping War and the End of the Qing Empire

The region of Guangxi province where the Taiping movement originated was an example of the entrenched social problems that

had been generating disorder through the empire for half a century. Agriculture in the region was unstable, and many made their living from arduous and despised trades such as carrying night-soil, producing charcoal, and mining. Economic distress was complicated by ethnic stratifications. A minority group, the Hakkas (originally migrants from north China), were frequently to be found in the lowlier trades, and tensions between themselves and the majority were rising. It is possible that the local economy had also been affected by the sharp rises and falls in the trade of opium, which after 1842 flooded the coastal and riverine portions of China, then collapsed as domestically grown opium began to dominate the market. The area was also close enough to Canton to feel the cultural as well as the economic impact of the growing number of Europeans and Americans in the treaty ports.

All these factors were significant in the experience of Hong Xiuquan (1813–64), the founder of the Taiping movement. He came from a humble Hakka background, and after years of study competed in the provincial Confucian examinations, hoping for a post in government. He failed the examinations repeatedly, however, and it appears that in his late thirties he suffered a nervous breakdown. Afterwards he spent some time in Canton, and there met both Chinese and American missionaries who inspired him with their teachings on Christianity. Hong, however, had his own

Plate 20 (facing page, top)   *The American Frederick Townsend Ward found some of the fame and fortune he craved in China before being felled by a Taiping musket ball in 1862, aged 30. Ward was part of an international network of mercenaries who had served in Crimea, particularly, before coming to China to help the Qing empire quash the Taipings. This portrait, done shortly before his death, shows the distinctive style of the Canton painters who worked for the international market but retained many Chinese elements of perspective and composition. (Essex Institute, Salem, MA)*

Plate 21 (facing page, bottom)   *Ward was buried in the regalia of an officer of the Eight Banners, including robe, Manchu cap, and boots of the sort depicted in all portraits of Manchus. (Essex Institute, Salem, MA)*

Plates 20–1   were previously published in Caleb Carr, *The Devil Soldier* (1992).

interpretation of what the Christian message was. He saw himself as the younger brother of Jesus, commissioned by God to found a new kingdom on earth, and drive the Manchu conquerors, the Qing, out of China. The result would be universal peace, and Hong later called his new religious movement the "Kingdom of Great Peace" (*Taiping tianguo*).

Beginning with a circle of friends and relatives, Hong quickly amassed a community of believers, primarily Hakkas, around him at Thistle Mountain. Their ideas and their practices alarmed the locality. They believed in the prophecy of dreams; Hong and his rivals for leadership in the movement went in and out of ecstatic trances; they claimed they could walk on air. They denounced the Manchus as creatures of Satan. News of the heterodoxy reached the government, and Qing troops were sent to disperse the Taipings and arrest their leaders. But to the shock of the court, the government troops were soundly defeated. Local loyalty to the Taipings spread quickly, their numbers multiplied, and they began to enlarge their domain. They forced the populations of captured villages to join their movement, and once people were absorbed their activities were strictly monitored. Men and women were segregated, and organized into work and military teams based on units of ten. Women were forbidden to bind their feet (foot-binding had never been a practice of the Hakkas), and participated fully in farming and laboring. There were also brigades of women soldiers who took the field against the Qing forces.

At first it appears that the Taipings relied upon Hakka particularism and the charismatic appeal of their religious doctrine to attract followers. But as their numbers and their power grew, they altered their methods of preaching and administering. They stopped enlisting Hakkas against the majority and began to enlist the majority against the Manchus, who in Taiping cosmology were the early manifestation of satanic forces. The outcome of the civil war would determine whether God or the Devil would rule China. As the movement grew, it spread to eastern and northern China. Panic preceded them, as villagers feared impressment into the Taiping work and military gangs and the elites recoiled in horror from the bizarre ideology of foreign gods, totalitarian rule, and able-bodied women. Local officials and landholders led the self-defense works, first repairing and strengthening village and town walls, then provisioning the communities within them, then arming and drilling the male residents. In the early 1850s these attempts at local defense were overwhelmed by the huge numbers the Taipings were able to muster in their campaigns. But as the Taipings had mastered the techniques of conquest and occupation, so the local communities began to achieve greater success with their defenses. When, in 1853, the Taiping armies crossed the Yangzi river and made their way to Nanjing, their momentum was slowing, and they were looking for a permanent base.

The fall of Nanjing to the Taipings sent waves of panic through the Qing capital at Peking. Nanjing had been an imperial capital in earlier times, and it was the British approach to this hallowed city that had forced the Qing court to agree to negotiate an end to the Opium War. To the nobles and elites of Peking, it was inconceivable that a bizarre religious cult had gathered a gigantic army and taken Nanjing. The assumption that the fall of Peking could not be far behind filled the streets of the capital with the high-laden carts of families moving themselves and their fortunes to more secure ground.

In fact, Qing military commanders were already gaining some ground in their attempts to stem further growth of the Taiping movement. Their successes were mainly due to the flexibility of the commanders of the imperial forces in the face of an unprecedented challenge. In the early years of the conflict bannermen were seconded from their regular positions to the new, irregular, mixed forces for combating the rebels. The earliest innovations of this kind were the two Grand Battalions made up of bannermen, Green Standard soldiers, and provincial militia, and mobilized to contain the Taipings south of the Yangzi if possible; later, bannermen and Green Standard soldiers, as well as foreign mercenaries, joined the armies organized by some provincial governors to combat the Taipings on a larger scale.

The Manchu Tacibu was reassigned from the Xianfeng (1851–61) emperor's own retinue to the new Hunan Army created by the provincial governor Zeng Guofan. Tacibu's skill and bravery provided Zeng with his earliest lessons – and later confidence – in the management of troops. By the time Tacibu died suddenly (perhaps of a heart attack) at the age of 39 in 1855, Zeng's Hunan Army had repeatedly prevented the Taipings from progressing northward, and had become the foundation of the imperial effort to suppress the rebellion. Other bannermen played similar roles, sometimes taking the unprecedented initiative of requesting leave from their garrison assignments to join the armies of the civilian

Chinese governors. Perhaps most famous among the banner elite working with the new organizations was Senggerinchin, a Mongol prince and descendent of Genghis Khan, who led a composite force in the first defeat of the Taipings in north China, in 1853. Senggerinchin quickly became a source of terror to the rebels. In victory he was as savage as in battle, piling up the severed ears and noses of his enemies to be sent to the capital as trophies. His talents were later directed against the British and French forces when they tried to breach the coast in the vicinity of the fort at Dagu, near Tianjin. To their surprise – and that of the Qing court – they were soundly repulsed by Senggerinchin, though they later found a way around him and menaced Peking, forcing the Xianfeng emperor to withdraw to the summer palace at Rehe. Senggerinchin was humiliated for his failure to keep the capital secure, but was recalled to combat the growing Nian rebellion in Shandong. There, as against the Taipings, he proved a terrible opponent – so terrible that a special squad of Nians ambushed him and assassinated him in 1865. The armies of Zeng Guofan and Li Hongzhang, another provincial governor, carried the war against the Nians to conclusion.

The military commanders were also powerfully backed by a group of civilian provincial governors who had studied the techniques developed by local militia forces for self-defense. In essence, certain of the provincial governors, foremost among them Zeng Guofan, combined their knowledge of civilian self-defense and local terrain with the interest of some traditional Qing soldiers in more efficient organization and the use of modern weaponry. The result was the organization of new, informal military units, in which many of the Qing hereditary soldiers, the bannermen, voluntarily served under civilian governors. The court agreed to special taxes to fund the new armies, and acknowledged the new combined leadership of the civilian and professional force. When the Taipings settled into Nanjing, these new armies had scored their first successes, and quickly surrounded Nanjing, hoping to starve out the Taipings.

This was not easily done. The Taipings had provisioned and fortified themselves well, and they had the advantage of several extremely brilliant young military commanders, such as Li Xiucheng, who at intervals mobilized enormous military forces that moved through nearby parts of eastern China, scavenging supplies and attempting to break the encirclement of Nanjing. For more than a decade the Taiping leadership remained ensconced at Nanjing, and their "Heavenly Kingdom" endured. Though the Qing forces had contained the rebellion, there was no certainty that they could eradicate it.

By 1856, Britain and France were concerned about the situation in China. The provisions of the treaties signed after the conclusion of the Opium War had not been implemented on the Chinese side, and European patience was wearing thin. Whether to support the intransigent Qing in the civil war, to take advantange of the situation to inflict punishment on them for neglecting their treaty obligations, or to support the Taipings in creating a new state that would abide by the agreements was a significant policy matter. European and American missionaries had visited Nanjing, curious to see what their fellow Christians were up to. The reports they sent home were shocking and, for the faithful, discouraging. Whatever the Taipings were practicing, it was not Christianity, and whatever they were reading, it was not the Bible. Hong Xiuquan and the other leaders appeared to lead lives of indulgence and abandon, and more than one missionary commented upon the homosexual practices of the Taiping rulers. Now having no fear of being accused of quashing an appealing Christian movement, the British and French considered the situation. Though the Taipings were not going to topple the Qing government, the outbreak in the 1850s of the Nian rebellion in northern China was ominous; a series of simultaneous large outbreaks might cause the empire to dissolve.

The European decision was to make a very swift, very brutal series of coastal attacks – a second opium war, called the Arrow War – which culminated in a British and French invasion of Peking in 1860 and destruction of the Qianlong emperor's rococo summer palace at Yuanming yuan. When that war was concluded, British and French forces, along with assorted mercenaries, joined the Qing in the campaign against the Taipings. Attempts to coordinate the international forces were sometimes riotous and sometimes tragic, but the injection of European weaponry and money aided in the quelling of both the Taiping War and the Nian rebellion during the 1860s.

The end to the Taiping War marked, in the eyes of many people, the actual end of the Qing empire, though the emperors continued on the throne until 1912. The material damage to the country was enormous. Estimates of deaths in the years of fighting between

1850 and 1864 range between twenty and thirty million. It ranks as the world's bloodiest civil war, and the greatest armed conflict before the twentieth century. The loss of life was due primarily to starvation and disease, since most engagements consisted of surrounding the enemy in a walled fortification and waiting until they starved, surrendered, or were so weakened that they could be vanquished easily. The sieges continued for months, and the populations of many cities found that after starving for a year under the occupation of the rebels they would be starved for another year under the occupation of the imperial forces. Reports of the eating of grass, leather, hemp, and human flesh were widespread. The dead were rarely buried properly, and epidemic disease was common in the war zone.

In addition, the area of early Taiping fighting was close to the regions of southwest China where bubonic plague had been lingering for centuries. The war ended in this region, too, and many Taiping adherents sought safety in the highlands of Laos and Annam. These areas soon showed infestation by plague, and within a few years the disease had reached Hongkong. From there it spread to Singapore, San Francisco, Calcutta, and London, so that the nineteenth century saw not only a brief revival of bubonic plague, but intense apprehension over the possibility of a major outbreak. In Europe and America, Chinese immigrants were regarded as likely carriers. They were occasionally quarantined, and their homes destroyed – a tactic which, in the case of San Francisco, only dispersed the rats carrying the parasite and magnified the reach of the disease. In 1882 Chinese immigration into the United States was banned by law.

Apart from the losses of life, the agricultural centers of China were devastated in the war. Many of the most intensely and successfully cultivated regions of central and eastern China were depopulated and laid barren after years of fighting. By the late nineteenth century some were still uninhabited, and the provincial population figures suggest that major portions of the country did not recover until the twentieth century. Cities, too, were very hard hit. Shanghai, which was primarily known as a foreign treaty port and had been very modest in size before the Taiping War, had its population multiplied many times by the arrival of refugees from the war-blasted nearby provinces of Zhejiang and Jiangsu. The city itself had been under attack by the Taipings, and with its bloated population endured months without food supplies. Major cultural centers in eastern China lost masterpieces of art and architecture, imperial libraries were burnt or their collections exposed to the weather, and not only books but the printing blocks used to make the books were destroyed.

Finally, the Qing government emerged from this civil war with no hope of achieving solvency again. Even before the uprising at Thistle Mountain, the Qing treasury had been bankrupted by the corruption of the late eighteenth century, the attempts of the early nineteenth-century government to restore waterworks and roads that had been neglected, declining yields from land taxes, and the geometrically increasing burden of indemnities demanded by Britain after its victory in the Opium War. By about 1850 the Qing government was taking in about a tenth of what it was spending. The civil war worsened this situation profoundly. Vast stretches of what had previously been very productive rice land were devastated, the population was dispersed, immediate relief for refugees was demanded, and the array of imperial, volunteer, foreign, and mercenary troops that had suppressed the Taipings was demanding that their unpaid wages and costs for provisions and weapons be made good. In addition, there were new indemnities to Britain and France after the Arrow War, on top of the unpaid indemnities from the Opium War.

Qing Territory and Hungry Empires

The treaty system in China resulted in the formal colonization of very small pockets of Qing territory, where foreign merchants, missionaries and their military guards lived apart from Qing law. But, as in the case of the Ottoman empire, the greatest territorial losses for the Qing resulted from the actual or nominal independence of the regions it had dominated. Britain and Russia were both active in attempts to eradicate the last vestiges of Qing sovereignty in Central Asia in the early 1800s, and in the late 1800s, France would force the court of Vietnam to end its vassalage to the Qing, while Britain encouraged Tibetan independence.

After the Taiping War, the Qing imperial lineage – usually under the control of one sort of regency or another – continued to preside over a series of regional governments, some growing stronger, more centralized and more industrialized, some growing weaker and poorer. Many of the weakest and poorest areas –

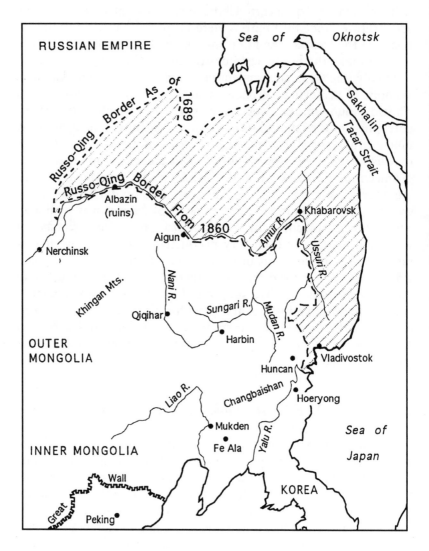

Map 2   *The Romanov–Qing boundaries in Northeast Asia as*
amended by the treaty of 1860.

Manchuria, Mongolia, Turkestan, and Tibet, for instance – were
at the borders, and as the Qing found their coastal barriers perfo-
rated by the military, political, and economic intrusions of first the
European and American powers, and later Japan, so it found the

Romanov empire applying increasing pressure on its Inner Asian and Central Asian frontiers. Combinations of banner and native troops in Manchuria repelled Russian incursions until 1860, when a treaty signed with Russia after the end of the second round of opium wars ceded the land that is now the Russian Maritime Province, and permitted development of the Russian trade city of Vladivostok. From that point Russian ambitions inside Manchuria were whetted, and the Romanovs would eventually discover that their most formidable opponent there was not the Qing, but the expansionist empire of Japan.

The key to Japanese expansion in Manchuria was Korea. Beginning soon after its own state reformation in 1868, Japan began initiating expansionist policies in Korea. There were small but violent conflicts between Japanese and Qing forces in Korea in the 1870s and 1880s, and in the 1890s Japan was sponsoring a violent movement for Korean national independence from China. By the end of the century Japan had by force or threatened force taken from the Qing the Liuqiu Islands (including Okinawa) and Taiwan, and had established military domination over Korea.

Central and Inner Asia, too, were profoundly affected by the structural decline of the Qing empire after 1800, since the area was the point of contact with all the empires. Tibet, for instance, had been noted since medieval times as the geographical key to domination of Central Asia. The Chinese, Mongolian, and Qing empires had all struggled for control of the land and its religious hierarchy. Now, as British interest in India deepened, British explorers, soldiers, and merchants began to turn their attention to nearby Tibet. British colonization of Tibet, which by the late nineteenth century appeared a possibility, would have amputated a large dependency of the Qing empire, and allowed direct British access to south and southwest China. As it happened, the British preferred to exercise indirect control, so that until 1910 Tibet was formally a part of the Qing empire but in reality a British protectorate. In 1910, Tibet declared independence from the Qing, which only meant a closer connection to Britain.

North of Tibet lay Turkestan, also formally a part of the Qing empire. By the 1840s both Russia and Britain were developing military strategies for its political domination. Though the intrigues of these governments produced several dramas and tragedies, they were of little effect in changing the overall political character of Turkestan. The caravan trade continued through the great cities of Central Asia, but it was no longer of continental significance. The city states of the region were ruled by independent, strongly Islamic, chiefs, who were hostile to attempts by foreign powers to dominate them. The Romanov empire, with its intense strategic interest in Turkestan, devoted the greatest wealth and energy to courting the leaders of Turkestan.

Their greatest obstacle in the period after the Taiping War was the Chinese governor Zuo Zongtang, who like Zeng Guofan and Li Hongzhang had trained himself in military tactics as well as bureaucratic administration. The weakening of the central Qing government and the distractions of the Taiping and Nian wars had encouraged several Muslim leaders of Shaanxi province, Gansu, and Turkestan to rise in challenge to Qing rule. Zuo Zongtang had undertaken to repacify the region, and came into direct confrontation with the economic morbidity of the empire. Upon arranging his battalions in Turkestan he realized that supplying them from Russia would be cheaper than transporting grain from central China. He found Russian merchants willing to bring in the supplies, but he had no money to purchase them, nor had the imperial government any means of finding it. Zuo suggested, repeatedly, that foreign banks in Shanghai be asked for the loans, and repeatedly he was opposed by Li Hongzhang, who thought there would be better uses for the money. Zuo at length prevailed, and managed to eradicate a portion of the independent Islamic regimes of the northwest. But one, under Yakub Beg, remained at Kashgar, and declared itself an independent state, gaining instant recognition from Russia and Britain – the two empires with designs upon Turkestan. Qing officials, including the Manchu Chonghou, were dispatched to persuade Russia and Britain to withdraw their recognition. These efforts were inconclusive, however, and Zuo Zongtang decided to retake Turkestan by force. In 1877 Yakub Beg committed suicide and Zuo's forces secured the region, which in 1884 was for the first time incorporated as a province – Xinjiang – of the Qing empire.

For most of the nineteenth century Mongolia and Manchuria were firmly under Qing control. Attempts at military invasion by the Romanov empire were defeated in Manchuria in the middle nineteenth century, even as the Qing empire was suffering disastrous defeats in coastal wars against Britain and France. But in the last years of the nineteenth century and first years of the twentieth, Mongolia and Manchuria would show a pattern reminiscent of that of Tibet and Turkestan in the early and middle nineteenth century: They were nominally governed by the Qing empire based in China, but in reality controlled by local rulers whom foreign powers – in these cases, Russia and Japan – tried unceasingly to co-opt or destroy. This created deep cultural and political divisions, as well as prolonged economic and military weakness. At the Ottoman and Qing peripheries in Central Asia, imperial control in all but name disintegrated over the course of the 1800s, leaving these areas as politically fragmented strategic vacuums into which Britain, in particular, attempted to intrude.

Illusions of Revival

With the Qing government so profoundly in their debt, Britain and France became active participants in the period of recovery in China that followed conclusion of the war. In order to ensure that the Qing government began repaying at least a portion of its debt to Britain, Robert Hart was installed as inspector-general of a newly-created Qing customs service. The revenues he collected were split between Britain and the Qing. Rutherford Alcock of Britain and Anson Burlingame of the United States put themselves in the employ of the Qing government as advisors and ambassadors, attempting to smooth communications between the Qing, Europe, and the United States while the imperial government started up the diplomatic machinery demanded by Europe in its treaties with the Qing.

The real work of the recovery, however, was managed by the civilian provincial governors who had come to the forefront in the struggle against the Taipings. In order to prosecute the war, they had gained from the Qing court permission to levy their own taxes, raise their own troops, and run their own bureaucracies. These special powers were not entirely rescinded when the war ended. Chief among these governors was Zeng Guofan, who oversaw not only programs to restore agriculture, communications, education, and publishing, but also attempts to initiate programs for reform and industrialization that would be necessary to regain some measure of independence for China. Like many provincial governors, Zeng preferred to look to the United States for models and aid, rather than Britain. He hired American advisors to run his arsenals for the manufacture of modern weapons, his shipyards, and his military academies. He sponsored a daring program in which promising Chinese boys were sent not to traditional academies to gain the Confucian educations that had previously been considered indispensable, but to Hartford, Connecticut, to be educated in English, science, mathematics, engineering, and history. They returned to China to assume some of the positions that foreign advisors had previously held in Zeng's industries and schools. Among the provincial governors, Zeng – whose death in 1871 deprived the country of one of its best hopes for leadership – was esteemed as the most capable, loyal, incorruptible, and flexible.

Much has been written on the period of recovery that the Qing empire experienced after the end of the civil wars in the 1860s, and much attention has been given to the great governors who, following the model of Zeng Guofan, used their ingenuity and regional authority to effect some degree of economic revitalization. Much has also been written about the role of foreign advisors and employees. Less has been said about the role of Manchu leaders, mostly but not exclusively aristocrats, who in the Tongzhi (1862–74) period in particular were the fulcrum upon which the lever of historical change turned.

Most famous at the time was Wenxiang, a man of comparatively humble background who distinguished himself in the 1850s' campaigns against the Taipings, but emerged as one of the most skilled negotiators with the foreign powers after the war. Wenxiang found the sudden appearence and extraordinary influence of the Western powers distasteful and frightening. But his advice was always to cooperate with these newcomers in any way that might strengthen the empire, and to temporize on everything else. He worked with Yixin [Prince Gong] to create the Foreign Office (*zongli yamen*), and with him established a strict principle for the department of abiding by treaty regulations (hoping never to provoke another retaliatory invasion of the Arrow War sort). At the same time, he so determinedly pressed the Western powers for a revision of those treaty regulations that he made himself an unwelcome figure, despite the fact that most Westerners who met him were in awe of his personal integrity and his brilliance. "I have never," remarked Sir Thomas Wade, "encountered a more formidable intellect." Wenxiang never achieved treaty revision (nor did anybody else until it was granted the National Government in 1946, as they were losing their own civil war to the Communists).

In other areas of reform Wenxiang had greater success. He was the originator of a plan to reduce the standing forces, including the Eight Banners, by as much as 90 percent over a ten-year period, a policy that was consonant with the general tendency of the emperors at mid-century to disembarrass themselves of the bannermen to the greatest extent possible. Wenxiang was convinced that the empire could achieve greater security with smaller, better-trained, better-armed units. He himself organized such a unit, the Peking Field Corps, which he led in successful campaigns against local bandits; the corps became the model for other new army units, most commanded by Chinese governors or their protégés. They were the beginning, however, of a regionalization of military organization that underwrote the "warlordism" that bedeviled attempts to reunite China in the early twentieth century.

A portion of the banner forces was reformed into elite units, under the leadership of Wenxiang, the Manchu aristocrat Ronglu, and others, that became the foundation of the New Armies who led the Revolution of 1911/12 and went on to form the vanguard of the forces of the warlord Yuan Shikai and many others. Nevertheless the Eight Banners themselves went the way of the banner officers' schools, becoming obsolete, decrepit, and overshadowed by the new forms to which they had given birth. Courses on armaments, both Qing and foreign, were added to the garrison officers' schools, and this inevitably led to limited technical studies by mid-century. Particularization of banner identity thereafter led to the banner schools becoming a source for the specialized military academies, language schools, and technical institutes of the later nineteenth century.

Concurrently, the development of hybrid forms of military organization, beginning with the Grand Battalions formed in Jiangnan to attempt to repulse the British invaders in 1841, created a new demand for the talents of translators, as banner officers assigned to these composite armies were required to maintain records both in Chinese and in Manchu, in order to keep the court informed – in the security language, Manchu – of the movements and internal power alignments within these forces. Indeed the Daoguang emperor, foreseeing renewed need for banner expertise in Manchu as the country's military organization became more complex, required all banner officers to prepare and sit for the Manchu examinations after 1843, a regulation which the court kept until the general attenuation of court administration of the garrisons in 1865. It has, moreover, been hypothesized on very good evidence that the Foreign Language Colleges (*tongwen guan*) established under the Office of Foreign Affairs were actually patterned after the banner officers' schools, and it is certainly true that they were both administered by garrison officials and attended almost exclusively by Manchu bannermen. By the end of the century the Foreign Language Colleges had added French, German, and Japanese to the original English course, and the old Russian shool in the Imperial City had been absorbed and reformed by the Foreign Language College at Peking. An expanded curriculum ultimately included mathematics, astronomy, and chemistry (an outgrowth of the identification of banner officers with percussion-cap manufacture), so that the Foreign Language College and its provincial branches took on the appearance of the forerunners of the Imperial University founded at Peking in 1896.

The reform programs of the Tongzhi "restoration" did not achieve lasting improvements. One reason was unrelenting foreign pressure. The increase of treaty ports led to a rise in foreign presence, and to increasing conflicts with the Chinese population. Incidents such as the Tianjin Massacre of 1870 – which broke out after a French officer fired a pistol at the Manchu official Chonghou in the middle of an altercation – led to increasing indemnities against the Chinese government. Indeed the Western powers had, as demonstrated in this instance, positive incentives to exploit petty differences with the Chinese in order to provoke crises, threaten invasions, and demand reparations or new privileges as settlement. The head of the Foreign Office, Yixin, actually lost his position after a war contrived by the French resulted in the severing of the traditional tributary relationship between China and Vietnam in 1884 (and colonization of Vietnam by France shortly thereafter).

Another reason was that the reforms were too little too late. They were always built upon a basic strategy of cutting expenditures, introducing modern technology to a reformed army, and shifting other expenses to localities. By these incremental changes, the Qing government would never be thrifty enough to eradicate its bottomless debts, and never be militarily strong enough to resist Western forces that were themselves undergoing dramatic technological advances and imperialist transformations. The incrementalism of these plans might have had some effect a century before, but were hopeless in the circumstances of the later nineteenth century.

More important, the nature of the reforms necessarily led to the dismantling of the empire. Indeed, after the Taiping War and its contemporary conflicts, the Qing "empire" was a court floating, as a lily pad, on a pond of increasingly self-contained regional regimes. Zeng Guofan had established the ethos of loyalty to the Qing emperors by these regional rulers, but it was only a matter of time before this would lose all credibility. Manchus – particularly Wenxiang – had themselves encouraged this independence, and created some of the basic military and bureaucratic innovations on which it was based. As the nineteenth century came to a close there was no consensus to be found among Manchus as to whether the emperors deserved the continued allegiance of the bannermen or anybody else.

This was primarily due to the emerging qualities of the empress dowager, Cixi. Though later reviled as a monster of corruption and arrogance, in the 1860s and 1870s Cixi had been instrumental in legitimating and facilitating the institutionalization of the discretionary powers of the provincial governors, some of whom became so powerful that they were managing Qing foreign policy as well as domestic affairs. She had played this early, constructive role first as a concubine to the Xianfeng emperor, who was impressed with her education and her understanding of political affairs, and often listened to her advice. Upon his death in 1862 her son, Zaichun, succeeded to the throne as the Tongzhi emperor. The boy emperor's regents recognized both Cixi and Ci'an – the widow of the Xianfeng emperor – as empresses. Both women immediately turned upon the regents, blaming them for allowing the invasion of Peking in 1860 and the destruction of the summer palace at Yuanming yuan. The imperial princes Yixin and Yihuan joined the empresses in the coup, and the primary regent, Sushun, was beheaded as a result of the purge. The Tongzhi emperor died young and without an heir; before he had breathed his last, Cixi had arranged for Yihuan's son Zaitian to be installed as the Guangxu emperor. Cixi and Ci'an controlled court affairs until Ci'an's death in 1881, after which Cixi ruled increasingly in the manner of a despot.

The reign of the Guangxu emperor was the downfall of Cixi. Unlike his two predecessors he did not die extremely young, though when he did die he left no heirs. In 1889 Cixi was forced to recognize the emperor's majority and approve his marriage, and in ensuing years a battle developed between the young emperor and the old dowager for power. At Yihuan's death in 1891 Zaitian became more adamant, insisting that eunuch influence at the court should be curtailed – a principle in accord with the strong beliefs of all the early Qing emperors, who had attributed the Ming downfall to eunuch interference. Zaitian also intended to cut the budget for the Imperial Household Department, which would have eliminated stipends for eunuchs and for a large number of remaining Chinese-martial officials as well. Cixi managed to quash these plans, but she could not do anything about the emperor's growing following among younger, reform-minded Manchus and Chinese. The Meiji Restoration in Japan, in which the young emperor Mutsuhito had become the icon for nationalist, progressive, industrializing change, was becoming an object of fascination and approbation.

This idea became most forceful after Japan's swift and unexpected defeat of the Qing navy in the war of 1895. The building of a modern navy had been the pet project of the imperial prince Yihuan, who had struggled for the diminishing proceeds of loans to the Qing to finance his shipyards and arsenals. The resulting force was large and on its face imposing. But the commanders and sailors were poorly trained, and the ships were – quite possibly due to Cixi's diversion of naval funds to her own pastimes, like the "marble boat" and the opera house at the Yihe summer palace – fraudulently supplied, sometimes with rice instead of gunpowder. When war broke out in 1894 between China and Japan over who would dominate Korea, Japanese ships sent most of the Chinese navy to the bottom of the sea. The Qing were forced to agree to the Treaty of Shimonoseki which in its first form gave Japan the island of Taiwan, the Pescadores, and unprecedented rights of direct investment and management in Chinese industries. Western powers, alarmed at the extraordinary privileges Japan had demanded, intervened to soften the terms, but China still was forced to cede Taiwan wholly to Japanese colonical rule.

Peking and other major cities were swept by open protests, led by examination candidates and other educated men, denouncing the settlement with Japan. On behalf of Cixi, Ronglu became one of the sponsors of the Peking Imperial University, which operated with a combined Chinese and foreign staff, intended to provide the modern training that would strengthen the country. Many of the staff, like the young Manchu reformer, Shoufu, were self-proclaimed progressives – Shoufu himself had been on a study tour of Japan, and was an advocate of constitutional government. The creation of the new university, however, was hardly found satisfactory by the dissidents. One of them, Kang Youwei, addressed to the young emperor a reform plan which gained the favor of the emperor's tutor Weng Tonghe, who within weeks arranged a meeting between Kang, his young follower Liang Qichao, and the emperor. Zaitian considered Kang and Liang among his advisors from that time, and by early 1898 had become resolved to launch a thoroughgoing revision of government that would inaugurate his accession to real rule. The program, in retrospect called the "Hundred Days' Reform," proposed that government expenditures would be streamlined; agriculture would be reformed; industries would be underwritten by the government; new educational policies would emphasize science and technology; the stipends to the aristocracy would be cut very severely; the Eight Banners would be abolished, with "useful employment" being found for the Manchus; and a consultative body would be formed that would eventually realize constitutional monarchy in China – as had already been established in Japan.

The empress dowager, who for two years had indulged the emperor's announced ambitions to rule in his own right and to transform the government, decided to move. The Guangxu emperor, she knew, had gone too far. Aristocrats and penniless bannermen alike, who had previously found the empress dowager an embarrassment and an evil, would now rally round her to protect their last hope of economic support, and to protest the "anti-Manchu" elements of Kang's proposed program – particularly the abandonment of numbering years by the reigns of the Qing emperors, and the ubiquitous rhetoric of Kang's Manchu-hating follower Tan Sitong. Ronglu ordered his soldiers to arrest the emperor and his reformers. Zaitian was incarcerated in the Forbidden City. Six of the reformers, including Tan Sitong, were netted, and within a short time beheaded. Kang Youwei and Liang Qichao, however, escaped to the international settlement at Shanghai, and later made their way to Japan. The Peking Imperial University was purged of reformist sympathizers, including Shoufu.

Reformist Manchus were silenced after the brutal repression of the Hundred Days' Reform. Cixi, and troglodytes such as the

Manchu official Gangyi – whose watchword was "Reform harms the Manchus and benefits only the Chinese" – became the most dominant features on the Manchu political landscape. Cixi had incurred the gratitude of bannermen who would have been left hopeless by the emperor's proposals. By this time a majority of the Manchu population had actually left the garrisons, but those who remained were fiercely loyal to the empress dowager, the first ruling figure in half a century to acknowledge, rather than attempt to disinherit, the bannermen. She encouraged them to join military clubs in order to improve their martial skills, and by the late 1890s many were members of these semi-subversive organizations, including the "Righteous and Harmonious Fists" – the Boxers. When a branch of the Boxers rose in rebellion in Shandong in 1897 it was quickly co-opted by the governor, Zhang Zhidong, and turned into a popular uprising for the purging of foreigners from China and the support of the Qing. Indeed it was a Manchu, one Encun of the Tiger Spirits Corps, who assassinated the German ambassador von Ketteler in Peking on June 29, 1900, setting off the sieges of the foreign delegations that, in the eyes of the Western press, marked the outbreak of the Boxer Rebellion. The emperor's brothers Zaiyi and Zaifeng were seen directing the Boxers in the attacks. As the armies of the Western allies approached Peking in August of 1900, Cixi – her prisoner, the Guangxu emperor, in tow – left for Xi'an. Shoufu committed suicide.

Though banner forces had until the middle nineteenth century kept Russia out of Manchuria, the Boxer Uprising gave the Romanov empire its opening to move into the sector and attempt its permanent occupation; Japanese disapproval of this plan eventually led to the Russo-Japanese war of 1904–5, which destroyed Russian imperial pretensions in Eastern Asia and solidified Japanese dominion in Korea and Manchuria. The Boxer Uprising also saddled the Qing government with an additional $470-million indemnity, and left the capital profoundly damaged. Zaiyi and Zaifeng finally capitulated to foreign pressure to promise a constitution, and on this condition invited Cixi to return to Peking. The Guangxu emperor was imprisoned by Cixi in a house within the Yihe summer palace, where he spent the rest of his life.

The period of "recovery" after the Taiping War marked a fundamental structural change in the Qing empire. Instead of a conquest regime dominated by a military caste and its civilian appointees, the empire was now directed by a consortium of reformist aristocrats and military men, independently powerful civilian governors, and a small number of foreign advisors. The decentralized pattern of governance was well adapted to the extreme variation in local conditions that characterized the period after the civil war, and the necessity to find local means to effect local improvements. But in the complex international situation, the Qing now lacked strong, central, unified leadership. The government was helpless in the face of increasing foreign challenge, especially from Japan, and the growing indemnities, territorial losses, and disintegration of border integrity that inevitably resulted. Moreover, the powers of taxation, legislation, and military command, once given to the provincial governors, could not be recovered once they had been granted. From the 1860s forward, the Qing empire devolved to a set of large power zones in which leadership was handed from governors to their protégés in a pattern that the Qing court could eventually only ritually legitimate.

The Pregnant Carcasses of the Eurasian Land Empires

As suggested earlier, the Qing and Ottoman empires had much in common – their shared traditions of Central Asian rulership and military servitude, their large land base, their complex problems of border management. Perhaps most critical to understanding their condition in the late nineteenth and very early twentieth centuries, however, is the degree to which each underwent a graduated debilitation by foreign powers and provided the material and political resources for the emergence of modern imperial organizations.

In the land-based empires of Eurasia, populations had increased very rapidly in the preceding hundred years, but now crop lands were expanding only slowly, and in some cases contracting because of soil exhaustion. Meanwhile, military expansion had overstretched the resources of their treasuries. As European and, later, American encroachment threatened these weakened orders, various responses arose. By the beginning of the nineteenth century the Moguls in India had allowed parts of their empire to be governed by the British East India Company. This was the beginning of a process that ended in the outright colonization of India by Britain.

In the Ottoman empire, early nineteenth-century attempts to de-stroy independent power bases in the military and religious estab-lishments in order to centralize imperial control resulted in repeated violence and only a tenuous government reform. In Rus-sia, the serfs were freed in the middle nineteenth century, in an attempt to expand the tax base and increase government revenues. At approximately the same time, the Qing empire was derolling large numbers of bannermen for the same reason. In all the Eura-sian land empires, deficit financing was practiced in order to maintain military preparedness and imperial splendor in the face of decreasing government income. The result was the indebtedness of these empires to the expanding sea empires of Europe, which desired colonies, low import taxes, and other privileges that they were now in a position to wrest from the land empires of Eurasia. In many instances, the economic pressures from Europe were supplemented by military confrontation. The Opium Wars in China, and the Crimean War on the shores of the Caspian Sea, were attempts to force land and political privileges from the Qing and Romanov empires respectively.

Many officials advised acceptance of European loans in the hope that time could be bought to make the governments more efficient and to bring modern technologies to the military. The result was a prolonged period of decline and weakness in the imperial governments before their colonization or destruction through war or revolution. In their last years both the Ottoman and Qing empires were satirized in the European press as the "sick men" of Europe and Asia, respectively. The Moguls did not lose formal control of India until 1857. Subsequently their imperial title (inspired by Genghis Khan) passed to Queen Victoria when she assumed her title as "Empress of India" in 1876. The Qing empire was destroyed in a civil war of 1911 and 1912, which resulted in the establishment of a nationalist republic but sparked decades of internal violence and disorder. The Ottoman empire dissolved in 1922, and though a strong nationalist government emerged in Turkey, the disintegration of the fringes of the Otto-man empire has produced nearly a century of violent turmoil in Eastern Europe and in the Middle East. The Romanov empire ended in 1917, followed by a series of governments and decades of political violence and economic dislocation.

In order to stabilize and strengthen themselves, these empires all attempted to learn the technological and managerial techniques that appeared to underlie the strength and aggressiveness of the European powers. At the same time, all were concerned to protect the traditional cultural values that legitimated the status of their elites and offered some symbols for national definition. The challenge of importing certain European goods, knowledge, and advisors while trying to limit their influence was complex, and ultimately created political instabilities. Perhaps more important, it inspired these empires to pursue programs of reform in the military and financial spheres, without undertaking more thoroughgoing restructuring of their economies and of their political life. In many cases there was indeed improvement, but it occurred in too small a degree and too slowly to rebalance the power between the great land-based empires of Eurasia and the increasingly expansive regimes of Europe and America.

By the middle 1800s, younger leaders in both the civil and military realms sometimes advised going to extremes in restructuring the state. Some argued for Euopean dress and education, and in many cases there was even a demand for radical restructuring of the government, in order to create constitutional monarchies resembling those of Great Britain, France, and the German states. These more extreme reform proposals were often supported by urban merchants and professionals, but were vigorously opposed by many members of the imperial families and their allies, by cultural traditionalists, and by most farmers and laborers. This tension between elite "Westernizers" and traditionalists, often accompanied by violence, was widespread in nineteenth-century Eurasia. It arose earliest in Russia, then, by the 1830s, was evident in the Ottoman empire. By the middle 1800s it affected India, and by the very late 1800s China began to show this split. This debate over the relationship of culture to power continued to trouble the societies of Eurasia, and in some form the debate continues today.

European merchants primarily demanded some natural resources from the living carcasses of the Eurasian empires, and markets for their finished goods. Apart from gaining mercantile and military bases that could be ruled on European principles, the European empires were not primarily interested in destroying the existing governments or ruling these countries directly. This aspect of the relationship was even stronger after the development of serious indebtedness of the Eurasian empires to Europe. The destruction of the traditional regimes of Eurasia would have meant the end of the profit and privilege that came to Europe from the loans it had made to the Eurasian empires. It was better, from the European perspective of the early 1800s, that the empires of Eurasia survive, though impoverished and, to Europe, militarily harmless. This outlook corresponded to a wish on the part of the traditional governments of Eurasia to survive. Imperial families jealously guarded their wealth and privileges, and in some cases resorted to increasingly predatory practices in order to preserve or even increase their wealth.

The legal process by which the Eurasian land empires were broken down had strong parallels. In the cases of both the Qing and the Ottomans, for instance, inhibitions against sudden aggrandizement by one of the new empires at the expense of the others were carefully instituted. The Treaty of Nanking that ended the Opium War in 1842, for example, guaranteed "most favored nation" status to Britain, meaning that any privileges granted to future signatories of treaties with China would also accrue to Britain. This would in effect preclude the colonization of Chinese territory, since giving land to one country would necessitate giving it to all. Similarly, the Treaty of Paris that ended the Crimean War in 1856 specifically guaranteed the territorial integrity of the Ottoman empire. This meant that Romanov expansion into Eastern Europe and into the Middle East was now blocked by the formal alliance of Britain and France with the Ottoman sultans. This, in turn, meant that the sultans were demonstrably dependent upon the cooperation and goodwill of Britain and France, and would no longer be in a position to reject British or French demands for privileges in trade or diplomacy. Finally, the terms gave Britain and France a means of checking each other's colonial ambitions in the Middle East; neither, according to Paris terms, was entitled to take Ottoman territory for its exclusive use.

The Qing rulers, like the Ottoman rulers, imagined for a time that this mutual distrust by the European powers would protect them against the individual ambitions of the European states. In the instance of China, this was referred to as "using the barbarians against the barbarians." But it actually meant that the Qing empire was continually embroiled in short, rather localized wars – or threatened wars – with aspiring participants in the "unequal treaty" system. With each round of treaties came a new round of privileges to be distributed among the European and American participants. The British, in their Treaty of Nanking, established their rights of residence in five Chinese "treaty ports," a very low tariff on imports, and a long-standing debt of the Qing empire to Britain in the form of an indemnity, or penalty for having initiated the war. Soon after, an American treaty established extraterritoriality, or the right of foreign residents in the treaty ports to live according to their own laws. It also legalized the right of foreigners to import opium to China. Later, French treaties established the rights of foreign missionaries to travel extensively in the Chinese countryside and preach their religion. With each round of treaties, the number of treaty ports grew, too, so that by the end of the nineteenth century there were more than ninety.

Synthesizing both domestic and international veiwpoints, the Crimean and Taiping Wars were watersheds in the loss of centralization and autonomy for the Ottoman and Qing empires, respectively. The processes bear some striking similarities, not least of which was that in each conflict the empire in question emerged as nominally victorious. In both cases the land-based Eurasian empires had experienced overextension, declining revenues, and social dislocation in the later eighteenth century, to which there had been a reformist response, if limited, from the state. Increasing pressure from Britain and France had deepened the financial woes and political tensions of the empires, and heightened elite awareness of the necessity for military reform. In the conflicts themselves, the financial obligations of the empires and the strategic advantages of their existence led to the formation of alliances with Britain and France. And in the aftermath of the conflicts, the empires experienced serious problems with decentralization, a loss of control over internal migration and over their borders, permanent indebtedness and inflation, a progressive loss of international and domestic credibility, and dependence upon foreign protection.

It is not surprising that the military technology, medicine, and education of Europe made such a vivid impact upon the elites of Eurasia in the nineteenth century. Europe and the United States themselves were often dazzled by the speed with which changes were wrought by the major military confrontations of mid-century, and by the speed with which the military dramas and their implications could be known. The Crimean War and the Taiping War were part of a set of very large and extremely bloody wars of the middle 1800s – including the American Civil War, and the Indian Mutiny, or "Sepoy Rebellion" – which saw the application of far more lethal technologies, the invention of new generations of killing machines, and the resulting slaughter of soldiers and civilians at a rate that had never been witnessed before. Improvements in rifle manufacture in the United States and Europe in the early 1800s meant that soldiers sent into these wars were supplied with accurate, breech-loading weapons, and in many cases with repeating pistols for closer combat. Rifles such as these actually helped ignite the Indian Mutiny in 1857, when word spread among the already disaffected Indian soldiers serving the British that the new weapons had to be lubricated with the fat – in packets that had to be torn open with the teeth – from animals whose slaughter was forbidden under Hindu and Muslim beliefs.

When deployed on a large scale, these infantry forces armed with rifles changed the strategic and the social structure of war. Heavy artillery could be placed well behind the lines at safer locations. Cavalry, once the preserve of the military elite, was suddenly far less effective against the lines of infantry who were often protected by perimeters of trenches and landmines. The hopelessness of cavalry in this new environment was commemorated in Alfred Tennyson's "Charge of the Light Brigade," a dramatic retelling of an incident at the Battle of Balaclava in the Crimean War.

Technologies and strategies employed on these battlefields quickly affected ensuing engagements, no matter where in the world they occurred. This was partly because of a new international network of soldiers who appeared on different continents in rapid succession, bringing with them not only access to but expertise in the new techniques. Some of these soldiers, such as General Charles Gordon, moved from battlefield to battlefield according to the contours of imperial interest. Gordon, for instance, was commissioned in the British army in 1852, then served in the Crimean War after Britain entered on the side of the Ottomans. Three years after the end of that conflict he had been dispatched to China, serving the British forces during the Arrow War and taking place in the sack of Peking in 1860 (playing a role in the humiliation of the redoubtable Senggerinchin). He stayed in China, seconded to the Qing imperial government, until the suppression of the Taipings in 1864, earning himself the nickname of "Chinese" Gordon. In later years he served as governor of territory along the Nile for the rulers of Egypt, and was killed there in 1885 attempting to lead his Egyptian troops in defense of the city of

Khartoum against the uprising of the local religious leader, the Mahdi.

Others who were part of this international military network were mercenaries from the beginnings of their careers, like the Americans Frederick Townsend Ward and Henry Burgevine. Both, looking for adventure, served under France in the Crimean War when they were in their early twenties. Later, both enlisted to serve the Qing imperial government in suppression of the Taipings. Ward, who earned the respect of the Qing military and civil elites, was made commander of the Ever Victorious Army of Western mercenaries who put their special skills at the service of the Qing. Building on their experience in the Crimean War, Ward and his colleagues drilled Qing imperial troops and militia in the use and care of modern rifles, in new patterns of fast-moving arms combat, and in the deployment of mines and early forms of hand grenades. Since both weapons and personnel rapidly changed hands between the loyalist and the Taiping troops, knowledge of Western warfare and weapons spread quickly throughout China as a result of the Western interventions. Ward was killed fighting on the Qing side in 1862, only 30 years of age, and was buried in the costume and with the full honors of a high-ranking Manchu soldier.

Fast communications were also a part of this military revolution. Steamships and railroads were often used to move large numbers of troops, supplies and artillery at previously unimaginable speed, and in many cases the telegraph could be used to accelerate communications between command centers and the battlefield. Equally important was the role of these communications in delivering information around the world concerning not only the battles and political implications of these wars, but the technologies they were using and advancing. In this way, the disintegrating Qing and Ottoman empires became the matrix in which the media and the images of modernity were formed.

Journalism can well be said to have had its start in this age, as the telegraph made it possible for readers in London to learn in detail of the war dramas in the Crimea or in China a week – or in some cases, days – after they had occurred. William Howard Russell's reports on the Crimean War and Andrew Wilson's coverage of the Taiping War permitted audiences to read gripping accounts of previously unimaginable carnage and moving heroism. They were soon accompanied by photographers who, like Matthew Brady in the American Civil War, made the reality of the

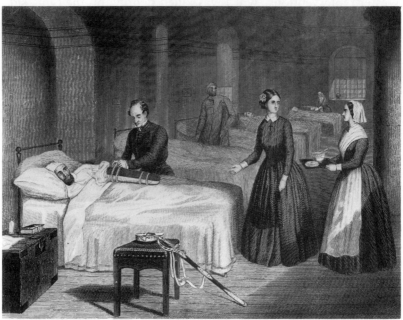

Plates 22–3 *Charles Gordon was, like Frederick Townsend Ward,*
part of a network of soldiers who shuttled across Eurasia in service
to the waning empires and European interests, spreading new

suffering more immediate and indelible. The implications for societies with growing journalistic enterprises were complex, as both jingoistic fantasies of Western superiority and internationally-minded pacifist movements drew inspiration from this new closeness to the fields of battle.

Print and photographic journalism also created new "stars" from these war experiences. Charles Gordon was one himself, but of equal stature was Florence Nightingale. In these great wars of the 1800s, the vast majority of deaths resulted from infections or unnecessary bleeding to death rather than the wounds themselves. Nightingale had, since her youth, distinguished herself for her interest in hospital management and nursing. She had gone to Prussia and to France to study advanced techniques, and was credited with leading a marked improvement in British health care before the outbreak of the Crimean War. As the public reacted to reports of the suffering, Nightingale was sent to the Crimea by the British government.

Nightingale's personal powers of leadership, self-sacrifice, and endurance were extensively reported by Russell and others, and her contributions were stunning: Within a year of her arrival the fatality rate in the military hospitals had dropped from 45 percent to under 5 percent. Her techniques for preventing septicemia and dysentery, and for promoting healing therapies, were quickly adopted by those working under and alongside her. Unfortunately, simultaneous wars such as the American Civil War, the Taiping War, and the Indian Mutiny benefited only in a limited way from Nightingale's innovations, though she was frequently consulted from afar by commanders on either side. On her return

weapons and tactics as they went. Among the new technologies of war was the telegraph, which not only speeded communications between command centers and the battlefields, but also made European and American audiences virtually instantly aware of the dramas unfolding in the distant locales. One result was the creation of celebrities of the new media. These stars included not only soldiers but those whose participation paralleled the escalation of war – particularly Florence Nightingale, whose involvement in the Crimean theater later had direct benefits for the hygiene of civilian hospitals in London. The Illustrated London News, *only one of the outlets of this new information age, carried these images of the lionized Gordon and Nightingale.*

to London, she established institutes for nursing that were quickly recognized as leaders in the world, and she herself was lionized by the British public, receiving the Order of Merit in 1907, three years before her death. Though women had never been absent from battlefields, Nightingale established a prominent, specialized, and professional function that, until very recently, has been the primary mode of female participation in modern war. The new efficiency of the killing machines of the 1800s made her work necessary, and the new efficiency of the era's communications made her techniques widely known. More to the point, Nightingale was a demonstration of the ways in which European civil life was changed by encounters with the end-stage of the Eurasian empires.

But the differences between the Qing and the Ottomans are illuminating. Though each was an enormous, overextended empire by the end of the eighteenth century, the Ottomans made an attempt to modernize their military and make their government more efficient before that time. Their proximity to Europe gave them direct experience with the Napoleonic era, and the rising nationalism of the nineteenth century. The intense struggle between France and Russia, particularly, gave the Ottomans a strategic position that made it distinctly to the advantage of France to side with them in their territorial struggles. For their part, the Ottomans were comparatively swift in their adaptation of aspects of French culture, military practices, and commercial institutions. This adaptability sustained Ottoman political credibility in Europe through the critical period of the war for Greek independence, and later allowed design and implementation of the reform program under Mahmud II that through the middle of the nineteenth century recentralized the state. On the strength of the recentralization, the secular programs that defined a civil sphere in Turkey and a concomitant consciousness of Turkish identity gave strength to the very nationalist movement that eventually helped destroy the empire.

Unlike the Ottomans, the Qing were not able to effect even a modest degree of recentralization and reform before the Taiping War. Suppression of the Taipings, Nians, and Muslims in Turkestan required the systematic dissolution of the traditional military structures, the regionalization of command and support, and finally the incorporation of foreign commanders, soldiers, and weapons into the "imperial" corpus. The alliance formed by Britain and France at this time would become more active in the nineteenth century, as the European powers and the United States intervened repeatedly to prevent colonization of Qing territory by Japan.

The Qing believed – unlike the Ottomans – until the middle of the nineteenth century that the Europeans were remote and only casually interested in trade. They knew little of the enormous fortunes being reaped in the early nineteenth century by European and American merchants smuggling opium into China. They did not know that silver gained in the illegal opium trade was financing part of the industrial transformation of Birmingham, England, and Providence, Rhode Island. But as Qing officials slowly learned, Britain was not so far away. It had colonies in India, where opium was grown. It had a major naval base at Singapore, through which it could transport opium to China and other parts of Eastern Asia. It was determined to right the trade imbalance that had occurred with China as a result of the tea trade, and opium seemed the key. The Qing insistence upon strictly limiting European trade to Canton and banning the opium trade altogether appeared to Britain an intolerable restraint upon trade, and a direct threat to Britain's economic health. The significance of naval power, which the Ottomans had appreciated but not learned to master in the Mediterranean and the Black Sea, was appreciated by the Qing much more slowly. Indeed, the difference between a naval invasion and piracy was not clear to Qing strategists until the Opium War was nearly ended.

As in the Ottoman territories, it was not necessary for Europeans or Americans to colonize the Qing in order to enjoy advantaged status. Neither the Ottoman nor the Qing lands were in need of "development" by colonial forces. They had pockets of wealth that needed only to be exploited, and this was best done through strategic alliances or diplomatic instruments, not by the expensive and risky methods of colonization. It is not a coincidence that both of the empires whose territorial integrity the European powers – and, in the case of China, the United States – swore themselves to defend were ultimately derided as the "sick men" of Eurasia, unable to defend themselves against their defenders, and kept in a state of low-grade survival to provide markets, raw materials, and strategic advantages to smaller, more dynamic nations.

European strategic interests in eastern Asia developed much more slowly than in the Middle East and Eastern Europe, but their expression, when it came, was much the same. Britain and France acted as financial guarantors and military guardians of the Ottoman and Qing, and resisted attempts by others to carve the central imperial territories into colonies. They were also wary of domestic challenges to the survival of these debtor states, and discouraged the development of nationalist, revolutionary movements. In the end this worked to the disadvantage of the imperial governments: The dynasties and foreign intervention became inextricably bound in the popular mind, and fueled the rising sentiments for rejection of both.

While the intrusion of the European powers framed both the attempts and the failures of the Ottoman and the Qing empires to reform themselves in the nineteenth century, the roots of reform and of the ability of survive the severe pressures of the nineteenth century were to be found in the empires themselves. As each neared the end of the eighteenth century, it found itself with lessening agricultural productivity, rising population, increasing migration to the cities, and a decentralizing political structure. In some areas, both empires struggled against intense movements for local autonomy. The arrival of Europeans after these developments changed the ways in which these empires responded to their internal challenges. They remained focused on attempts to marginally improve military strength while gradually making finances more efficient. These reform programs could not, however, outpace the destructive forces of economic decline, social turmoil, and intrusion by Europe and the United States (and, in the Qing case, Japan). By the end of the nineteenth century, the Qing and Ottoman empires were both disintegrating under the pressures of external invasion by European powers, and of internal political radicalization that led to rising movements for nationalist revolution.

7

Epilogue: The Manchus in the Twentieth Century

Three vivid impressions remain in Western culture of Manchus in the twentieth century. One is that of Manchukuo, the puppet state of the Japanese military that controlled Manchuria from 1932 to 1945. The second is Fu Manchu, the imaginary villain combining in his character as well as his name the legendary "savagery" of the "Tartars" with the treacherous, lecherous, "oriental" stereotypes beloved in the West of the 1930s and 1940s. The third is the narcissistic fantasy animating Bernardo Bertolucci's film *The Last Emperor*, in which an effete man seeks to recapture the closed world of total self-indulgence he knew as a child, and becomes the abused tool of those who, never having experienced the rarities that he alone has enjoyed, will forever be his inferiors.

These impressions are all related, of course, and should first of all be put into this perspective: There are now, and will probably continue to be, millions of Manchus. Far more, in the past two hundred years, have been very poor than very rich, and over the generations they have experienced China's occasional fits of xenophobic rages. Some have been outstanding novelists, calligraphers, historians, and actors, but most have been quite ordinary people.

It is a question for historians, sociologists, and Manchus themselves whether there would be any modern Manchu identity without the Taiping War. For the first time, the Taipings introduced an ethnic vocabulary, providing the modern terms *hanzu*, for the ethnic "Chinese," *manzu* for the "Manchus," and *mengzu* for the Mongols. At a time when the Qing court was attempting to make a majority of bannermen feel unwelcome in the garrisons and enticing them to go out into the world and melt away, the Taipings

Plates 24–6 *The earliest Fu Manchu stories by Sax Roehmer
(Arthur Sarsfield Ward) were clearly intended to offer the hero,
Nyland Smith, as a successor to Sherlock Holmes. Fu Manchu was
a shadowy Professor Moriarty figure, haunting London's old
Chinatown, and rarely seen. When glimpsed, however, he was
clearly not Chinese – the early stories described him as having
"bright green eyes and neutral-colored hair." Similarly, these early
illustrations are not intended to depict a stereotypical "Chinese."
Rather, Fu Manchu in these stories represents a stereotyped combination of "Tartar" savagery with the cosmopolitan heartlessness of
the new global criminal class. Chinese were almost invariably his
victims, particularly those struggling to overcome the criminal
temptations that, in Roehmer's world, permeated east London and
all the other ghettos. When Hollywood decided to bring Fu
Manchu to the screen the character was recast as strictly Chinese, in
the fashion of an evil Charlie Chan. On these grounds, the government of the Republic of China lobbied successfully against the early
projects for filming the stories, and ever since Fu Manchu has been
cited as an illustration of the denigrating Western caricaturing of
the Chinese.* (Collier's Magazine, 1913)

identified the Manchus as a people, and as an enemy. Not only did they make the identification, they acted it out, hunting Manchus or Manchu look-alikes down and murdering them like animals. Under these pressures, Manchu bannermen were quickly able to see themselves as Manchus first and as bannermen second; many left the garrisons for the duration of the war to serve in any army unit, whether run by Chinese civilians, by foreign mercenaries, or by imperial commanders, that would crush the racially-oriented movement that threatened them and their families.

This experience was repeated in the nationalist revolution that destroyed the empire and created the first modern Chinese republic. Racial invective against the Manchus poured forth from the treaty ports (the extra-territorial enclaves) where prior to a judicial revision in 1903 Qing subjects could denounce the empire with no fear of reprisals. In the aftermath of the Chinese defeat by Japan in 1895, the deficits of the Manchus were denounced large. Lu Haodong patented the formula by establishing that either the Manchus could survive, or the Chinese – not both. He called the Manchus the "target of vengeance ... It must be understood that today, without exterminating the Qing, the Chinese nation can under no circumstances be restored." The juvenile radical Zou Rong, in his *Revolutionary Army* of 1902 (for which he was eventually imprisoned by the international authorities), had many colorful ways of demanding the extermination of the "bandit spawn of Jianzhou," calling frankly and gleefully for race war against the conquerors.

Even nationalist leaders who would some day cultivate a gentlemanly rhetoric of enlightened, inclusive politics that was calculated to gain the sympathy of the Western powers could, in earlier days, crank out the crudest forms of hate speech. Liang Qichao (1873–1929), before he was a noted liberal, wrote "Whenever I read accounts of the conquest of China by the Manchus, my eyes overflow with warm tears . . . If there were a way to save the nation and at the same time help us to take revenge against the Manchus, I would certainly be delighted to follow it." And Sun Yatsen, generally celebrated as the father of the Chinese republic, before reaching the epiphany of his "Brotherhood of the Five Races," opined, "Our ancestors refused to submit to the Manchus. Close your eyes and imagine the picture of the bitter battles, when rivers of blood flowed and the bodies of the fallen covered the fields, and you will realize that the conscience of our ancestors is clear."[1]

At the time of these statements in the late 1890s, it was a conscious tactic on the part of nationalist firebrands to create one consolidated object of vilification out of the various realities of the garrison populations, the Manchu reformist elite, and the court still in the stranglehold of the Empress Dowager. Historical fact – such as that the great massacres of the conquest, like the conquest itself, were largely the work of the majority Ming deserters, not the minority bannermen – was not of interest. Nor was contemporary reality: Revolutionaries blared on interminably about the parasitical bannermen receiving silver and grain rations while the Chinese starved in their hovels, when in fact material supplies to the garrisons had, with few exceptions, stopped generations before, and actual bannermen lived as beggars, rickshaw pullers (a life immortalized in the work of the great Manchu novelist Lao She),[2] prostitutes, night-soil carriers, and jugglers, and in other employments of the extremely poor. Many were homeless and died of exposure in the winter nights, or of starvation in times of drought – exactly like their Chinese neighbors.

The deliberate distortion of the condition of most Manchus at the end of the nineteenth century had one distinct advantage to radical nationalists, and one distinct disadvantage. By refusing to identify the enemy as the Qing court exclusively, revolutionaries were well poised to reject Qing promises of radical political reform in the early years of the twentieth century. As Cixi's government promised a constitution, restructured its bureaucratic departments, and modernized the military, all could be rejected as meaningless: It was the nature of the Manchus that was at issue, and as Manchus the members of the Qing court were necessarily predatory and untruthful. The court was incapable of reform, and revolution was by definition the only possible course. There was, at a slightly earlier point, a cost: The energies, talents, and political capacities of reformist Manchus in the generation of Shoufu were ruthlessly excluded from the reform campaigns from the time of Kang Youwei on, and the possibility of a broad-based coalition for profound, systematic political change was pre-empted.

Whatever the political wisdom of the deliberate racism of the nationalist movement, the cost to living Manchus – and Mongols, Muslims, and others who were not to be welcomed in the new society – was high. It was to be expected that high-ranking Manchus would, in the period of radicalization of the Chinese nationalist movement between 1905 and 1911, be targets for assassination. They were sometimes killed by sharpshooters, but more often by bomb specialists who pioneered the terrorist techniques with which we are all familiar today. But when the revolution broke out in earnest in 1911, nationalists and their supporters from the local "secret societies" proved their racial hatred in earnest, the world following all in telegraphed dispatches from the Western press: At Wuhan, where the revolution began, the search for "Manchus" went on for days after the capture of the city. A British reporter described "the streets deserted and the corpses of Manchus lying in all directions, fifty bodies being heaped together outside one gate alone. The Rebel troops are still hunting for Manchus, of whom 800 are reported to have been killed." There was no pretense that nationalist troops were rooting out those likely to fight to preserve the empire. On the contrary, at Yichang, near Wuhan, the fighting had been relatively light. Yet seventeen Manchu women and children were rounded up, and several days after the fighting had concluded they were publicly executed to, in the words of the Hunan Provisional Government, "placate the troops." The climax came at Xi'an, in November, where the garrison community of 20,000 people were cut off from food supplies for weeks. Finally, the patience of the local secret society exhausted, the revolutionary troops broke into the compound, and within three days had killed the entire emaciated population.

The final settlement of the war, in February of 1912, provided for the safety of Manchus and their property. But few Manchus expected the provisions (which were rescinded in 1924) to be observed. A small number of Manchus made their way back to Manchuria, where loyalist warlords proclaimed they would be safe. A vast majority, however, had neither the means nor the inclination to abscond to a country that was foreign to them. They chose the easier strategy of lying low, answering few questions about their family histories, getting along, and staying out of politics. There is greater security, perhaps, for the present population of nearly ten million Manchus in the People's Republic of China, who are only slightly less than one out of a hundred people in the country.[3]

This is the collective experience of many modern ethnic groups, as has been the rediscovery of Manchu "identity" by recent generations of people who now choose to identify themselves as Manchu, whether in China or in Taiwan. Many speak of parents and grandparents who acted all their lives as if they had a guilty secret, and on their deathbeds would suddenly recite banner and lineage details revealing their Manchu ancestry. Some of the younger people claim to be tortured by the historical accounts of the massacres at Yangzhou and Jiading during the conquest, others are angered by the claim that conquering emperors – whether Khubikii Khan or the Kangxi emperor – are never given any credit for having achieved anything beneficial to China. Most, however, express only relief at being able, as their parents and grandparents were not, to simply say they have Manchu ancestors, and have it be just a prosaic fact of life (something Manchus in the time of the Qianlong emperor may well have longed for as they groaned under his endless prescriptions for more Manchu, more riding and shooting, more worship of the Aisin Gioro spirits).

Such relief is indeed new, and the saga of the "last emperor" is part of the reason why. Far from being the diffident, sensually-crazed esthete imprisoned by the crudity of modern politics of the Bertolucci fantasy, Puyi showed a surprisingly acute ability to manipulate his limited options. It was not his interior world he longed to return to, but a real exterior world that, despite his efforts, remained very slightly beyond his grasp.

By the time she died in November of 1908, Cixi had probably already arranged for the Guangxu emperor to expire before her, and had certainly guaranteed that Puyi – the 3-year-old son of Zaifeng – would be the new emperor. As regent, Zaifeng (who had inherited his father's title of Prince Chun) selected the reign name Xuantong for the child, and continued his program of creating grand new military commands and reserving them to himself and his brothers – behaviors he had carefully modeled on those of the Hohenstaufen dynasty of Wilhelm II. He was interrupted, however, by the outbreak of the revolution in October of 1911. The war, as indicated above, went badly for the Qing side, but not catastrophically. The dynasty had supporters among powerful northern governors, and a negotiated settlement was reached. Puyi would abdicate as emperor, but the imperial lineage would retain its property, it would continue to reside in the northern half of the Forbidden City, the Imperial Household Department and the Eight Banners would continue in truncated form (supported by subsidies from the republic's budget), and the Articles of Favorable Treatment would guarantee the property and political rights of Manchus, Mongols, Tibetans, and Muslims. Restrictions were also put on the sort of public role Puyi could in future assume: He could not give out rewards, make political pronouncements, or appear outside the Forbidden City without permission from the government.

The inability of republican leaders to create a unified order permitted many forms of political mayhem to continue, one of which was persisting attempts to restore Puyi to power. Some were, in one way or another, funded or otherwise encouraged by Japanese agents. This was the case, for instance, in the abortive restorationist movements of the Mongol prince Babojab and Manchu prince Shanqi, who despite some Japanese funding and a vague promise of Japanese military support were never able to coordinate their followers into a single uprising; Babojab was killed by the troops of the local warlord in 1916, and Shanqi escaped to Lushun in Manchuria to live under Japanese protection until his death in 1921. His daughter Jin Bihui, who took the name Kawashima Yoshiko, had a bizarre career afterward as a cabaret singer and amateur spy. In 1917, the loyalist "pigtail general" Zhang Xun was able to exploit a juncture in local politics to have his troops occupy the Forbidden City and restore Puyi to the throne for about two weeks. The occasion, if contemporary accounts can be believed, was festive. Entrepreneurs rushed to produce and sell souvenirs of the event, and people dragged traditional Qing robes out of storage to parade around the streets. The fun ended when troops of the warlord Duan Qirui, flying biplanes over the Forbidden City, dropped enough shells to drive Zhang's troops out into the streets, where they were arrested. This comic opera episode aside, Chinese political activists like Jiang Kanghu, intellectuals like Hu Shi, and world pacifists like Rabindranath Tagore could not divest themselves of the idea that in Puyi there might, in fact, be the possibility of restoring peace to China with a constitutional monarchy. They often got sufficient inspiration to come back, but nobody got enough to take up the cause.

As Puyi neared his twentieth birthday, matters relating to the Forbidden City and to the imperial property became serious. By the Articles of Favorable Treatment, the lineage did not own the Forbidden City; they had in fact agreed to vacate it at their earliest convenience and repair to the Yihe summer palace at Haidian on the outskirts of Peking. They never made the transfer, and part of the reason was obviously a wish to remain close to what still survived of the invaluable imperial treasures, which had over the centuries accumulated both at Mukden (now again Shenyang) and at Peking. These, according to the articles, were the property of the imperial lineage. But the vast majority had been seized in the revolution by the nationalist armies, and much was even on display in a part of the Forbidden City where Puyi was not generally permitted to go. According to the contemporary testimony of Puyi's British tutor Reginald Johnston, the estimated value of the treasures in 1916 was something over four million Mexican dollars, of which items totalling about $500,000 were in the possession of the imperial lineage. That meant the republic owed Puyi and his relatives about three and a half million Mexican dollars.

The total estimate was a staggering sum for the time; but in the end it was the $500,000 which precipitated a small crisis. Puyi's tutors, including but not limited to Johnston, urged him to assume rule (that is, destroy Zaifeng's regency), and use the money himself. Their advice was that he use it for public charities and to create a good image for himself, possibly to excite enthusiasm for a restoration, but more likely to make himself a glamorous figure who would attract international prestige and affection (from which many rewards could flow). Puyi liked the idea of getting control of the money, though he found the idea of giving it away to charities rather stale and unprofitable. A buyer, on the other hand, could easily be found (the American multi-millionaire J.P. Morgan had already expressed interest), and the useless goods converted to cash. Puyi was more attracted to the idea of going to live in Europe as a private citizen, being a university student, seeing the world, even having fun.

Prince Chun put his foot down, and he was not the only one opposed to the plan. A good-sized faction of the eunuchs in the Imperial Household Department were also opposed, immediately inciting the suspicion of Puyi's supporters. What were these eunuchs hiding, other than the long-rumored truth that they had surreptitiously pilfered the imperial treasures, carting them in small doses around to the antique shops of Nanchang Street, and lining their own pockets as the prized possessions of the Kangxi and Qianlong emperors were boxed up to become the mantel ornaments and garden sprites of rich Westerners? As Puyi announced his intention of getting to the bottom of the matter in 1923, one of the palaces in the Forbidden City that had been a primary warehouse for the collection burned to the ground. Its contents, if any, could not afterwards be ascertained.

A greater calamity was awaiting. While the great treasure hunt had been going on in the Forbidden City, the contest between the warlords of Fengtian (formerly Liaodong) and Zhili provinces had been going on without. In 1924 a truce was declared, and the warlord Feng Yuxiang assumed control of Peking. The republic now had the means to kick the imperial entourage out of the Forbidden City, abrogate the Articles of Favorable Treatment, and declare the imperial treasures to be the property of the nation. The inmates of the Forbidden City were turned out into the streets, the imperial lineage, Puyi, and his tutors all repairing to Tianjin, where they would live in the Japanese concession.

The plan Puyi had nursed since childhood of being a rich, private person had been snatched away, and all accounts indicate that for a long time he and his entourage lived in collective depression at the villa in Tianjin. He had already been introduced to the agents of the deepening Japanese economic and military domination of Manchuria, but could not work up much interest in their cause. In 1928, however, there occurred an event which galvanized him. In the course of warlording, the local potentate Sun Dianying had allowed his troops to desecrate the imperial tombs at Dongling, where the Qianlong emperor, the dowager empress Cixi, Ci'an, and other members of the Aisin Gioro were buried. The tombs had been burst into, the main sacrificial hall strafed by machine-gun fire. Explosives had been applied to the outer doors of the mausolea of the Qianlong emperor and of Cixi, and the remains broken down with axes. The caskets had been smashed open, the bodies danced about and eventually torn to pieces, the grave-goods carted away. On hearing the report, Puyi was pale and shaken. His former lack of interest in politics had been transformed into a wish to avenge the desecration of his ancestors.

Less than four years later, Puyi – now Henry Puyi – was installed at Mukden as president of the Republic of Manchukuo. Japanese troops had, in 1931, exploited an explosion on a railroad track to seize control of Shenyang and the rest of Fengtian province. Now Shenyang was Mukden again, and an Aisin Gioro was living in the imperial palaces built by Nurgaci and Hung Taiji. Around him, a Japanese military occupation that did not shrink from unspeakable brutality was maturing. There has never been evidence of to what degree Puyi did or did not know of the particulars of the Manchukuo enforcement mechanisms. What is certain is that he was an eager participant in the Manchukuo project, that he saw it as having some historical justice, and that the fact that the Japanese were playing the leading role was a necessary unpleasantness.

Puyi was not much of a puppet. The Japanese made it clear that they intended to upgrade him from president to emperor – which he found suitable – but that he should recognize the Japanese emperor as his superior. This he found less suitable, and clearly chafed at public occasions on which he (a tall and in bearing somewhat dignified person) was supposed to act the ritual inferior to the small Hirohito. When possible, Puyi was disobedient. The Japanese propaganda ministry had specifically rejected his plans to wear traditional Qing robes and execute the traditional shamanic and Buddhist rituals at the time of his enthronement as the Kangde emperor of the Manchukuo empire in 1934, but he did so anyway. Surely, however, Puyi knew how far he could push; before and after his arrival in Manchuria, ambitious collaborators with the Japanese had been eliminated without compunction when they became an inconvenience.

When Japan was defeated, the Soviet Union occupied Manchuria (which they saw a justice of their own). Puyi was taken into custody by the Soviets in 1946. When at length the allied authorities decided against trying him as a war criminal and the latest civil war in China was concluded, Puyi was turned over to the People's Republic of China for imprisonment in 1950. He spent most of the years of his Chinese imprisonment at Fushun, where his family had forged the early foundations of their empire. It was now a grimy center of coal and iron production, feeding China's incipient industrialization.

It was during his imprisonment in Manchuria that Puyi's controversial "autobiography" was produced. Whether it is regarded as Puyi's own composition surely depends upon one's definition of composing, and there are questions about the origins of the autobiography that will never be resolved. Certainly they were the result of forced writing, in combination with structured debriefing. In *The Last Emperor*, by some irony the inquisitor was played by Ying Ruocheng – often hailed as China's greatest actor – who is himself a Manchu, the scion of generations of Manchu writers and scholars. Whether Puyi ever experienced the soul-searing confrontation with himself that the film depicts is a matter for skepticism, it being so central to the coerced tale of a feudal master repenting of his ways and surrendering himself to the good of the people, and so necessary to the tale that the Chinese authorities insisted Bertolucci tell.

Puyi was released from prison in 1959, after a rather short period of incarceration for a high-ranking icon of Japanese imperialism in China. Of course the theory of Chinese imprisonment is not based on how long it takes to avenge a wrong against society, but how long it takes to transform the consciousness of a backward person into that of a right-thinking one. But the release of Puyi was patently political, and thereby hangs its lesson: Though in the eyes of so many historians until recently the Manchus have evaporated from existence, the People's Republic of China believed that the imprisonment of the former Manchu emperor had political weight. The independent-minded governors of the industrially-advanced provinces of Manchuria had recently been deposed, suspected of conspiring with the Soviet Union to compromise the Chinese border. In 1959, new border conflicts with the Soviet Union were imminent – indeed, a complete break in relations was possible. The release of Puyi could be construed as a bid for the goodwill of the Manchus (at the time, about 2.4 million) of the region, but history gives no reason to take such a narrow view: The early Qing state had been built upon regional solidarity, not Manchu sympathies (which could not have existed then), and there is evidence that regionalism in Manchuria had remained strong since Nurgaci's time. In any event, the break with the Soviet Union did indeed come, and Manchuria did indeed remain Chinese.

Puyi's life after his release was not entirely private – indeed it could hardly have served the needs of the state if it had been. He was, like other token "minorities," made a prominent member of the National People's Congress, the non-legislative, perpetually consultative branch of the state. Through the early 1960s, he lived as a gardener, married a nurse, and was reunited with his younger brother Pucheng, who had also been imprisoned and improved. But Puyi's end – a surprise to those who have seen *The Last Emperor*, no doubt – did not come as transformation into a butterfly. Official accounts stated tersely that he died of cancer during the Cultural Revolution, at the age of 60. It is at least equally possible that other reports are true, and that he was murdered by Red Guards in 1967. This was certainly the case for the Uigur historian Jian Bozan; or the Manchu novelist Lao She, who was beaten and drowned by Red Guards during this period; or for many other scholars, writers, and artists who were identifiable "minorities." Periods of political radicalization in China are hazardous for those who are not of the majority, since they are likely to harbor sentiments of ethnicity, to feel a link with history that would impede their socialist transformation, or to look skeptically on life from the margins to which the society has assigned them. How much worse for the former emperor of the Manchus.

Reign Periods of the Aisin Gioro Rulers

Nurgaci	*beile* of the Jianzhou	1582–1616
	khan of the Khorchin Mongols	1606–16
	khan of the Jianzhou federation	1616–18
	khan of the Jin (reign: Tianming)	1618–26
Hung Taiji	khan of the Jin (reign: Tiancong)	1627–35
	emperor of the Qing	1636–43
	(reign: Chongde)	
Fulin	(reign: Shunzhi)	1644–61
Xuanye	(reign: Kangxi)	1662–1722
Yinzhen	(reign: Yongzheng)	1723–35
Hongli	(reign: Qianlong)	1736–95
Yongyan	(reign: Jiaging)	1796–1820
Minning	(reign: Daoguang)	1821–50
Yizhu	(reign: Xianfeng)	1851–61
Zaichun	(reign: Tongzhi)	1862–74
Zaitian	(reign: Guangxu)	1875–1908
Puyi	(reign: Xuantong)	1909–12
	president of Manchukuo	1932–34
	emperor of Manchukuo	1934–45
	(reign: Kangde)	

Cherished Soldiers

The exact date of the introduction of the term *ujen cooha* and its precise meaning are unresolved. I have myself changed my idea about the meaning of this term, as well as its linguistic, social, and ideological affinities. Liu Chia-chü proposed that the term might mean that the soldiers in question were armored and sent ahead of the invading Jurchens/Manchus as "cannon fodder." See "The Creation of the Chinese Banners in the Early Ch'ing," p. 60. The practice of driving captives ahead of the invading army was traditional and attested, but given the high value placed on armor, it hardly seems that such protection would be lavished on those treated this way, and as a consequence this does not appear a strong possibility for the origin of the term. *Ujen* seems to mean "heavy" in the sense of laboring under a burden, like a pack animal or like a team of men attempting to drag, position, and operate a cannon – and the Jurchens first acquired their cannons at Fushun. I have previously suggested that it might, alternatively, mean "slow," in the sense of unmounted soldiers, carrying their own provisions; Manchus, of course, rode and had their provisions carried by slaves.

Having studied Jin Qizong's citations from Jurchen and thought anew about related words in Manchu, and having considered the context from which the term *ujen cooha* emerged, I now have a different understanding of it. Jurchen *udzə*, like Manchu *ujen*, meant both "heavy" and "important, emphasized, serious, valuable, respected." Jin (*Nuzhen wen cidian*, pp. 100–1) cites two verbs, evidently variants of each other, *udzəbimei* and *udzubimai*, both meaning "to respect." They are reflected in Manchu *ujelembi*, whose meanings Jerry Norman cites as "1. to be heavy,

2. to act respectfully, to treat respectfully, 3. to be serious, to act in a serious manner, 4. to act generously, 5. to value highly" (*A Concise Manchu – English Lexicon*, p. 292). The root of these words is also related to Jurchen *udzu-dzi-ru*, "to nourish, cherish, raise," reflected in Manchu *ujimbi*, which has the same meaning. As is discussed above (see chapter 3), this puts these words in extreme intimacy with Nurgaci's usual description of himself as "raising, nourishing, cherishing" (*ujire, ujikini*, etc.) the "various nations" (*geren gurun*). I suggest below that the original object of Nurgaci's cherishing was not the *geren gurun* but the *ujen cooha*.

Whatever the origins of this name, it was eventually generalized to the Chinese-martial banners and throughout the Qing period remained a quaint way of referring to them. See also Mou Ranxun, "Mingmo xiyang dapao you Ming ru Hou Jin kaolue."

Ujen cooha is often equated with *hanjun baqi* – the Chinese-martial Eight Banners – but this association took some time to become established in the records. In the Jin history from which the term was taken, it had been a modified noun (or a compound noun), meaning the "army of the Han (i.e. north China) people." In the Eight Banners, however, *hanjun* is an adjective, used to describe either a Chinese-martial division of the Eight Banners (*hanjun baqi*) or Chinese-martial bannermen associated with that division (*hanjun qiren*). It was not used in the Qing official records to mean "Han army" and aside from some idiosyncratic instances it has no grammatical equivalent in the appellations for the Manchu and Mongol banners (there is no *manjun* or *mengjun*); its equivalents are simply *manzhou* (*manzhou baqi*) and *menggu* (*menggu baqi*). This book argues the value of distinguishing the *hanjun* from what in the middle seventeenth century was readily identifiable as the "Chinese" population, and it is useful to have a word to aid in making that distinction. "Chinese-martial," a substantive noun (like secretary[ies]-general, court[s]-martial, etc.) that lends itself to the adjectival uses of *hanjun*, has seemed to me to suggest the grammatical functions, the meaning, and the flavor of *hanjun*. Though "martial Chinese" would be equally good and grammatically interchangeable, it would not preserve the word order of the original, which is merely a nicety in any case. Only the grammatical peculiarities of the English word "Chinese" prevents "Chinese-martial" from changing its form with respect to adjective/noun or singular/plural usage. If there is a value beyond convenience in the invention of this translation, it is the opportunity to dispel the notion that *hanjun*, in its Qing form, is a noun meaning "Chinese army," when, despite its form, it is an adjective meaning "martial Chinese" – that is, Chinese-martial.

Lest I be accused of inconsistency here, readers should be aware that I do not endorse the usage "Chinese martials," which occurs in the published version of an essay authored by me ("Manchu Education") and appearing in Elman and Woodside, *Education and Society in Late Imperial China, 1600–1900*. I am at a loss to account for either the grammatical or the lexical logic behind the editing in this particular instance.

A Glossary of Names and Terms

Words that appear in **bold type** within entries have their own entries in this glossary

beile: In **Nurgaci**'s youth, this was the normal title for a headman in Manchuria, and the magnitude of powers it indicated ranged from very small to just short of what would be necessary to be recognized as a **khan**. The word itself is clearly imported, probably from early Turkic languages, and is related to the modern Turkish word *beg*, which has a similar meaning. In **Jurchen**, the word was *begile*, which suggests that it was for some reason adopted into Jurchen in a declined form – possibly as a plural (as is often assumed), or more likely with the Turkic suffix *-lar* meaning "like, in the style of." It may, in this sense, share ancestry with Russian *boyar*, and is certainly an early cousin of the modern **Manchu** word for a headman, *bogiya*.

The normal plural for this loanword would be *beise* in Manchu, but as in the case of *taise* the word was used as a singular for the title of a minor prince – particularly Mongols who married daughters of Nurgaci and were thus imperial sons-in-law (*efu*).

Changbaishan: A mountain range whose height and position at the confluence of the Korean, Russian, and Manchurian borders has made it a prominent spot in the history of Northeast Asian peoples. According to the history of the Northern Wei, early inhabitants called the mountains "Tutai," but from late Han times the Chinese called its central peak, probably because of its volcanic crater, the "incomplete mountain" (*buxian shan*). The Northern Wei themselves called the range, for its appearence, the

"Great White Mountains" (*taibai shan*) or "Ever White Mountains" (*changbai shan*). It was the southernmost marker of the boundaries of **Parhae**, and the easternmost marker of the Jianzhou **Jurchens** in the 1400s. In the eighteenth century, the **Qing** court would attempt to construct a romantic lore of centuries of unbroken contact with their putative "ancestral" region at Changbaishan. In standard **Manchu**, the range is "Šanggiyan-alin," or sometimes "Sanyan-alin" (in either case, "the white mountains"). In English the Chinese name is sometimes translated as 'the long white mountain," using an alternative meaning of Chinese *chang*. The region is now a UNESCO preserve.

Eight Banners (Chinese *baqi*, **Manchu** *jakūn gūša*): The idea of organizing military units into "banners" (because each carried a distinctive flag) was imported into Manchuria via the Ming practice of organizing the military according to this terminology. It is convenient to think of the "Eight Banners" as being the socio-military organizational foundation of the **Qing** state from the time of **Nurgaci** to 1924, when they were officially disbanded by Yuan Shikai. But it should also be remembered that the early history of the banners is tangled. Conventionally the creation of four banners (yellow, white, blue, and red) is dated from 1601, when Nurgaci made four of his kinsmen the "lords" of these banners. But the testimony of Sin Chung-il suggests that units were already organized and carrying their banners in 1595. In 1616, each of the four banners was split into two, one being the "plain" banner and the other being "bordered."

The banners were made up of "companies' (Chinese *zuoling*, Manchu *niru*) that were originally based upon *mukūn*. From the earliest times Nurgaci's supporters included immigrants who were not members of *mukūn*, and were organized into a separate company of their own, probably from the first carrying a black flag. In the early 1600s these units were known as the *ujen cooha* (see appendix II), and in 1642 were officially incorporated into the Eight Banners as the Chinese-martial banners.

The Eight Banners were really twenty-four banners plus some odd companies. By the middle seventeenth century there were eight Manchu banners, eight Mongol banners, and eight Chinese-martial banners, each with a different set of companies under it. There were also special banners created for the New Manchus, and capitulating Muslims of Turkestan.

Hung Taiji (also romanized according to Chinese renderings: Hong Taiji, Hongtaiji, and Huang Taiji – the last an erroneous but common corruption of the name): Born 1592, died 1643 at Mukden, the eighth son of **Nurgaci**. This name is a mystery. It means "Prince Hung," and is probably not a name but a title. The man to whom it is applied – the second **Jin khan** and first **Qing** emperor – is referred to in early **Manchu** records as 'the fourth *beile*" (*duici beile*), which is not a name either. Some writers have, on the basis of a historiographical misunderstanding, assigned him the wrong name of "Abahai." The fact is that the exact original name is not known, nor are the reasons why it is not known known. He was the creator of the Qing empire.

Jin: Meaning "Gold," or "Golden," the name chose as the dynastic appellation of the **Jurchen** empire (1121–1234). According to the imperial history, written in Chinese, the name was chosen because of the fairness of the Jurchen people, though whether this is supposed to refer to their complexion or their traditional white clothing is not clear. In any case, it is not probable that the name was chosen to refer to any of the physical attributes of the Jurchens. The original seat of Jurchen power, and the location of the early capital Shangjing, was on the Achun River (now called the Ashi, a tributary of the Songari), whose name resembled the word for "gold" (*anchun*) in the Jurchen language. If it is necessary to explain why a people would want to call themselves "Golden," the explanation probably lies here.

Jurchen: The people using this name in the tenth century were certainly inheritors of the cultural traditions of the **Mohe**, and the name may have been related. On the other hand, early forms of the name "Jurchen," if one allows for some wide variation, may be present in records of the earlier Tang period, and so it is possible that "Jurchen" existed as an independent name, or some variation of "Mohe," well before the emergence of the Jurchens as a politically distinct people in the **Liao** period (late eleventh to twelfth centuries). In the early twelfth century the Jurchens under Agūda created an empire in Manchuria and wrested control of northern China from the Liao empire of the Kitans.

During and after the **Jin** empire, Jurchen groups were widely dispersed through Manchuria and northern China, and their cultures also varied. The eastern Jurchens, including the Jianzhou Jurchens from whom **Nurgaci** arose, continued to use the name, but not the written language. The name was officially discontinued in 1635.

khan (**Manchu** *han*): The term "khan," in one form or another, has a long history in Manchuria. It is possible that it was known as a term for a high ruler in the Korean peninsula in the fourth century. By the Tang period, certainly, the term "khan" was very familiar in Manchuria; a Kitan rebel leader styled himself "the khan who is inferior to no one" in the late 600s.

In **Nurgaci**'s youth the title was a rare and exalted one, and it was not applied to Nurgaci himself until the submission of the Khorchin Mongols to him in 1606. Even after that, he was still known to his **Jurchen** subjects as a *beile* until 1616, when he assumed the title "khan" at the same time as he declared the founding of the state.

The origins of the word are very obscure. Attempts have been made to link it to the West Asian term *shah*, which would imply a very early origin, corresponding to the period of Indo-European domination of Central Eurasia, before 2500 BCE. A possibly related interpretation connects it to the title for the ruler of the Xiongnu, which appears in the Chinese histories (in modern transliteration) as *shanyu*. An alternative hypothesis gives "khan" an eastern origin, deriving it from the Chinese word (in modern transliteration) *guan*, "official." The idea is that it might have gotten abroad as a common name for the ancient Chinese office of hegemon, *ba*, during the Western Zhou period (*c*.1050–487 BCE). The ancient Chinese hegemon was, like the khan, a *primus inter pares*, whose role was highlighted in times of war and otherwise intended to be weak. Since this is very much the way that khans functioned among the Turkic peoples, the Mongols in some periods, and the peoples of Manchuria, this interpretation, if correct, has identified an almost unique stability of meaning – for any word – over a very long period of time. In any event, in one form or another the term "khan" was ubiquitous through Eurasia as early as the fifth century CE.

Among the Mongols (most likely after the death of Genghis), the title of khan developed a more specialized offspring, *khaghan* – the "khan of khans" (very likely inspired by the Iranian title of *shahan shah*, "shah of shahs"), or the "Great Khan." See Lawrence Krader, "Qan-Qaɣan and the Beginnings of Mongol Kingship," for a summary of the debates on etymologies and relationships of the Mongolian terms *khan* and *khaghan*. Though the supreme title might not have been applied to Genghis until after his death, it appears that *khaghan* may have been the older of the two words, and that it is present in attestations from languages at the two extremes of the geographical spectrum, Old Bulgarian and Korean. Evidence from Jurchen supports this, as Jin Qizong cites the Jurchen disyllabic *ha-(g)an*, which appears on the stele of the Yongning temple (*Nuzhen wen cidian*, p. 122). In Manchu, however, the distinction between *khan* and *khaghan* is unknown – the single word *han* could have resulted from a contraction of the weak consonant. More important, it suggests that use of the title was not a direct borrowing from the imperial Mongols, but represented a separate political terminology among the post-imperial Jurchens of Manchuria.

Liao: The empire of the Kitans, established in 907 and destroyed by the **Jurchens** in 1121. The political federation upon which the state was founded originated near the Liao River in Manchuria. The word *liao* in Chinese also means "iron," and so had many resonances with the economic history and the political ideologies of Manchuria and Central Asia.

Manchu (Manchu *manju*, Chinese *manzhou*): The name "Manchu" did not come into offical use until 1635. Early **Qing** records do not state the meaning of the name or the reasons for its adoption. One of the earliest attempts to explain the name related it to Manjušri, a manifestation of the Buddha which figured in some of the imperial cult rituals of the Qing. This term is supposed to have accrued to the Qing court through its early association with Tibet, which each year submitted a written greeting addressing the Qing emperor as Manjušri.

"Manchu" occurs as a title or element in a title of headmen as early, it seems, as the **Mohe**, who may have called their headmen *damofo manju*, and the great Chinese historian Meng Sen speculated that the name of the rival of **Möngke Temür**, Li Manzhu, may really have been a title signifying the status of Li as the rightful headman of the Jianzhou federation. In this reasoning, "Manchu" would have been the title adopted by **Nurgaci**'s ancestors after they had displaced Li from power in the 1400s. The Ming, then, may have mistakenly generalized the title to the people as a whole, and this may have been legitimated by **Hung Taiji**'s policy in 1635.

The official Qing explanation – not offered until the eighteenth century – for the name "Manchu" was that it had originally been the name of a tribe that had joined the Jianzhou federation at some point, and it may even have been the name of a small river in the region. Unfortunately, no evidence confirming any aspect of this explanation can be found.

Chinese historians have a tradition of explaining the introduction of the Manchu name as clouding the **Jurchen** identity of the state, in order, evidently, to obscure the fact that the Jurchens had been tributaries of the Ming court and therefore could not be legitimate rulers over China. It could hardly be that the Qing rulers assumed that anybody would "forget" the Jurchen origins of the state, which the Qing themselves emphasized repeatedly, and which in any case they would hardly have regarded as compromising their right to rule. It is likely that "Manchu" was familiar among the Jurchens before its official adoption as a national name in 1635. Quite possibly there was some etymological connection to very ancient terms for headmen, perhaps as early as Mohe times, and its use in 1635 may have been intended to identify the Manchus as, literally, the *Herrenvolk* within the state. But as of this moment, all is flimsy speculation.

Mohe: The direct descendants of the **Wuji**, and probably sharing the same name. During the Tang period the Mohe were gradually distilled into two large groups, the Heishui in northern Manchuria and the Sumo in the south (ancestors of the **Parhae**). The Mohe predated the Parhae, but a portion persisted through the Parhae period and later formed the early **Jurchens**.

Möngke Temür: A Mongolian name meaning "enduring iron," and used by several leaders of Manchuria and Mongolia. One of them was the leader of the Odori **Jurchens**, forerunners of the Jianzhou federation. Möngke Temür was killed in northern Korea in 1434, evidently while rooting out other Jurchens who were obnoxious to the Korean court. His younger brother Fanca later led the Odori north and west into southern Manchuria, where they settled for some time before moving westward again and settling near the Ming province of Liaodong. The title granted by the Ming court to Möngke Temür, "Commandant" (*dudu*) of his federation, passed to his son Dongshan, and was later assumed by his great-great-great-grandson, **Nurgaci**.

mukūn: Early discussions of **Manchu** kinship have provided the

Qing neologism *halamukūn* as the usual term for a "clan," or lineage (see Shirokogoroff, *Social Organization of the Manchus*, and Ling Chunsheng, *Songhuijiang xiayou de hezhe zu*). This, it has been suggested, was cognate to Chinese *shizu*, which also suggests the latter word as a unit of the former: That is, that *hala* (or *shi*) is a "clan" and *mukūn* (or *zu*) a sub-clan, or lineage. In fact *mukūn* is the older of the two Manchu terms, and (like *zu*) was originally not a word that unambiguously indicated a blood-related group. *Hala* came later to indicate federations of *mukūn*, and in the Qing period *mukūn* remained the normal word for a lineage or extended family, with *hala* being an infrequently-invoked reference to the totality of people sharing a lineage name (whether they were actually related or not).

Jurchen *mouke* (from Chinese transcription in the Jin history) was ancestral to the modern Manchu word. It did not, as Tao Jingshen thought, mean "one hundred" (the word for one hundred, *tanggū*, was the same in Jurchen as it is in Manchu), but meant what *mukūn* means – a cooperative (later kin) group.

Nurgaci (also romanized Nurhaci, Nurhachi, Nurhachu): Born 1559 died 1626 at Mukden. From 1582 he worked to unite and lead the Jianzhou **Jurchens**; from 1586 he was recognized as *beile*: in 1595 he styled himself "lord" (*zhu, ejen*) of the "Jianzhou Garrison Officers and the Wildmen." From 1606 he was recognized as **khan** of the Khorchin Mongols; in 1616 he declared himself khan (*han*) of the Jurchens; and in 1618 he announced the name of his state as **Jin**. In 1621 he added most of the former Ming Manchurian province of Liaodong to his territories. He died attempting to conquer western Liaodong.

Parhae (Bohai): Though evidently related to **Mohe** in sound, the actual characters for the name "Bohai" came from one of the Chosŏn Commandaries established in Korea in Han times. See chapter 2.

Puyŏ: Putative founders of the Paekche and Koguryŏ states in the Korean peninsula of the first century CE.

Qing: The dynastic name of the empire founded by **Hung Taiji**. The name in Chinese means "pure," "clear," "brilliant," as these might relate to water, and is not a surprising dynastic epithet (since it would relate cyclically to the "fire" connotations of the Ming dynasty name, and cosmologically explain the Qing conquest through the defeat of fire by water). It has also been supposed to have Buddhist overtones (as water imagery suggests reflection, perspicacity, and enlightenment), and may have been chosen as complementary to the dynasty's connections to the Bodhisattva Manjušri (see chapter 7).

"Qing," it should be noted, is the name of several rivers in Manchuria, and the battle of the Qing River in 1619 was an important one in **Nurgaci**'s campaigns to win Liaodong. It is the subject of one of the illustrations in the **Manchu** annals, and whatever the larger connotations of the name, it may first have become a part of the Latter **Jin** lore on account of its figuring in these early battles. Like "Jin," it is a name to which big ideas can rapidly accrue.

The Manchu historian Jinliang insisted that in Shenyang there was a placard in both Chinese and Manchu, in which Chinese *Qing* was used to translate Manchu *aisin*, "gold." He hypothesized that the names of the Latter Jin – Nurgaci's state – and of the Qing – Hung Taiji's state – were not substantially different.

This placard no longer exists, and if it did its significance would be difficult to decipher. Unfortunately, Hung Taiji did not explain his intentions in promulgating either the Manchu national name or the Qing dynasty name. Evidence for the exact meaning, in either case, has not yet been adduced.

Sibo (Chinese *Xibo*): The Sibo people speak a dialect of the language now recognized as **Manchu**, and though closely related to the Manchus have had a distinct history. There have been frequent attempts to link their name to the Xianbei people, from whom the Toba (Tabghach) people who founded the Northern Wei dynasty arose. If this is correct, then the ancestors of the Sibo were not Tungusic speakers, but used a language that was either Turkic or proto-Mongolian. There is the difficulty of many centuries intervening between the Xianbei and Sibo, during which there is virtually no evidence of a "Sibo" people.

During the past six centuries the Sibo have been Tungusic speakers, and they were well known to Russians moving toward the Pacific, who named Siberia after them. The Manchus conquered the Sibo in the 1640s, incorporating them into the banners as "New Manchus." This designation aided in the preservation of a distinct Sibo identity within the banners, and they were famous for their garrison community at Yili, in Xinjiang, where they continued to speak their language and practice a rather traditional culture to the end of the **Qing** period. Many of the modern speakers of "Manchu" are actually Sibo, who have injected their accent into our contemporary understanding of what Manchu sounds like.

taiji/taise: A Mongolian title for "prince," from Chinese *taizi*. In the **Manchu** annals, this title was normally affixed to the names of the sons of **Nurgaci** who were also *beiles* in his **khan**ate, or owners of the Eight Banners. The normal plural for this loanword would be *taise*, but it was used as a singular in the title of Nurgaci's son Cuyen when he was appointed co-ruler.

Uriangkha: Often thought of as Mongols, they may have been of **Jurchen** origin. In any case, they were probably carriers of a Mongolian influence to Jurchens settled in Heilongjiang after the fall of the Jurchen **Jin** empire, and were a distinctive element in the formation of the eastern Jurchen peoples of the Yuan and Ming periods. The Uriangkha were not the first people of indeterminate origin to come out of Manchuria and later be identified as "Mongol." The Toba, who probably originated in the area of the Xing'an ranges, were called *xianbei* by the Chinese, which was thought to indicate a Tungusic origin. Later scholars, however, at one time or another called them Turkic, and now prefer the term "proto-Mongol." Though separated by a few centuries in time, the Toba and the Uriangkha appeared in roughly the same area of Manchuria and their development shows many of the same ambiguities; it is possible that the early Uriangkha were descendents of the Toba remnants.

The name occurs in the annals of the early **Liao** as "Wenlianggai" and "Wolanggai." This was supposed to be a place name, but it was also the lineage name of the great Mongol commander Sübüdei, who menaced Eastern Europe in 1241. Several references in the imperial history of the Liao empire of the Kitans indicate the presence of Uriangkha in Liaodong and the vicinity of the Shira Muren in the early tenth century. By the time of the Ming empire (after 1368) the Uriangkha were situated well north and west of that region, and by the late Ming they were identified as part of the "western" Mongol alliance. Though the Ming recognized the Uriangkha as part of the contemporary Mongol alliance, they thought that the origins of the Uriangkha lay in the Yuezhi people (usually thought to be Sogdians) of the period after the fall of the Han empire.

Since early times a Jurchen or Tungusic origin for the

Uriangkha has been assumed. They were probably associated with or part of the **Mohe** peoples in the Tang–**Parhae** era. During the Yuan empire of the Mongols, Rashid ad-Dīn described them as "forest peoples," which suggests more the Jurchens than the Mongols. In the fifteenth century, the connection of the Uriangkha with the Jurchens remained strong – so strong that the Korean court dealing with **Möngke Temür** and other headmen called them all *orankha*, which in Korean became synonymous with "savage." While the Jurchens were taking the Uriangkha name southward with them, it was also being taking into Siberia and the extremes of Northeastern Asia by other peoples, including the Tuvin, Tubalar, Sayan, and Yakuts.

Wuji: The Chinese tradition that the Yilou, Wuji, **Mohe**, and **Jurchen** were all descendents of the "Sushen" mentioned in Chinese records of the Zhou period (*c.*1050 BCE to 221 BCE) has no direct evidence to support it, which does not prevent its being repeated from time to time by modern scholars.

This is the earliest name for a people who can be confidently identified as precedessors of the **Jurchens**. They were a prominent people in Manchuria during the period of the Northern Wei dynasty. Many scholars, from **Qing** times on, have noted that this name, in its modern variation, is close to the **Manchu** word *weji*, meaning a forest or forest dweller, and have suggested this as an etymology. But it is not likely that is related to any modern word. Its contemporary pronunciation probably was similar to or the same word as **mohe**.

Notes

1 The Paradox of the Manchus

1 In the Wade-Giles romanization used very commonly before 1979, this is "Ch'ing," and in the *pinyin* romanization favored by the People's Republic of China and standard in Western publishing since 1979, "Qing." This was the dynastic name established by the founders of the empire in 1636. The antecedent state, the khanate established under Nurgaci in 1618, was in its own time known as Jin (in *pinyin*; in Wade-Giles, "Chin,") which meant "Gold," and historians now refer to the period between 1616 and 1636 as that of the "Latter Jin" or "Later Jin" (in Chinese, *Hou Jin*) acknowledging the earlier Jurchen empire from which Nurgaci appeared to have taken the name. Thus there are several choices of dates for fixing the beginning of the Qing era: establishment of Nurgaci's khanate in 1616, the promulgation of the imperial name in 1636, or the conquest of Beijing in 1644. There is also some ambiguity about the end of the Qing period. Most historians choose to date it from establishment of the provisional republican government in late 1911, though the last Qing emperor, the child Puyi, did not abdicate until February of 1912.

2 See for instance the memoirs of Pierre Joseph d'Orleans (1641–98), *History of the two Tartar conquerors of China*, and of Joseph-Marie Amiot, *Éloge de la ville de Moukden, poème composé par Kien-Long, empereur de la Chine et de la Tartarie, actuellement régnant.*

3 D.O. Morgan, "Edward Gibbon and the East," p. 88.

4 Very little of this early scholarship is available in English. A hint of it lingers in the translation of Li Chien-nung's progressive work, *The Political History of China*, pp. 3–10.

5 As noted in a later chapter, there is a large literative on the Taipings, but the most recent study is Jonathan D. Spence, *God's Chinese Son.*

6 This has been a ubiquitous paradigm in modern China studies, but for elaboration on this particular point see Crossley in Bentley (ed.), *The Routledge Companion to Historiography.*

7 The Banners were the original military and social administration of the Nurgaci state, and were continued and elaborated under the empire. They later became the definitive institutions in the emergence of the "Manchus" as a people in the Qing period. There is a very large international secondary literature on the Eight Banners. For recent studies see Mark Elliott, "Resident Aliens: The Manchu Experience in China, 1644–1760;" P.K. Crossley, *Orphan Warriors*; and Kaye Soon Im, *The Rise and Decline of the Eight Banner Garrisons in the Ch'ing Period (1644–1911)*.

8 This is the modern province of Liaoning, in southwest Manchuria. During the Qing and Republican eras it was called Fengtian.

9 The history of this subgroup of the conquest elite is the subject of the first part of P.K. Crossley, *A Translucent Mirror*.

10 It appears that the original manuscript was lost long ago, but the text was preserved by being entered into the annals of the Yi kingdom, the *Yijo sillŏk*, and a reproduction of a damaged hand copy is also available. Sin's report has been briefly summarized by Giovanni Stary, "Die Struktur der Ersten Residenz des Mandschukans Nurgaci," pp. 103–9. In 1977 a new, corrected, and partially restored edition by Xu Huanpu was published (in *jiantizi*).

11 See also Morgan, *The Mongols*, p. 30. For Fletcher's best-known work published in his lifetime see "China and Central Asia, 1368–1884" in Fairbank, *The Chinese World Order*; "Ch'ing Inner Asia *c.*1800" in *The Cambridge History of China* [Vol. 10, part I]; and "The Mongols: Ecological and Social Perspectives" in *Harvard Journal of Asiatic Studies* [1986]. Much of Fletcher's work remained in manuscript at the time of his death, and has since been revised for publication by other authors. See particularly the work revised, reshaped, and edited by Beatrice Manz, *Studies on Chines and Islamic Inner Asia* (Aldershot and Brookfield, VT, 1995), which for the first time presents in complete form Fletcher's remarkable discoveries on the connections between the religious cultures of West Asia and China in the eighteenth and nineteenth centuries. See also "A Bibliography of Published and Unpublished Work" printed in the issue of *Late Imperial China* dedicated to Fletcher – 6:2 December, 1985.

12 For a much more detailed description of the policies and practices relating to the Manchu language in the Qing period, see Pamela Kyle Crossley and Evelyn Sakakida Rawski, "A Profile of the Manchu Language."

13 For an English translation see Lo Kuan-chung, *Three Kingdoms*.

14 For an English translation see Clement Egerton, *The Golden Lotus*.

15 See Crossley, *Orphan Warriors*, pp. 82–6, 251 f.n. 18–21.

2 Shamans and "Clans": The Origins of the Manchus

1 To avoid confusion I use the name "Heilongjiang" only to refer to the easternmost Chinese province; the river that the Chinese also call Heilongjiang I call Amur, a name familiar to most Western readers. Though the reader will readily understand that "Manchuria" is used anachronistically in much of this chapter, I have nevertheless chosen to use it because it is

familiar, and consistently refers to the region indicated here. What is important is that Manchus were not called Manchus because they came from Manchuria – it is rather that in modern times the ancestral region of the Manchus has begun to be called Manchuria.

2 Shirokogoroff, *Social Organization of the Manchus*, p. 16.

3 *Ibid.*, p. 31 (italics in the original).

4 *Qingshi gao* 1:1. Versions of the legend, all identical except for inclusion or exclusion of certain details, may also be found in *Manzhou shilu* (based upon the *Manju i yargiyan kooli*) 1, and *Donghua lu* 1. See also "Introduction to the Qing Foundation Myth."

5 On the background and content of this folk epic, see Chuang Chi-fan [Ehuang Jifa], *Nisan saman i bithe*, and Margaret Nowak and Stephen Current, *The Tale of the Nisan Shamaness*.

6 See for example work in progress by Gari Ledyward on the relationship between Mongolian Phags-pa script and *han'gul*.

7 Beginning in the early 1400s, the Ming tributary authorities granted military ranks to Manchurian leaders, as if they were officers in garrisons. On the workings of this system, see Monis Rossabi, *The Jurchens of the Yüan and Ming*.

8 Cited in Yan Chongnian, *Nurhachi zhuan*, pp. 134, 182–3.

9 The inspiration for this innovation may well have come from the *han'gul* script of Korea. This has been hypothesized by J.P.R. King and others. See King, "The Korean Elements in the Manchu Script Reform of 1632," pp. 252–86.

10 Giovanni Stary, "A New Subdivision of Manchu Literature: Some Proposals," p. 289.

3 The Enigma of Nurgaci

1 Lao Che in the film is a sort of modern-day Fu Manchu, but the selection of name is interesting. It appears to have been inspired by the hardly villainous but obviously Manchu novelist known as Lao She (see Epilogue).

2 The personal name of Qing Taizu, the dynastic founder, has been spelled various ways. "Nurgaci" is the plain transliteration from Manchu according to the Möllendorf system, which has now become standard through its use in Tamura Jitsuzo et al.'s *Kotai Shimbun kan yakukai* (1966) and Jerry Norman's *A Concise Manchu–English Lexicon* (1978).

3 Xiaohan de gushi, pp. 122–5, in Ubingga et al., *Manzu minjian gushi xuan*.

4 Joseph F. Fletcher Jr, Turco-mongolian Tradition in the Ottoman Empire, pp. 240–1.

5 That is, cardinal as in the points of a compass. Later records suggest that there were four *hōšoi beile*, as in the points of a Western compass, but there were, as will be discussed below, eight – as in the eight cardinal points of the shamanic compass of northeastern Asia.

6 This aspect of royal banqueting, which would continue in increasingly elaborate form among the Qing, was an ancient custom of the Jurchens. In 1163

Jin Shizong had complained that the old custom of entertaining banqueters with exhibitions of riding and archery was being abandoned for more sedentary pursuits; see Herbert Franke, "Some Folkloristic Data in the Dynastic History of the Chin (1115–1234)," p. 137. Riding displays of the Jin period often included polo. In origin the imperial shooting displays may have remembered the religious rituals of the Kitans; see Franke, "Some Folkloristic Data," p. 148.

7 Translated in Gertrande Roth [Li], "The Manchu–Chinese Relationship," p. 9.

4 The Qing Expansion

1 From the Manchu archives in the old style, *Jiu manzhou dang yizhu*, document 2564.
2 From Pamela Kyle Crossley, *Orphan Warriors*, p. 52.

5 The Gilded Age of Qianlong

1 This is connected to an elaborate subplot involving the manner in which the Yongzheng emperor originally came to the throne; very likely that event was touched by various degrees of corruption, distortion and possibly murder. It has been dealt with extensively (and contentiously) in Silas Wu, *Passage to Power*, and Pei Huang, *Autocracy at Work*.
2 See also Bawden, pp. 81–186.
3 *Mongghol Borjigid Oboghü teüke*. Translated and cited by Bawden, p. 114.
4 Cited and translated in Bawden; transliterations changed to be consistent with the present text.

7 Epilogue: The Manchus in the Twentieth Century

1 See also Pamela Kyle Crossley, *Orphan Warriors*, p. 61.
2 Lao She, the literary name of Shu Qingchun (of the Sumuru lineage), wrote many very vivid novels of working-class life in turn-of-the-century Beijing. In most of them the identity of the characters as Manchus is implied (most famously in *Rickshaw Boy*), but it is explicit in the posthumous, incomplete novel translated into English as *The Plain Red Banner*.
3 Liu Xianzhao, *Zhongguo minzu wenti yanjiu*, p. 342.

Bibliography

Abe Takeo. Shinchō to ka i shishō. *Jimbun kagaku* 1:3 (December, 1946), 150–4.
——. *Shindai shi no kenkyū.* (Tokyo, 1971).
Augi. *Qing kaiguo fanglue.* (Taipei, 1966, photo reprint of QL bingwu original).
Augi et al. *Qinding manzhou yuanliu kao.* (Taipei, 1966, photo reprint of 1783 original).
Aisin Gioro Puyi [Aixinjueluo Puyi]. *Wode qian bansheng.* (Peking, 1977).
Ahmad, Zairuddin. *Sino–Tibetan Relations in the Seventeenth Century.* (Rome, 1970).
Amiot [Amyot], Joseph-Marie. *Éloge de la ville de Moukden, poème composé par Kien-Long, empereur de la Chine et de la Tartarie, actuellement regnant.* (Paris, 1770).
Bartlett, Beatrice S. *Monarchs and Ministers: The Grand Council in Mid-Ch'ing China, 1723–1820.* (Berkeley, 1991).
Belov Y.A. The Xinhai Revolution and the Question of Struggle against the Manzhou. In S.L. Tikhvinsky (ed.), *Manchzhurskoe vladichestvo v Kitae.* (Moscow, 1983).
Bentley, Michael (ed.). *The Routledge Companion to Historiography.* (London, 1996).
Bol, Peter K. Seeking Common Ground: Han Literati under Jurchen Rule. *Harvard Journal of Asiatic Studies* 47 (December, 1987), 461–538.
Borokh, L.N. (D. Skvirsky, trans.). Anti-Manzhou Ideas of the First Chinese Bourgeois Revolutionaries (Lu Huadong Confession). In S.L. Tikhvinsky (ed.), *Manchzhurskoe vladichestvo v Kitae.* (Moscow, 1983).

Brackman, Arnold C. *The Prisoner of Peking*. (New York, 1975).
Brunnert, H.S. and V.V. Hagelstrom (Beltchenko and Moran, trans.). *Present Day Political Organization of China*. (Shanghai, 1911).
Ch'en Chieh-hsien [Chen Jiexian]. *Manzhou congkan*. (Taipei, 1963).
Ch'en Ching-fang [Chen Jingfang]. *Qingmo Man Han zhengzhi quanli xiaozhang zhi yanjiu*. (Taipei, 1961).
Ch'en Wen-shih [Chen Wenshi] (P.K. Crossley, trans.). The Creation of the Manchu Niru. In P. Huang (ed.), *Chinese Studies in History*, XIV, No. 4 (White Plains, 1981) – originally published as "Manzhou baqi niulu de goucheng," *Dalu zazhi* 31:9 and 31:10 (1965).
———. Qingdai Manren zhengzhi canyu. *Zhongyang yanjiuyuan lishi yuyan yenjiusuo jikan* 48:4 (1977), 529–94.
Ch'oe Hak-kyun. *Kugyok Mongmun Manju sillok* (2 vols). (Seoul, 1992).
Chai Yü-shu [Zhai Yushu]. *Qingdai Xinjiang zhufang bingzhi de yanjiu*. (Taipei, 1969).
Chan Hok-lam. *Legitimation in Imperial China: Discussions under the Jurchen Chin Dynasty*. (Seattle, 1985).
Chuang Chi-fa [Zhuang Jifa]. *Nisan šaman i bithe*. (Taipei, 1978).
Cinggertai et al. *Qidan xiaozi yanjiu*. (Peking, 1985).
Cleaves, Francis W. A Mongolian Rescript of the Fifth Year of Degedü Erdem-tü (1640). *Harvard Journal of Asiatic Studies* 46 (June, 1986), 181–200.
Crossley, Pamela Kyle. *Manzhou yuanliu kao* and the Formalization of the Manchu Heritage. *Journal of Asian Studies* 46:4 (1987), 761–90.
———. *Orphan Warriors: Three Manchu Generations and the End of the Qing World*. (Princeton, 1990).
———. Thinking About Ethnicity in Early Modern China. *Late Imperial China* 11:1 (June, 1990), 1–35.
———. The Rulerships of China: A Review Article. *American Historical Review* 97:5 (December, 1992), 1468–83.
Crossley, Pamela Kyle and Evelyn Sakakida Rawski. A Profile of the Manchu Language. *Harvard Journal of Asiatic Studies* 53:1 (June, 1993), 63–88.
Deng Shaozhen. Shilun Ming yu Hou Jin zhanzheng de yuanyin ji qi xingzhi. *Minzu yanjiu* 5 (1980).

——. *Nurhachi ping zhuan* [*Critical Biography of Nurgaci*]. (Shenyang, 1985).

Du Jiaji. Qingdai baqi lingshu wenti kaochao. *Minzu yanjiu* 5 (1987), 91.

Egerton, Clement. *The Golden Lotus: A Translation, from the Chinese Original of the Novel Chin Ping Mei*. (London, 1972).

Elliott, Mark. Bannerman and Townsman: Ethnic Tension in Nineteenth-Century Jiangnan. *Late Imperial China* 11:1 (June, 1990), 36–74.

——. Resident Aliens: The Manchu Experince in China, 1644–1760. Doctoral dissertation, University of California. (Berkeley, 1993).

Etō Toshio. *Manshū bunka shi jo no ichi shinwa*. (Tokyo, 1934).

——. *Dattan* [*Tatars*]. (Tokyo, 1956).

Fairbank, John K. (ed.). *The Chinese World Order*. (Cambridge, 1968).

—— (ed.). *The Cambridge History of China, Vol. 11: Late Ch'ing, 1800–1911, Part I*. (Cambridge, 1978).

—— (ed.). *The Cambridge History of China, Vol. 11: Late Ch'ing, 1800–1911, Part II*. (Cambridge, 1980).

Farquhar, David. The Origins of the Manchus' Mongolian Policy. In J.K. Fairbank (ed.), *The Chinese World Order: Traditional China's Foreign Relations*. (Cambridge, 1968).

——. Emperor as Boddhisattva in the Governance of the Ch'ing Empire. *Harvard Journal of Asiatic Studies* 38:1 (June, 1978), 5–34.

Feng Erkang. *Yongzheng zhuan*. (Peking, 1985).

Fletcher, Joseph Francis Jr. Manchu Sources. In Donald D. Leslie et al., *Essays on the Sources for Chinese History*. (Canberra, 1973).

Franke, Herbert. Chinese Texts on the Jurchen: A Translation of the Jurchen Monograph in the San-ch'ao hui-pien. *Zentralasiatische Studien* 9 (1975), 119–86.

——. Etymologische Bemerkungen zu den Vokabularen der Jurcen-Sprache. In Weiers, Michael and Giovanni Stary (eds), *Florilegia Manjurica in Memoriam Walter Fuchs*. (Weisbaden, 1982).

——. Some Folkloristic Data in the Dynastic History of the Chin (1115–1234). In Alvin Cohen (ed.), *Legend, Love and Religion in China*.

Fu Guijiu. Donghua lu zuozhe xinzheng. *Lishi yanjiu* 5 (1984), 168–70.

Fu Kedong. Baqi huji zhidu chucao. *Minzu yanjiu* 6 (1983), 34–43.

Fu Tsung-mou [Fu Zongmou]. Qingchu yizheng tizhi zhi yanjiu. *Guoli Zhengzhi Daxue xuebao* 11 (May, 1965), 245–95.

Goodrich, Luther C. and Chao-ying Fang. *Dictionary of Ming Biography* (2 vols). (New York, 1976).

Grousset, René (Naomi Walford, trans.). *The Empire of the Steppes: A History of Central Asia.* (New Brunswick NJ, 1970).

Grube, Wilhelm, *Die Sprache und Schriften der Jučen.* (Leipzig, 1896).

Grupper, Samuel Martin. The Manchu Imperial Cult of the Early Ch'ing Dynasty: Texts and Studies on the Tantric Sanctuary of Mahakala at Mukden. Doctoral dissertation, Indiana University. (1980).

——. Review of Sagaster, *Die Weisse Geschichte. Mongolian Studies* 7 (1981–2), 127–33.

Guan Dedong and Zhou Zhongming. *Zidi shu congchao* (2 vols). Peking, 1984).

Guan Xiaolian. Manwen laodang de xiufu yu chongchao. *Lishi dang'an* 3 (1987), 125–9.

Guang Dong. Jiufuquan de chansheng, fuzhan he xiaowang chu cao. *Minzu yanjiu* 2 (1985), 19–28.

Guo Chengkang. Qingchu niulu de shumu. *Qingshi yanjiu tongshun* 1 (1987), 31–5.

——. Shixi Qing wangchao ruguan qian dui hanzu de chengce. *Minzu yanjiu* 3, 15–22.

Guy, R. Kent. *The Emperor's Four Treasuries: Scholars and the State in the Late Ch'ien-lung Era.* (Cambridge, 1987).

Halkovic, Stephen A., Jr. *The Mongols of the West.* (Bloomington, 1985).

Hao, Yen-p'ing and K.C. Liu. The Importance of the Archival Palace Memorials of the Ch'ing Dynasty: *The Secret Palace Memorials of the Kuang-hsü Period, 1875–1908. Ch'ing-shih wen-t'i* 3:1 (1971), 71–94.

Harrell, Stevan, Susan Naquin and Ju Deyuan. Lineage Genealogy: The Genealogical Records of the Qing Imperial Lineage. *Late Imperial China* 6:2 (December 1985), 37–47.

He Hai. Baqi zidi de xingrong yu "huangdu" Beijing. *Yandu* 6 (1986), 36–7.

Hiu Lie. *Die Manschu-Sprachkunde in Korea*. (Bloomington, 1972).

Hongli [Qing Gaozong Shun Huangdi]. *Han i araha Mukden i fujurun bithe, Yuzhi Shengjing fu*. Wuying dian edition, 1748.

Hua Li. Qingdai de Man Meng lianyin. *Minzu yanjiu* 2 (1983), 45–54.

Huang, Pei. *Autocracy at Work: A Study of the Yung-cheng Period, 1723–1735*. (Bloomington, 1974).

Hummel, Arthur W. et al. *Eminent Chinese of the Ch'ing Period*. (Washington DC, 1943).

Ilyushechkin, V.P. Anti-Manzhou Edge of the Taiping Peasant War. In S.L. Tikhvinsky (ed.), *Manchzhurskoe vladichestvo v Kitae*. (Moscow, 1983).

Im, Kaye Soon. *The Rise and Decline of the Eight-Banner Garrisons in the Ch'ing Period (1644–1911): A Study of the Kuang-chou, Hang-chou, and Ching-chou Garrisons*. (Ann Arbor MI, 1981).

Ishida Mikinosuke. Joshin-go kenkyū no shin shiryō. *Tōa bunkashi sōkō*. (Tokyo, 1973, first published 1940).

Ji Dachun. Lun Songyun. *Minzu yanjiu* 3 (1988), 71–9.

Jiang Liangqi. *Donghua lu*. (Peking, 1980, reprint of Qianlong eidtion).

Jin Guangping and Jin Qizong. *Nuzhen yuyan wenzi yanjiu*. (Peking, 1980).

Jin Qizong. *Nuzhen wen cidian*. (Peking, 1984).

Kahn, Harold L. *Monarchy in the Emperor's Eyes: Image and Reality in the Ch'ien-lung Reign*. (Cambridge, 1971).

Kanda Nobuo. Shinshō no *yizheng daren* ni tsuite. In *Wada Hakushi kenreki kinen tōyōshi ronsō*. (Reprinted, Tokyo, 1951).

——. Shinshō no beile ni tsuite. *Tōyō gakuhō* 40:4 (March, 1958), 349–71.

——. Remarks on *Emu tanggū orin sakda-i gisun sarkiyan*. In Sungyun, *Emu tanggū orin sakda-i gisun sarkiyan*. (Wiesbaden, 1983).

Kanda Nobuo and Matsumura Jun. *Hakki tsushi retsuden sakuin*. (Tokyo, 1965).

Kanda Nobuo et al. (trans. and annotators). The Secret Chronicles of the Manchu Dynasty. *Tongki fuka sindaha hergen i dangse* vols I–VII. (Tokyo, 1956).

Kanda Shinobu (Wang Ling, trans.). Qingchao de *Guoshi liezhuan* he *Erchen zhuan*. *Qingshi yanjiu tongshun* 3 (1986), 57–60.

Kane, Daniel. *The Sino-Jurchen Vocabulary of the Bureau of Interpreters*. (Bloomington, 1989).

Kessler, Lawrence. Ethnic Composition of Provincial Leadership during the Ch'ing Dynasty. *Journal of Asian Studies* 28:3 (May, 1969), 489–511.

——. *K'ang-hsi and the Consolidation of Ch'ing Rule, 1661–1684*. (Chicago, 1976).

King, J.R.P. The Korean Elements in the Manchu Script Reform of 1632. *Central Asiatic Journal* 31:3–4 (1987), 252–86.

Kiyose, Gisaburo N. *A Study of the Jurchen Language and Script: Reconstruction and Decipherment*. (Kyoto, 1977).

Klaproth, Jules. *Chrestomathie Mandchou, ou Recueil de Textes Mandchou*. (Paris, 1828).

Kostyaeva, A.S. The "Down with the Qing" Slogan in the Pingxiang Uprising of 1906. In S.L. Tikhvinsky (ed.), *Manchzhurskoe vladichestvo v Kitae*. (Moscow, 1983).

Krader, Lawrence. Qan-Qaɣan and the Beginnings of Mongol Kingship. *Central Asiatic Journal I* 1 (1955), 17–35.

Kuhn, Philip A. *Rebellion and its Enemies in Late Imperial China: Militarization and Social Structure, 1796–1864*. (Cambridge MA, 1970).

Kwong, Luke S.K. *A Mosaic of the Hundred Days: Personalities, Politics and Ideas of 1898*. (Cambridge, 1984).

——. On "The 1898 Reforms Revisited": A Rejoinder. *Late Imperial China* 8:1 (June, 1987), 214–19.

Lee, Ki-Baik (E. Wagner, trans.). *A New History of Korea*. (Cambridge, 1984).

Lee, Peter H. *Songs of Flying Dragons: A Critical Reading*. (Honolulu, 1977).

Lee, Robert H.G. *The Manchurian Frontier in Ch'ing History*. (Cambridge, 1970).

Lei Fangsheng. Jingzhou qixue de shimo ji qi tedian. *Minzu yanjiu* 3 (1984), 57–9.

Leung, Man-Kam. Mongolian Language Education and Examinations in Peking and Other Metropolitan Areas During the Manchu Dynasty in China (1644–1911). *Canada–Mongolia Review/Revue Canada–Mongolie* 1:1 (1975), 29–44.

Levin, Maksim Grigor'evich (H.N. Michael, trans.). *Ethnic Origins of the Peoples of Northeastern Asia*. (Toronto, 1963).

Li Chien-nung (Ssu-yu Tēng and Jeremy Ingalls, trans. and eds). *The Political History of China*. (New York, 1956).

Li Hsüeh-chih [Li Xuezhi]. *Cong jige manwen mingci tantao manzhou (nuzhen) minzu de shehui zuzhi*. (Taipei, 1981).

Li Qiao. Baqi shengji wenti shulue. *Lishi dang'an* 1 (1981), 91–7.

Li Xinda. Ru Guan qian de baqi bingshu wenti. *Qingshi luncong* 3 (1982), 155–63.

Li Zhiting. Ming Qing zhanzheng yu Qingchu lishi fazhan shi. *Qingshi yanjiu tongshun* 1 (1988), 7–12.

Ling Chunsheng. *Songhuajiang xiayou de hezhe zu* (2 vols). (Nanking, 1934).

Liu Chia-chü (Liu Jiaju) (P.K. Crossley, trans.). The Creation of the Chinese Banners in the Early Ch'ing. *Chinese Studies in History* XIV, No. 4 (1981), 47–75 – originally published as "Qingchu hanjun baqi de zhaojian," *Dalu zazhi* 34:11 and 34:12 (1967).

Liu Guang'an. A Short Treatise on the Ethnic Legislation of the Qing Dynasty. *Social Sciences in China* 4 (Winter 1990), 97–117 (from *Zhongguo shehui kesue* 6 (1989)).

Liu Qinghua. Manzu xingshi shulue. *Minzu yanjiu* 1 (1983), 64–71.

Liu Xiamin. Qing kaiguo chu zhengfu zhu bu jiangyu kao. *Yanjing xuebao* 23:6 (1936), reprinted in *Qingshi luncong* 1 (1977), 107–46.

Liu Xianzhao. *Zhongguo minzu wenti yanjiu*. (Peking, 1993).

Lo Kuan-chung (Moss Roberts, trans. and annotator). *Three Kingdoms: A Historical Novel Attributed to Luo Guanzhong*. (Berkeley, 1991).

Lü Guangtian. Qingdai buteha daxing Ewenke ren de Baqi jiegou. *Minzu yanjiu* 3 (1983), 23–31.

Lui, Adam Yuen-chung. The Ch'ing Civil Service: Promotions, Demotions, Transfers, Leaves, Dismissals and Retirements. *Journal of Oriental Studies* 8:2 (1970), 333–56.

——. The Imperial College (*Kuo-tzu-chien*) in the Early Ch'ing (1644–1795). *Papers on Far Eastern History* 10 (1974), 147–66.

——. Syllabus of the Provincial Examination (*hsiang-shih*) under the Early Ch'ing (1644–1795). *Modern Asian Studies* 8:3 (1974), 391–6.

——. Censor, Regent and Emperor in the Early Manchu Period

(1644–1660). *Papers on Far Eastern History* 17 (1978), 81–102.

——. Manchu–Chinese Relations and the Imperial "Equal Treatment" Policy, 1651–1660. *Journal of Asian History* 19:2 (1985), 143–65.

Ma Wensheng. Fu'an Dong Yi kao. Wanli period, reprinted in Shen, *Qing ru guan qian shiliao xunji* #1.

Mair, Victor H. Perso-Turkic Bakshi = Mandarin Po-shih: Learned Doctor. *Journal of Turkish Studies* 16 (1992), 117–27.

Mancall, Mark. *Russia and China: Their Diplomatic Relations to 1728.* (Cambridge, 1971).

Manzu jianshi. (Peking, 1979).

Meadows, Thomas T. *Translations from the Manchu with the Original Texts.* (Canton, 1849).

Meng Sen. Baqi zhidu kaoshi. *Lishi yanjiusuo jikan* VI:3 (1936), 343–412.

——. *Qing chu san da yi'an kaoshi.* (photo reprint in Jindai Zhongguo shiao congkan series, Shen Yün-lung [Shen Yunlong] (ed.), Taipei, 1966).

——. *Qingshi qianji.* (Taipei, n.d.).

Mitamura Taisuke, *Shinchō zenshi no kenkyū.* (Kyoto, 1965).

Miyake Shunjō, *Tōhoku Ajia kōkugaku no kenkyū.* (Tokyo, 1975).

Mo Dongyin. Qingchu manzu de saman jiao. In *Manzu shi luncong* (originally Peking, 1958, reprinted Peking, 1979).

Morgan, D.O. Edward Gibbon and the East. *Iran* XXXIII (1995), 85–92.

Mou Ranxun. Mingmo xiyang dapao you Ming ru Hou Jin kaolue: II. *Mingbao yuekan* (October, 1982).

Naquin, Susan. *Millenarian Rebellion in China: The Eight Trigrams Uprising of 1813.* (New Haven, 1976).

Naquin, Susan and Evelyn S. Rawski. *Chinese Society in the Eighteenth Century.* (New Haven, 1987).

Nivison, David. Ho-shen and his accusers: Ideology and Political Behavior in the Eighteenth Century. In David S. Nivison and Arthur R. Wright (eds), *Confucianism in Action.* (Stanford, 1959).

Norman, Jerry. *A Concise Manchu–English Lexicon.* (Seattle, 1978).

Nowak, Margaret and Stephen Current. *The Tale of the Nisan Shamaness.* (Seattle, 1977).

Okada Hidehiro. How Hong Taiji Came to the Throne. *Central Asiatic Journal* 23:3–4 (1979), 250–9.

——. Mandarin, A Language of the Manchus; How Altaic? In Martin Gimm, Giovanni Stary and Michael Weiers (eds), *Historische und bibliographische Studien zur Mandschuforschung* (third volume in the series *Aetas Manjurica*). (Wiesbaden, 1992).

Onogawa Hidemi. Yōsei tei to Taigi kakumeiroku. *Tōyōshi kenkyū* 18:3 (December, 1959), 99–123.

——. *Shimmatsu seiji shisō kenkyū*. (Kyoto, 1960).

Ortai et al. *Baqi tongzhi* [chuji]. (Original edition 1739).

Oxnam, Robert B. *Ruling from Horseback: Manchu Politics in the Oboi Regency, 1661–1669*. (Chicago, 1970).

Peng Bo. *Manzu*. (Peking, 1985).

Peng Guodong. *Qing shi kaiguo qian ji*. (Taipei, 1969).

Polachek, James. *The Inner Opium War*. (Cambridge, 1992).

Qiang Xiangshun and Tong Tuo. *Shengjing huanggong*. (Peking, 1987).

Qingdai dang'an shiliao congbian vol. 11. (Peking, 1982).

De Quincey, Thomas. (Charles W. French, ed.). *Revolt of the Tartars; or, Flight of the Kalmuck Khan and his People from the Russian territories to the Frontiers of China*. (Chicago, 1899).

Rossabi, Morris. *The Jurchens in the Yüan and Ming*. (Ithaca NY, 1982).

Roth [Li], Gertraude. The Rise of the Early Manchu State: A Portrait Drawn from Manchu Sources to 1636. Doctoral dissertation, Harvard University. (1975).

——. The Manchu–Chinese Relationship. In Jonathan D. Spence and J. Wills (eds), *From Ming to Ch'ing: Conquest, Region and Continuity in Seventeenth-Century China*. (New Haven, 1979).

Samuel, Geoffrey. *Civilized Shamans: Buddhism in Tibetan Societies*. (Washington DC, 1993).

Saunders, John B. de C.M. and Francis R. Lee. *The Manchu Anatomy and its Historical Origin, with Annotations and Translations*. (Taipei, 1981).

Serruys, Henry. *Sino–Jürched Relations in the Yung-lo Period (1403–1424)*. (Wiesbaden, 1955).

Shavkunov, Ernst Vladimirovich. *Gosudarstvo Bokhai i pamyatniki ego kulturi v primor'e*. (Moscow, 1968).

Shirokogoroff, Sergei Mikhailovitch. *Social Organization of the*

Manchus: A Study of the Manchu Clan Organization. (Shanghai, 1924).

Sin Chung-il [Shen Zhongyi]. *Kŏnju jichŏng dorŏk.* (Taipei, 1971, photo reprint of 1597 original).

———. (Xu Huanpu, ed.). *Jianzhou jicheng tulu.* (Shenyang, 1979).

Sinor, Denis. The Inner Asian Warriors. *Journal of the American Oriental Society* 101:2 (April–June 1981), 133–44.

Snellgrove, D.A. The Notion of Divine Kingship in Tantric Buddhism. In *The Sacral Kingship.* (Leiden, 1959).

Song Ki-Joong. The Study of Foreign Languages in the Yi Dynasty (1392–1910). *Bulletin of the Korean Research Center: Journal of the Social Sciences and Humanities* 54 (December, 1981), 1–45; 55 (June, 1982), 1–63.

Spence, Jonathan D. *Ts'ao Yin and the K'ang-hsi Emperor: Bondservant and Master.* (New Haven, 1966).

———. *The Search for Modern China.* (New York, 1989).

———. *God's Chinese Son.* (New York, 1996).

Spence, Jonathan D. and J. Wills (eds). *From Ming to Ch'ing: Conquest, Region and Continuity in Seventeenth-Century China.* (New Haven, 1979).

Stary, Giovanni. A New Subdivision of Manchu Literature: Some Proposals. *Central Asiatic Journal* 31:3–4 (1987), 287–96.

———. *China's ёrste Gesandte in Rußland.* (Wiesbaden, 1976).

———. Die Struktur der Ersten Risidenz des Mandschukans Nurgaci. *Central Asiatic Journal* XXV (1985), 103–9.

———. L'Ode di Mukden' dell'imperator Ch'ien-lung: Nuovi spunti per un analisi della tecnica versificatoria mancese. *Cina* 17, 235–51.

———. The Manchu Emperor "Abahai": Analysis of an Historiographic Mistake. *Central Asiatic Journal* 28:3–4 (1984), 296–9 – originally published in *Cina* 18 (1982), 157–62.

Struve, Lynn. *The Southern Ming, 1644–1662.* (New Haven, 1984).

———. *Voices from the Ming–Qing Cataclysm: China in Tiger's Jaws.* (New Haven, 1993).

Sudō Yoshiyuki. Shinchō ni okeru Manshū chūbō no toku shusei ni kansuru ichi kōsatsu. *Tōhoku gakuho* 11:1, 176–203.

Sun Wenliang. *Nurhachi pingzhuan.* (Shenyang, 1985).

Sun Xiao'en. *Guangxu pingzhuan.* (Shenyang, 1985).

Sun Zhentao et al. *Erchen zhuan* (undated colophon). (Guoshi guan shanben, 1785).

Sungyun. *Emu tanggū orin sakda-i gisun sarkiyan, Bai er lao ren yulu.* (Taipei, 1982, reprint of 1791? original).

Tamura Jitsuzo et al. *Kotai Shimbun kan yakukai.* (Kyoto, 1966).

Tao Jinshen. *The Jurchen in Twelfth-Century China: A Study of Sinicization.* (Seattle, 1976).

Telford, Ted A. and Michael H. Finegan. Qing Archival Materials from the Number One Historical Archives on Microfilm at the Genealogical Society of Utah. *Late Imperial China* 9:2 (December, 1988), 86–114.

Teng, Ssu-yü. *Historiography of the Taiping Rebellion.* (Cambridge, 1972).

Tieliang et al. *[Qinding] Baqi tongzhi,* 1977 (Taipei reprint, 1966).

Tong Jingren. *Suiyuan cheng zhufang zhi.* (Huhehaote, 1984, revision of 1958 original).

——. *Huhehaote manzu jianshi.* (Huhehaote, 1987).

Torbert, Preston M. *The Ch'ing Imperial Household Department: A Study of its Organization and Principal Functions, 1662–1796.* (Cambridge, 1977).

Ubingga, Li Wengang, Yu Zhixian and Jin Tianyi. *Manzu minjian gushi xuan.* (Shanghai, 1982, 1983).

Vorob'ev, M.V. *Chzhurchzheni i gosudarstvo Czin' (X v.–1234 g.) Istoricheskii Ocherk.* (Moscow, 1975).

Wakeman, Frederic, Jr. *The Great Enterprise: The Manchu Reconstruction of Imperial Order in Seventeenth-Century China.* (Berkeley, 1985).

Wang Xiuchou [Wang Hsiu-ch'u] (L. Mao, trans.). A Memoir of a Ten Days' Massacre in Yangzhow. *T'ien-hsia Monthly* 4:5, 515–37.

Wang Zongyan. *Du Qingshi gao za ji.* (Hongkong, 1977).

Weins, Mi-chu. Anti-Manchu Thought during the Ch'ing. *Papers on China,* vol. 22A (Harvard East Asian Research Center; May 1969), 1–24.

Widmer, Eric. *The Russian Ecclesiastical Mission in Peking during the Eighteenth Century.* (Cambridge, 1976).

Wilhelm, Hellmut. A Note on the Migration of the Uriangkhai. In Omeljan Pritsak (ed.), *Studia Altaica* (1957).

Wright, Mary C. *The Last Stand of Chinese Conservatism: The T'ung-Chih Restoration, 1862–1874.* (New York, 1966).

—— (ed.). *China in Revolution: The First Phase, 1900–1913.* (New Haven, 1968).

Wu ti Qingwen jian. (Peking, 1957, photo repring of Qianlong period original).

Wu Yuanfeng, Zhao Zhiqiang, Xibo zu you Kharqin Menggu qi bianru Manzhou baqi shimo. *Minzu yanjiu* 5 (1984), 60–55.

Wu, Silas. *Passage to Power: K'ang-hsi and his Heir Apparent, 1661–1722.* (Cambridge, 1979).

Wylie, Alexander. *Translation of the Ts'ing Wan K'e Mung.* (Shanghai, 1855).

Xu Zengzhong. Zeng Jing fan Qing an yu Qing Shizong Yizheng tongzhe quanguo de da zheng fangzhen. *Qingshi luncong* 5 (April, 1984), 158–78.

Yan Chongnian. *Nurhachi zhuan.* (Peking, 1983).

Yanai Watari. *Wulianghai ji dadan kao* (translation of the 1914 original, *Orankai sanei meisho kō*).

Yang Lien-sheng. The Organization of Chinese Offical Historiography. In Beasley and Pulleyblank (eds), *Historians of China and Japan.* (London, 1961).

Yang Qijiao. *Yongzheng di ji qi mizhe zhidu yanjiu.* (Hongkong, 1981).

Yang Xuechen and Zhou Yuanlian. *Qingdai baqi wanggong guizu xingxhuai shi.* (Shenyang, 1986).

Yang Yang, Sun Yuchang and Zhang Ke. Mingdai liuren zai Dongbei. *Lishi yanjiu* 4 (1985), 54–88.

——, Yuan Lukun and Fu Langyun. *Mingdai Nurgan dusi ji qi weisuo yanjiu.* (Zhumazhen [Henan], 1981).

Yang Yulian. Mingdai houqi de Liaodong mashi yu Nuzhenzu de xingqi. *Minzu yanjiu* 5 (1980), 27–32.

Yinzhen [Qing Shizong]. *Dayi juemi lu.* (Taipei, 1966, photo reprint in Jindai Zhongguo shiao congkan series, Shen Yün-lung [Shen Yunlong] (ed.)).

Zhang Bofeng. *Qingdai gedi jiangjun dutong dachen deng nianbiao, 1796–1911.* (Peking, 1977).

Zhang Jinfan and Guo Chengkang. *Qing ru guan qian guojia falu zhidu shi.* (Shenyang, 1988).

Zhang Shucai. Zai tan Cao Fu zui zhi yuanyuin ji Cao jia zhi qi jie. *Lishi dang'an* 2, 80–8.

Zhao Erxun. *Manzhou mingchen zhuan.* (Taipei, 1928).

Zhou Yuanlian. *Qingchao kaiguo shi yanjiu.* (Shenyang, 1981).

——. Guanyu baqi zhidu de jige wenti. *Qingshi luncong* 3 (1982), 140–54.

Zhu Chengru. Qing ru guan qian hou Liao Shen diqu de Man (Nuzhen) Han renkou jiaoliu. In Bai Shouyi (ed.), *Qingshi guoji xueshu taolun hui.* (Shenyang, 1990).

Zhu Fangzu and Huang Fengqi. Liaodai keju zhidushulue. In Chen Shu (ed.), *Liao Jin shi lunji* vol. 3 (Peking, 1987).

Zhu Xizu. *Hou Jin guohan xingshi kao.* (Peiping, 1932).

Index

Adun (Kim Adun, Ado) 45
Afghanistan 34, 80
agriculture 17, 28, 40, 41, 43, 52, 56, 91, 97, 134–5, 140, 164; foreign crops 134–5 (*see also* environmental decay, population)
Aisin Gioro lineage 7, 23, 30, 31, 32, 44, 55, 65, 78, 79, 84, 87, 103, 115, 119, 122, 125, 138, 139, 154, 180, 195, 196, 198; female influence in 76, 78, 138 (*see also* Ajige, Cuyen, Daišan, Degelei, Dorgon, Fulin, Giocangga, Hongli, Hung Taiji, Manggüldai, Minning, Möngke Temür, Murgaci, *ninggū da*, Nurgaci, Pucheng, Puyi, Shanqi, Soocangga, Surgaci, Taksi, Tanggudai, Utai, Xuanye, Yihuan, Yixin, Yoto, Zaichun, Zaifeng, Zaitian, Zaiyi)
Ajige 67
Albazinians (Cossacks) 81, 104 (*see also* Eight Banners, Russia)
Alcock, Rutherford 169
Alexander, William 144
Altaic theory 33–6, 39
Altan Khan 95, 96, 98 (*see also* Mongols, Americans, British 143; in China trade 142; in opium trade 154; Native 3, 19, 24, 34, 35, 102 (*see also* mercenaries, United States of America)
Amherst, William Pitt 150
Amin 63, 67, 77
Amur river 8, 14, 16, 101, 102, 103, 124, 217n1
Amursana 121 (*see also* Mongols, Turkestan)
Amyot, Joseph-Marie 139, 140, 146 (*see also* Jesuits)

Arabic language or script 33
Articles of Favorable Treatment 194, 195, 196, 198
Ašoka 112, 120 (*see also* Buddhism)
Atai 51
Attiret, Jean-Denis 131, 139 (*see also* Jesuits)

Babojab 196
banishment 101–2, 156
Bartholin, Thomas 92
beile 42, 43, 44, 53, 54, 60, 62, 63, 69, 81, 206; *hošoi beile* 64, 67, 75
Benoist, Michel 136
Book of Documents 132 (*see also* Confucianism)
Borjigid lineage 76, 162 (*see also* Lomi, Senggerinchin, Xiaozhuang Wen)
British East India Company (BEIC) 105, 119, 140, 143, 148, 150, 177
British empire 9, 147, 150; George III 143, 146, 147; Royal Navy 155, 156; Victoria as Empress of India 178
Buddhism 18, 24, 35, 37, 67, 88, 98, 108, 114, 115; *čakravartin* 112, 113–14, 120; living Buddhas 118; Mahākāla 77, 112, 119; Sa-skya pa 24, 112, 113; Vaisrana 119 (*see also* Dalai Lama, *dhāraṇī*, Panchen Lama, Tibet)
Bujantai of Ula 58, 62, 63, 64
Burgevine, Henry 183
Burlingame, Anson 169

calendar – *see* mathematics
cannibalism 164
Canton (Guangzhou) 91, 143, 148, 159
Cao Xueqin 126